LAW FROM BELOW

Recent Titles from the Moral Traditions Series

David Cloutier, Andrea Vicini, SJ, and Darlene Weaver, Editors

The Structures of Virtue and Vice
Daniel J. Daly

The Aesthetics of Solidarity: Our Lady of Guadalupe and American Democracy
Nichole M. Flores

Radical Sufficiency: Work, Livelihood, and a US Catholic Economic Ethic
Christine Firer Hinze

Tragic Dilemmas in Christian Ethics
Kate Jackson-Meyer

The Fullness of Free Time: Leisure and Recreation in the Moral Life
Connor Kelly

Beyond Biology: Rethinking Parenthood in the Catholic Tradition
Jacob M. Kohlhaas

Beyond Virtue Ethics: A Contemporary Ethic of Ancient Spiritual Struggle
Stephen M. Meawad

Growing in Virtue: Aquinas on Habit
William C. Mattison III

Reenvisioning Sexual Ethics: A Feminist Christian Account
Karen Peterson-Iyer

Tomorrow's Troubles: Risk, Anxiety, and Prudence in an Age of Algorithmic Governance
Paul Scherz

Wealth, Virtue, and Moral Luck: Christian Ethics in an Age of Inequality
Kate Ward

LAW FROM BELOW

HOW THE THOUGHT *of* Francisco Suárez, SJ, CAN RENEW CONTEMPORARY LEGAL ENGAGEMENT

Elisabeth Rain Kincaid

GEORGETOWN UNIVERSITY PRESS / WASHINGTON, DC

© 2024 Georgetown University Press. All rights reserved. No part of this book may be reproduced or utilized in any form or by any means, electronic or mechanical, including photocopying and recording, or by any information storage and retrieval system, without permission in writing from the publisher.

The publisher is not responsible for third-party websites or their content. URL links were active at time of publication.

Library of Congress Cataloging-in-Publication Data

Names: Kincaid, Elisabeth Rain, author.
Title: Law from below : how the thought of Francisco Suárez, SJ, can renew contemporary legal engagement / Elisabeth Rain Kincaid.
Description: Washington, DC : Georgetown University Press, [2024] | Series: Moral traditions series. | Includes bibliographical references and index.
Identifiers: LCCN 2023013722 (print) | LCCN 2023013723 (ebook) | ISBN 9781647124052 (hardcover) | ISBN 9781647124069 (paperback) | ISBN 9781647124076 (ebook)
Subjects: LCSH: Suárez, Francisco, 1548-1617. | Law—Philosophy. | Political theology.
Classification: LCC K230.S8454 K56 2024 (print) | LCC K230.S8454 (ebook) | DDC 340/.1—dc23/eng/20230929
LC record available at https://lccn.loc.gov/2023013722

♾ This paper meets the requirements of ANSI/NISO Z39.48-1992 (Permanence of Paper).

25 24   9 8 7 6 5 4 3 2   First printing

Printed in the United States of America

Cover design by Trudi Gershenov
Interior design by BookComp, Inc.

Contents

Acknowledgments vii

Introduction 1

1 Political Theology's Loss of Law: Why Francisco Suárez Matters 10

2 Law as Activity: Suárez's Theory of Law from Below 48

3 Suárez and Modernity: Critics and Concerns 83

4 The Work of the People: The Power of Custom for Positive Lawmaking 109

5 Doubts and Deliberation: Communal Engagement in Legal Interpretation 144

6 Falling between the Legal Cracks: Practices of Equity in the Face of Injustice 173

Conclusion 208

Index 215

About the Author 221

Acknowledgments

The long drawn-out process of bringing this book to publication has only been possible because of wise and supportive friends and colleagues. In many ways, much of the joy of the process has been the encouragement and support of many friends along the way. First, Jean Porter has been a consistently kind, supportive, responsive, and wise academic director and seamlessly continues to be a support and encouragement in bringing this book to print. Jerry McKenny has been a wonderful mentor in every area of academic life, and many areas of personal life as well over my time at Notre Dame and through my teaching career. I'm grateful to so many other colleagues involved in the process of retrieving Francisco Suárez. John Robinson of Notre Dame Law School provided incredibly helpful guidance on many topics, from jurisprudence to Suárez to Latin translation. Robin Lovin first piqued my interest in the relationship between law and theology in the early modern period and has continued to remain a kind and supportive guide and teacher. Charlie Curran, Beka Miles, Steve Long, Dallas Gingles, Bruce Marshall, and the late and much-missed William Abraham from Southern Methodist University all offered invaluable support, advice, and encouragement in the various revision stages of the process.

One of the great and unexpected joys of life as a theologian has been the wonderful community of spiritual and intellectual friends I have encountered. I'm especially grateful to Michael Altenburger, Garwood Anderson, Kirsten Anderson, Matthew Lee Anderson, Neil Arner, Stewart Clem, Michael Cover, Jordan DeGuire, OP, Brian Dunkle, SJ, Thomas Esposito, O.Cist., Phil Ganir, SJ, Craig Iffland, Kyle Lambelet, David Lantigua, Michael Magree, SJ, Julie Dolan Mitchell, David Elliot, Nathan O'Halloran, SJ, Matthew Olver, Paul Scherz, and Paul Wheatley, for words of wisdom and encouragement at various points in the process as well the gift of their friendships. I am also grateful to graduate assistants Micah Hogan and Alejandra Arguello and to Valerie Alombro for their careful review of this manuscript. Aaron Pidel, SJ, has provided me with many crucial resources on Suárez and insights into the Ignatian tradition as well as exhortation and encouragement. Lorraine Cuddeback-Geddeon has been a wonderful companion at conferences and throughout encounters with all the mysteries of the academic life. I am also especially grateful to David Cloutier for his incredibly able editorial assistance and to Andrea Vicini, SJ, for helping me formulate my early book proposals, as well the very helpful feedback from several anonymous reviewers.

Along with this academic support, I am grateful to the Nanovic Institute for granting me the Paul G. Tobin Fellowship, funding a year of writing that eventually led to this book. The Episcopal Church Foundation provided important financial support through its ECF Fellows Program and the Nanovic Institute and Notre Dame's Rome Global Gateway program funded a research trip to Rome, which gave me the opportunity to read more on Suárez in both the archives of the Jesuit Curia in Rome and the Pontifical Gregorian University Library.

I have been supported and encouraged and prayed for many years by so many, but especially Jenny Reynolds, Carrie Boren Headington, Risa Gross, and Anna Schroeder. I thank my in-laws, Barbara and Sam Kincaid, for being constant encouragers and gracious grandparents, providing countless hours of child care to give me time to write. My parents, John and Ellen Rain, have lifted my spirits when I was discouraged, always been willing to talk about my research, encouraged me to love reading and learning, and prayed for me and supported me. Dad read every word of this manuscript and provided many helpful stylistic inputs. My children, Sam and Mary Clare, have provided laughter, a tolerance of sleepless nights, and a continual reminder of God's abundance. Finally, I say thank you to my husband, Thomas, who has supported me every step of the way in studying theology and encouraging my writing at great personal sacrifice.

Introduction

In 1613 King James I, the Protestant ruler of England, Scotland, and Ireland, ordered an eagerly anticipated theological treatise to be tossed onto the flames in a public bonfire at the cemetery of St. Paul's Cathedral in London. Within six months the French Parlement in Paris, eager to curry favor with its Catholic king, Louis XIII, would order that the same treatise be burned on the doorsteps of all of the Jesuit houses in Paris.[1] Upon receiving the news that his work had met such a fiery demise, the author of the treatise, Francisco Suárez, SJ, wrote to his friend from his retirement in Lisbon: "May it please God that the fate of my book might also be mine, and that I may confirm with my blood and life the doctrines which up to now I have defended only with my pen."[2] The controversy occasioned by the book amply demonstrated that if either James or Louis could wrest Suárez from the domains of the Spanish king, his person might suffer the same fiery fate as his work.

A retired theology professor writing scholastic treatises on theological jurisprudence seems an unlikely person to have united two of the most powerful Catholic and Protestant rulers of the day in such extreme actions of shared revulsion. However, both King James and King Louis believed that Suárez's *Defensio* articulated a theory of law that posed a significant theological threat to their claims to hold absolute lawmaking authority. Their concern was justified. Suárez specifically developed his theory of popular engagement with law by the people by offering theories and resources for communal engagement with law in order to challenge the new divine rights theorists of his day. In both the polemical *Defensio* and the more theoretical *De Legibus*, Suárez drew upon both Thomistic theory and secular and ecclesiastical jurisprudence to describe law not as a static command issued by rulers and imposed upon the people, but rather as the ever-developing product of dialectical engagement between the sovereign and the people.

Several generations later Suárez's legal theories caused controversy again, as they provided theological justification for Latin American Jesuits advocating for freedom from European domination and a lifting up of the voices of *mestizo* and Indigenous communities.[3] In Suárez these theologians and advocates found a vision of the power of the community that explained and justified their struggle against unjust rulers and that provided concrete methods by which citizens could challenge unjust laws. Throughout this book I argue that Suárez's theology of law is just as relevant today for challenging the law-making claims and legal enactments of new autocratic powers and rulers.

In the current political situation we are seeing a revival and strengthening of the historical narrative that law is imposed only from above, specifically by the chief executive acting upon some sort of perceived populist mandate. We can see an especially clear example of this dangerous authoritarian turn in a speech made by then–attorney general of the United States William Barr on November 15, 2019. In his speech Barr relies on assertions of executive privilege during the war on terror in the previous Bush and Obama administrations to argue for a view of law that returns to the royal absolutism of James I. In this address to the Federalist Society, Barr argued that seventeenth-century British legal theory was notable for its long-term muzzling of the authority of the king by the Whiggish parliament, which assumed sovereign powers at the cost of the executive.[4] Barr's revisionist twist on this reading includes the claim that the goal of the Founding Fathers when drafting the constitution was a restoration of the power of the chief executive that had been lost in the transition to parliamentary government even before the Glorious Revolution of 1689, which saw the deposition of James II, the last of the Stuart kings. Barr claims that in order to reverse this development in the new United States, the executive branch must be given much more than simply the power to execute the laws determined by legislators. Barr describes the legal regime envisioned by the founders as instead motivated by pragmatic concerns for swift, united decision-making in government. He argues that under the terms of the constitution, the executive branch is granted power outside the rule of law: the power to handle essential sovereign functions—such as the conduct of foreign relations and the prosecution of war—which by their very nature cannot be directed by a preexisting legal regime but rather demand speed, secrecy, unity of purpose, and prudent judgment to meet contingent circumstances.

In addition, Barr argues that the third element of executive power is the power to act swiftly in situations where the well-being of the nation might be compromised "but on which the law is either silent or inadequate." The fourth element places the executive above the reach of the law, granting powers of "internal management" needed to protect the executive branch's powers. In this description of the president's power, Barr explicitly looks backward, reclaiming some of the royal absolutism of James I to justify the use of executive power *against or above the rule of law* in the United States today.[5] Not only does Barr have no sense that there might be any way in which the people can be involved in changing law to make it more just; he explicitly seeks to remove great swaths of power from the people's democratically elected representatives in Congress and from judges in courts who might protect minority groups against majorities.

Rather than rebuking these broad claims of executive power, some Christians provide theological window dressing to justify this type of lawmaking power grab. For example, American evangelist Franklin Graham has given theological articulation to this approach, rebuking politicians who question President Trump's integrity or commitment to the rule of law on the grounds that he is "just trying to protect our nation."[6] According to Graham, Trump's policies should be unconditionally supported because they benefit Christians, since the policies enhance economic stability, which can fund ministry, and provide "protections" for Christians.[7] Graham expresses no concerns about possible violations of the rule of law as long as actions advance what Graham believes are worthy ends. In addition, he clearly has no conception that the people themselves can work to reform unjust laws or advance the common good. Rather, Graham has explicitly placed all confidence and authority in the hands of the ruler whom some evangelicals argue that God has appointed—a Cyrus who will restore the promised land of America to the holy people of Israel.[8] Graham, alongside another evangelical public figure, Eric Metaxas, has gone so far as to claim that Christians who oppose Trump and his expansion of executive power may even be victims of demonic possession.[9] In considering these arguments, Esther Reed's warning regarding the danger of viewing law as something only imposed from above seems especially prescient. Unless Christians are able to "to develop an ethic of law beyond sect and compromise—neither retreating from the responsibilities of Christian witness and mission with respect to the human activity of law-making nor allowing the insidious temptations of our own age so to impair our judgment so that, to cite Ernst Bloch's observations on Reformation theologies of natural law, we ally ourselves with the Neros, having 'too little of anything, of Christ and of his community.'"[10]

Although few boldly promote this type of executive absolutism, the understanding of law as imposed only from above and with possibilities of response that are strictly binary—obedience or disobedience—has not only permeated legal and political discourse but also defines and limits most of contemporary theological discourse surrounding law and politics. Such permeation is not surprising, since this concept of law appears prominently in early modern and modern political theology and theology of law. Using Barr's nostalgic gaze back to the days of Stuart absolutism, we will examine how closely his and Graham's viewpoints and theological justifications parallel the claims made by James I, his royal chaplain, Lancelot Andrewes, and his intellectual heir, Thomas Hobbes. Many political theologians would agree that this understanding of the relationships between rulers, subjects, and the law is a morally and theologically problematic resurrection of the Eusebian heresy. However, due to this limited view of law as imposed only from above, many twentieth-century political theologians have focused primarily on changing laws using the tools of the political system and have given little consideration to possible engagement by citizens to directly change law by their actions. Rather, they often focus instead on making law more just by working outside the legal and political system, through various strategies of activism and civil disobedience. Although these are very important forms of citizen engagement, focusing on them to the exclusion of other forms of engagement limits the responses to unjust laws that are available to Christians.

The goal of this book is to describe a political theology that provides an additional mode of engagement with unjust laws: the theology of Francisco Suárez, which was developed to combat an authoritarian view of law and may be successfully retrieved to provide a constructive model of legal engagement for Christians today, including the possibility that communities may work to change law from the ground up as they function within the legal system, not outside it. Suggesting that the retrieval of the theological jurisprudence of an early modern Spanish Jesuit can provide answers to the legal challenges of our contemporary context may seem counterintuitive. Perhaps the contemporary equivalent of the kings' fiery destruction of Suárez's work has been the depiction of him as a much-pilloried pivotal figure in the "decline to modernity" narratives.[11] When his legal work is considered, he is often described as a voluntarist focused on the will of the monarch and the obliging power of law, rather than a proponent of the lawmaking power of the community.[12] Even those who support the community's original possession of political power generally have focused on the moment of political inception, rather than the idea of law in a state of continuing development.[13]

In contrast to these claims, Suárez, one of the most influential legal scholars of the early modern period (his works influenced Grotius and John Locke, among others), is an appropriate figure for this type of retrieval because his historical context positions him as a bridge figure engaged in the challenges that accompanied the formation of the idea of nation-state and the accompanying dangers of growing state authority. Suárez to a large degree shares the moral, theological, and legal suppositions of many of our own contemporaries. His theory of law thus provides a theologically serious way to mount a counternarrative to the theory of law handed down exclusively from above, while still acknowledging the good that can be found in the rule of law and its imposition by a legislative authority. He acknowledges the crucial contribution of citizens toward improving laws' moral content without removing the importance of law's inherent authority or the role of the lawgiver.

Suárez's theory is relevant today because it explains the ability of an individual community to improve or moderate law imposed from above in order to protect justice and the common good without denying the entire legal system's authority or independent legitimacy. Not only does Suárez offer a robust and theologically grounded explanation of law's formation and development; he also describes the processes and practices by which people can change law to make it more just. Under his theory of law the community is empowered to participate directly in legal formation in ways that go beyond both civil disobedience (to force the ruler to change the law) and recourse to the ballot box (to vote the ruler out). Instead, Suárez argues for an intrinsic lawmaking power held by the people alone, which they can never completely alienate or delegate. The people are not limited to exercising this power only through the obvious moments of legal and political engagement, such as through protest or by voting or taking a case to court. Rather, Suárez describes how the quotidian actions of ordinary people, working within their small local communities, actually have the power to change law within existing legal structures.

Suárez's theory of law is engaged by both exegetical and descriptive work and constructive retrieval. Although this focus is primarily theological, such a consideration of how Suárez's theory of law might apply to a modern society draws upon philosophers of law as his primary interlocutors, both because philosophy of law offers rich resources for different well-developed understandings of law and also out of a belief that the proper understanding of law should be able to engage, at least to a certain degree, in secular legal as well as theological discourse and withstand pragmatic and philosophical challenges from outside the theological realm. These legal philosophers have been useful conversation partners in a genuine retrieval of Suárez. However, as a work of theology, there are questions and discussions among some legal philosophers not fully considered or engaged.

While this is a historical retrieval of Suárez's view of law, the focus is primarily constructive. In addition, although this is a work of political theology, the approach taken is somewhat different and more granular than many works of contemporary political theology. I do not consider the nature of the state itself, that is, whether it is desacralized or is the last remaining vessel of the sacred within the contemporary polis. I do not consider which form of government is most appropriate for Christians, nor the relationships between religion, public policy, and constitutional law or the Church's role in the public square. Recovering Suárez's views of law could affect discussions of all of these issues, but the narrow focus here is upon Suárez's works and specific contemporary examples in which Christians have successfully deployed the practical techniques he describes in order to make laws more just.

I also consider here the failure of contemporary political theology—by focusing on civil disobedience only—to provide new theories of how Christians can work within the legal system to challenge unjust laws and improve problematic ones. I provide some brief background information on Suárez to demonstrate why he shares many of the concerns of our day regarding the need for laws to promote justice and the common good in the face of autocratic government promulgation. I also examine his investment in protecting the voices of minority communities against governmental imposition of restrictive or discriminatory laws.

Chapter 2 contains a discussion of how Suárez's theory of law provides an understanding of law suitable for retrieval in our own time. He offers a synthesis of Thomas Aquinas's legal theory and relies on juristic and canon law sources in order to address the challenges of early modern political theory, not as imposed from above but as developed through dialectical discernment between ruler and citizen. Chapter 3 considers the place of Suárez within theological and philosophical analysis in order to argue that his work presents an important development of the Thomistic tradition rather than a rejection of it. Included are a review of the problematic readings of Suárez that have contributed to this rejection view and a constructive argument that demonstrates the connection between Suárez's understanding of law and contemporary Catholic social teaching.

Chapters 4, 5, and 6 consider how Suárez's reflections on communal engagement with civil law through custom, statutory interpretation, and equity can be applied in our own time. Many of Suárez's suggested practices are already being used in ad hoc ways, arising from within Christian communities, such as community organizers and supporters of the sanctuary movement. These practices include Suárez's theory of interpretation and reception, which claims that local communities, not just courts and legislators, should be involved in determining the most just meaning of law. His theory of the development of custom creates room for engaging multiple approaches to improving laws, from the popular level as well as the explicitly legal and political levels, and demonstrates that resistance can take the form of working for cultural change rather than only via rejection or disobedience. His explanation of practices stemming from the virtue of equity stresses the importance of a single act to motivate communal change and legal improvement. In concluding I consider the importance of the Church in this specific type of legal engagement. I do not argue that these tools of engagement nullify or devalue the most prominent modes of engagement with law in our nation's political discourse, that is, voting, recourse to the court system, and civil disobedience. Rather, developing these modes of engagement expands the tool kit of constructive options for Christians to make law more just.

By considering both Suárez's theory of law and some modern examples of constructive communal practices of legal change I hope to provide modern Christians with helpful tools to develop more theorized modes of constructive and creative engagement with law (rather than a rejection of law) and enable us to better challenge the rise of authoritarians and autocrats in our own day.

A Note on the Sources Used

The definitive collection of Francisco Suárez's works—although still not quite complete—is the so-called *Vives* edition: Francisco Suárez, *Opera Omnia* (Paris: Apud Ludovicum Vives, 1856–78). The publication of a bilingual (Spanish and Latin) critical edition of *De Legibus* has been ongoing at the Consejo Superio de Investigationes Científicas in Madrid since 1972. Volumes 1 to 4 of the series were edited by Luciano Pereña Vicente: Francisco Suárez, *Tractatus de legibus ac Deo legislatore,* ed. Luciano Pereña Vicente (Madrid: Consejo Superior de Investigaciones Científicas, 1972).

The project was restarted in 2010 under a new editorial team. Book 6, on interpretation, was edited by C. Baciero and Jesús María García Añoveros and published in 2012: Francisco Suárez, *Tractatus de legibus ac Deo legislatore,* ed. C. Baciero (Madrid: Consejo Superior de Investigaciones Científicas, 2012). Whenever possible I have relied on this edition; when citing volumes 1 through 4, the translations are my own.

In the chapter on custom, a subject contained in book 7 and which has not yet been published in a critical edition, I rely primarily on the translations from *Selections from Three Works of Francisco Suárez, S.J.,* trans. Gwladys L. Williams, Ammi Brown, and John Waldron (Oxford: Clarendon, 1944; rprt.:

8 Introduction

Indianapolis, IN: Liberty Fund, 2013) and consulted the *Vives* edition to confirm the translations.

When citing Suárez's *Defensio* I use the translation found in Francisco Suárez, *Defense of the Catholic Faith Against the Errors of Anglicanism*, trans. Peter L. P. Simpson (Createspace, 2012), consulting the Latin edition of *Vives Opera Omnia* to ensure correct translations. See Francisco Suárez, *Defensio Fidei Catholicae et Apostolicae contra Errores Anglicanae Secta*, in *Opera Omnia*, vol. 24 (Paris: Apud Ludovicum Vives, 1856–78). When referencing Suárez's other works, specifically *de Sacramentis* and *de Religione*, I rely upon the *Vives* collection.

Notes

1. Joseph Fichter, *Man of Spain: Francis Suárez* (New York: MacMillan, 1940), 300–301.
2. Fichter, 302.
3. Enrique Dussell, "Las Casas, Vitoria, and Suárez: 1514–1617," in *Human Rights from a Third World Perspective: Critique, History and International Law*, ed. José-Manuel Barreto (United Kingdom: Cambridge Scholars Publishing, 2013), 204–5.
4. William Barr, "Barbara K. Olson Memorial Lecture," Washington, DC, November 15, 2019, https://www.justice.gov/opa/speech/attorney-general-william-p-barr-delivers-19th-annual-barbara-k-olson-memorial-lecture.
5. While Barr's yearning for the days of royal absolutism might seem odd in the context of contemporary democratic politics, the rhetoric of kingship has gained increasing traction in certain evangelical and nationalist political circles connected to the Trump administration. See Katherine Stewart, "Why Trump Reigns as King Cyrus," *New York Times*, December 31, 2018, https://www.nytimes.com/2018/12/31/opinion/trump-evangelicals-cyrus-king.html.
6. Caitlin Burke, "Franklin Graham: 'Shame on Republicans and Democrats' Who Don't Support Trump's Security Initiatives," November 2, 2017, https://www1.cbn.com/cbnnews/us/2017/november/franklin-graham-shame-on-republicans-and-democrats-who-dont-support-trumps-security-initiatives.
7. "Franklin Graham Praises President Trump for Defending Christianity," *CBN News*, January 21, 2018, https://www1.cbn.com/cbnnews/us/2018/january/franklin-graham-praises-president-trump-for-defending-christianity.
8. For further examples of this type of apocalyptic rhetoric regarding the Trump presidency, see Michael J. Mooney, "Trump's Apostle," *Texas Monthly*, August 2019, accessed at https://www.texasmonthly.com/articles/donald-trump-defender-dallas-pastor-robert-jeffress/.
9. Peter Wehner, "Are Trump's Critics Demonically Possessed?," *The Atlantic*, November 15, 2019, https://www.theatlantic.com/ideas/archive/2019/11/to-trumps-evangelicals-everyone-else-is-a-sinner/602569/.
10. Esther D. Reed, "Richard Hooker, Eternal Law and the Human Exercise of Authority," *Journal of Anglican Studies* 4, no. 2 (2006): 219.
11. A number of these claims are discussed in chapter 3. For additional descriptions and typologies of these modern critiques of Suárez, see Robert Miner, "Suárez as a Founder

of Modernity: Reflections on a *Topos* in Recent Historiography," *History of Philosophy Quarterly* 18, no. 1 (January 2001): 20. See also Richard Cross, "Duns Scotus and Suárez at the Origins of Modernity," in *Deconstructing Radical Orthodoxy*, ed. Wayne Hankey and Douglas Hedley (United Kingdom: Ashgate, 2005), 85–102.

12. See, for example, Thomas E. Davitt, SJ, *The Nature of Law* (St. Louis, MO: B. Herder, 1951), 39. See also William Daniel, *The Purely Penal Law Theory in Spanish Theologians* (Rome: Gregorian Biblical Bookshop, 1968), 88. See also J. B. Schneewind, "Modern Moral Philosophy from Beginning to End," in *Essays on the History of Moral Philosophy*, ed. J. B. Schneewind (Oxford: Oxford University Press, 2009), 92–93.

13. See, e.g.: Charles McCoy, "Note on the Problem of the Origin of Political Authority," *The Thomist* 16, no. 1 (1953): 71–81; and J. P. Sommerville, "From Suárez to Filmer: A Re-Appraisal," *Historical Journal* 25, no. 3 (September 1982): 525–40. Sommerville argues that Suárez's statement of political authority is "far more radically constitutionalist than is usually supposed" (525). However, he ends his description of Suárez's theory with the claim that "Suárez vigorously asserted that the original community was a direct democracy, but argued that although natural law gave the people political power, it did not oblige them to keep it" (530).

1

Political Theology's Loss of Law

WHY FRANCISCO SUÁREZ MATTERS

In 1993 the auxiliary bishop of Argentina, Jorge Bergoglio, published an essay commemorating the early Jesuit missionary martyrs in Paraguay. In examining their mission and martyrdom, Bergoglio repeatedly asks: What was their "project of the heart" (*"proyecto de un corazón"*)?[1] These three Jesuits, he argues, risked their lives because of their conviction that they were called to a unique missionary project informed by the Jesuit understanding of the transforming reality of the Incarnation of Jesus Christ as revealed both through the gospel and in the world. In Bergoglio's words, they were involved in *"una proyecto de libertad, de liberación cristiana."*[2] The project of Christian liberation undertaken by these missionaries was not a freedom from or rejection of the culture of the villages in which the missionaries proclaimed the gospel. Rather, by bringing the gospel to the village, they in turn, in accordance with "justice," opened themselves to the culture of the *pueblo* where they evangelized. This mutual openness between the missionaries and the pueblo ensured that the culture and "the seeds of the Gospel . . . in these places, would flourish equally and distinctly." In his eulogy Bergoglio articulates both his understanding of Jesuit missiology and, more broadly, an explication of the proper relationship between culture and the gospel and between the natural and the supernatural.

Bergoglio connects the Jesuit missionary approach directly to political theology. Specifically, he traces it to the thought of Francisco Suárez. This Jesuit missionary endeavor occurred, in his words, at "the grand moment" of Suárez. He suggests that in fact it is likely some of these missionary martyrs had been Suárez's students at some point in their formation. Bergoglio claims that the key to their understanding of the connection between culture and the proclamation of the gospel developed from Suárez's understanding of political power, specifically his theory of the corporate location of the "deposit of power." Rather than being entrusted to the ruler, political power remains in the hands of the people, who choose the ruler who will seek the common good. The wise ruler, therefore, is obligated to not betray the "life and culture of the people," but rather to understand his role as listening and learning from it. This understanding of the mutuality between ruler and people also informed the Jesuits' approach to their mission within the Church. They understood the natural and the supernatural as interrelated, not oppositional, and functioning within a justice of exchange exemplified by an openness to receiving wisdom from the pueblo without losing sight of the unique mission of the Church to proclaim the gospel to the pueblo.

A further examination of Bergoglio's writings as Pope Francis shows that the influence of this vision of culture, politics, and mission was adapted from the South American Jesuits' reception of Suárez. To begin, however, consider the crucial themes that Bergoglio argues these Jesuit missionaries retrieved from Suárez: the location of political power in the people and the necessity of a just exchange between those in authority and the community. Specifically, this concept of just exchange in the formation of "law from below" and the possibilities it provides for popular engagement in lawmaking goes beyond the ballot box, rights claims, and civil disobedience. In the face of the contemporary lure of authoritarianism, it is more important than ever to consider all of the constructive tools provided by the tradition of Christian reflection upon law—including the possibility that communities may work to change law "from the ground up" by functioning within the legal system, not just outside of it. The legal theory of Francisco Suárez, which was developed to directly combat an authoritarian view of law, may be successfully retrieved to provide a constructive model of legal engagement for Christians today.

First we must consider how the details of Suárez's own life story and thought create the possibility for his awareness of the importance of just laws, engaging especially with his concerns about many important issues present in our own time. Retrieving this understanding of popular engagement in the lawmaking process can supplement and expand contemporary discourse in political theology.

Suárez's Life and Intellectual Development

Suárez's life was shaped from birth by the quickly changing world of early modern Europe. He was born in Granada, Spain, in 1548, a little more than fifty years after the city was conquered and taken from the last Moorish king by Isabella of Castile and Ferdinand of Aragon.[3] Suárez's family were upwardly mobile merchants and courtiers who had deep connections to the Catholic Church. Suárez's maternal uncle, Francisco de Toledo, was one of the early members of the Society of Jesus and the first Jesuit elevated to cardinal. Several of Suárez's sisters entered religious orders and his brother Diego was also a Jesuit priest.

Suárez began his education with a study of canon law, and at age sixteen applied to enter the Society of Jesus. Despite early concerns about his intellectual aptitude (which some biographical accounts describe as dramatically improving after his continued pleas to the Virgin Mary for intercession), he was eventually accepted into the Jesuits and began the standard theological and philosophical formation. During his studies at Salamanca he was exposed to the revival of Iberian Thomism that followed upon the teaching of the Dominican Francisco de Vitoria. Suárez later became one of the most famous of a generation of Jesuit Thomists raised up in this Salamancan tradition. After graduation he began a teaching career in Spain's universities and in schools run by the society, including at Avila, Valladolid, Alcalá, Salamanca, Rome (at the Collegio Romano), and, for the last two decades of his career, at the University of Coimbra in Portugal. Although he did not begin publishing written works until his early forties, Suárez had a truly prodigious scholarly output. The complete edition of his works runs to twenty-six volumes.

The range of Suárez's works is truly phenomenal, covering a multitude of subjects, including law, metaphysics, philosophy, sacramental theology, dogmatic theology, Mariology, systematic theology, moral theology, ecclesiology, canon law, angelology, spiritual theology, and even a polemical work criticizing James I. Although his work does not perfectly mirror all the topics found in Aquinas's *Summa Theologiae*, Suárez's Thomistic training is evident in the shape of his theological corpus.[4] When he died at age seventy in 1617, he left an additional nine completed works that were published posthumously.

Suárez's academic career was dogged by various controversies. Part of his apparent attraction to controversy was his methodological approach. Although committed to engagement with the scholastic canon, he argued that his students should begin their theological and philosophical reflections not by repeating the received opinion but rather by considering each problem from the ground up. He wanted them to learn how to "look at things more from the root" (*"mirar las cosas mas de raiz"*).[5] These theological controversies involved the Immaculate Conception, epistolary confession, arguments involving human freedom, conflict with the Dominicans over what constituted acceptable appropriations of Aquinas, and a staunch defense of the Jesuit approach to the religious life.[6] At one point Suárez was even reported to the Inquisition authorities by one of his former teachers for allegedly holding heretical views.[7] However, despite these challenges, by the time of his death Suárez was regarded as a leading theologian of the Catholic Reformation and was even granted the title *Doctor Eximius* by Pope Paul V.

It is not surprising that Suárez was so often involved in controversy, since he lived in an age of controversy. The political and theological controversies of his day proved to be a crucible for the development of his theology and philosophy, especially his engagement with legal philosophy and contemporary political theology. Although he adhered to the scholastic methods and grounded his work in the tradition of Aquinas and medieval legal thought, both civil and ecclesiastical, he did not shy away from bringing the resources of this tradition to bear upon the questions that were dividing Europe. His engagement with new political, cultural, and legal challenges required that he build new theories based on the foundations of political theology and legal thought he had received. In both his theological foundation and his engagement with new challenges, he followed in the footsteps of his Dominican predecessors in the School of Salamanca.

When developing his theories of law, Suárez also had to engage with new challenges arising from global exploration. The immense cultural changes that arose from the Spanish encounter with South American and Pacific Islander civilizations directly impacted him from a very early age. As a second-generation member of the Jesuit order, his spiritual formation was deeply influenced by a new awareness of a world that extended beyond Europe and the Mediterranean. While other older religious orders shared a "Great Commission" commitment to mission, the Jesuits from their founding instituted a type of worldwide attention as part of their charism. Jesuits always viewed their charge "to help souls" as being a global mandate. Any Jesuit could be sent anywhere on mission: whether to India, China, South America, Africa, the Middle East, or islands of the Pacific, every Jesuit had to be prepared for mission work anywhere in the rapidly expanding world.[8] Suárez's brother Baltazar also entered the Jesuit order and eventually was sent to the Philippines as a missionary, only to die shortly after his arrival.[9] This global emphasis in Suárez's formation meant that his theological reflections would extend beyond Christian Europe and take into account the realities of different religions and cultures spread around the globe.

Not only his formation as a Jesuit but his time spent in Salamanca also exposed Suárez to the challenges of globalization and imperialism. He arrived at Salamanca one generation after the great theological disputes in the university community had taken place, when Dominicans Domingo de Soto and Francisco de Vitoria challenged the Spanish Crown, beginning with Vitoria's great lecture, "*De Indis*," delivered in 1537. Suárez was taught by professors who were aware of the atrocities perpetrated by the Spanish in South America and Latin America as well as the theological objections to this behavior. They possessed a keen sense of duty and responsibility and understood that part of their role as theologians involved a mandate to challenge the injustice of laws enacted by the Crown. Suárez, through his long association with the University of Salamanca, would come to view his own work as part of this heritage of challenge and resistance to legal injustice.[10] In addition, this legacy undoubtedly influenced Suárez's repeated arguments for the validity of laws issued by non-Christian rulers and the limited impact of the laws imposed by Christian rulers on the religious practices of non-Christians.[11]

Suárez extended his concerns regarding who was capable of possessing political and spiritual authority to include women. Growing up in Spain, Suárez saw strong women rulers and leaders in action. In Granada, he likely would have heard repeated stories lauding the wisdom and power of Queen Isabella, the Catholic liberating queen of Castile, who occupies a unique place in the Spanish political consciousness. It was Isabella, not her husband, Ferdinand, whom Spaniards believe provides the truest example of the godly monarch. Isabella's daughter Juana ruled as sovereign queen for the first seven years of Suárez's life. Following Juana's death, her son Philip II married Mary Tudor, the sovereign queen of England, as part of a Spain-orchestrated political strategy to return England to the fold of the Catholic faith. Given these formative experiences, it is not surprising that in his work *De Legibus*, Suárez explicitly argues that women can hold political authority at every level, even over their own husbands. In this instance he rejects the authority of Aquinas. In fact, although he draws on Aquinas for support of some of his claims regarding women as God's image-bearers, he carefully neglects to include any of Aquinas's arguments regarding natural female inferiority.[12] In addition to supporting women's ability to hold various forms of political authority, Suárez also supported women exercising various forms of spiritual authority. Rather than joining in the condemnation of Teresa of Avila's mysticism and leadership of her order of Carmelite nuns because she was a woman, he was a supporter of Saint Teresa's efforts from early on in his priestly ministry. He served as a spiritual director for the sisters in Valladolid while working as a professor there.[13] At some point early in his career Suárez also became acquainted with Teresa personally. Years later, as part of her canonization process after her death and shortly before his own, he testified to the impact this relationship had had upon him, convincing him of her personal sanctity and the orthodoxy of her spiritual writings. In supporting

Teresa's work and eventual canonization, Suárez was making a similar choice to expand the spheres in which women's authority could be exercised.

Suárez was deeply and personally impacted by the struggles of Spain's ethnic and religious minority communities to challenge cruel and dictatorial laws. Growing up in Granada, he was surrounded by visual reminders of centuries in which the three primary religious groups of Spain had lived together under Moorish rule. In fact, he grew up literally next door to a family of Morisco descent: the Granada Venegas. This experience gave him valuable first-hand knowledge of the challenges that even converts to Christianity faced under Spanish rule. Suárez was able to put this personal experience to good use in his later career as a theologian and jurist, when he contributed a lengthy defense of the induction of the leader of the Granada Venega family into a Christian chivalric order. In this legal document Suárez writes that to hold that descent from a non-Christian family justifies exclusion from opportunities such as membership in the chivalric orders available to Christians or to doubt the sincerity of their faith is a sin against both justice and charity.[14] In fact, he claims that this type of exclusion explicitly violates Saint Paul's stricture to the early Christians that "in Christ there is no Gentile or Jew, barbarian or Scythian, slave or free"; rather, in Christ we are all one (Col 3:11; Romans 10:12).[15]

Perhaps Suárez sympathized so much with the plight of the Venega family because it was similar to his own family's story. Although the Suárez family had connections with the court and other influential figures in Granada, their position was far from secure. Like many other early members of the Society of Jesus, Suárez was of *converso* descent. His family had migrated from Toledo to Granada, not simply to take advantage of the economic opportunities of the Reconquista but to escape the known fact in Toledo of their Jewish heritage. This history of Jewish descent later resurfaced in an inquisitorial procedure when his maternal uncle, Cardinal Francisco de Toledo, attempted to testify in defense of the converso archbishop of Toledo. The inquisitor argued that Toledo should be excluded from the process because of his own descent from a "notorious" Jewish family in Cordoba.[16] His grandfather had been tried for allegedly engaging in Jewish religious practices. His grandmother and great-grandparents suffered the ultimate penalty and were burned at the stake. Despite these revelations, the Suárez family's "secret" was hidden from the outside world as much as possible but must have haunted Suárez, who saw the emphasis on blood purity grow stronger over the course of his lifetime. This awareness of how easily his voice could be silenced or his family suffer because of unjust laws must have lent poignancy and urgency to

Suárez's claims about the power of each specific community, non-Christian as well as Christian, to challenge unjust laws.

However, despite his insights and theological acuity, Suárez was far from a complete moral hero. During his own lifetime his adherence to the asceticism of Jesuit life was questioned. While his own life-long struggles with ill health necessitated some avoidance of an unduly rigorous rule of life, his confreres at various Jesuit residences complained about his lifestyle, including his disengagement from the communal life and a habit of maintaining his own (much better) food supplies.[17] Sadly, he allegedly committed the cardinal sin for academics of secreting away to his own study too many library books and not returning them. In addition to these personal flaws, he did not always stand against the prevailing wind of popular opinion. This was especially apparent in his engagement with the *limpieza de sangre* (cleanliness of blood) movement in Spain and within the Society of Jesus. Instead of speaking out to protect his fellow confreres of Jewish descent, Suárez argued in support of the Jesuit General Congregation V's ability to limit entry to the Jesuits based on Jewish origin. At times this support has been understood as motivated by racism, especially among authors unaware of Suárez's own converso origins. However, Robert Maryks argues convincingly that, given the Suárez family's experience, Suárez's acquiescence more likely arose from fear for his own position within the order and in Spain itself, and should be understood as a desperate attempt at self-preservation, not anti-Semitism.[18] In another moral miss, despite his strong support of female political authority, he lacked the insight to see the benefits of women religious acting in an apostolic role, not simply as cloistered sisters, and thus withheld support for Mary Ward's Institute, an English female order whose rule incorporates insights from Jesuit spirituality and apostolic practices.[19]

Suárez's personal moral failings (his cause for canonization flourished at one point but failed to gain momentum or reach a conclusion) does not necessarily detract from the value of his ideas. Rather, as a proponent of an "everyday" type of political engagement for everyday people, Suárez appears to be the type of person who is right there with us, working things out, flawed and failing like the rest of us.

Suárez's own life created the occasion for him to consider many of the questions that are significant for discussions of political theology today. Some current approaches taken regarding lawmaking authority demonstrate that the contemporary discourse could benefit from the retrieval of Suárez's theory of theological jurisprudence. Suárez's understanding of the possession and use of political power for the development of law offers political, communal, and ecclesial insights for the actions of Christians in the world today, just as it informed the missionary activity of the Jesuit martyrs. An examination of his theory of political power can help explain the role of the people in the development of law from below and provide an alternative mode of political and legal engagement by which Christians and other people of goodwill may act in the world to promote justice and the common good. This approach takes seriously both the actions of the people in creating and shaping law and the role of law in promoting the common good holding together natural and cultural ethical discernment with the unique witness of the Church. An understanding of the role of the people in both the reception of and the formation of law provides an underexplored alternative means for engaging with various contemporary political theologies.

Law and Political Theology Today

The perception of law as only imposed from the top down has informed much of the twentieth- and twenty-first-century understanding of law within political theology, even among those who reject William Barr's explicit and approving retrieval of divine right. Barr's absolutist view of executive authority was reintroduced into contemporary discourse through engagement with the work of Carl Schmitt. In 1930s Germany, Schmitt attempted to address the perceived weakness of democracy by drawing on the theories of Thomas Hobbes and denying early modern political theorists such as Robert Bellarmine, in order to reject the claim that power can be granted indirectly to a ruler.[20] Rather, Schmitt argued that a sovereign's power should be understood as absolute and direct, imposed fully from above. Schmitt does acknowledge an exception granted to the rule of law, but such an exception can only be established by the sovereign. The power to suspend other laws and to establish a "state of exception"—when the restraint of laws would no longer apply to a sovereign's sheer will—is one of the key markers of the sovereign's identity.[21]

In his essay considering whether or not Americans have a "right to break the law," legal philosopher Ronald Dworkin argues that such a theory of law has pervaded much of the discourse regarding law even among those who would consciously reject the authoritarian Hobbesian and Schmittian strains. Dworkin also clearly identifies the limited responses that will arise from the view that law can only be imposed from above. He begins by identifying two general approaches to law: "The conservatives, as I shall call them, seem to disapprove of any act of disobedience; they appear satisfied when such acts are prosecuted, and disappointed when convictions are reversed.

The other group, the liberals, are much more sympathetic to at least some cases of disobedience; they sometimes disapprove of prosecutions and celebrate acquittals."[22] However, upon closer study, Dworkin finds that the two camps are actually united on the same principle that underlies these apparently opposed stances: "In a democracy . . . each citizen has a general moral duty to obey all the laws, even though he would like some of them changed. He owes that duty to his fellow citizens, who obey laws that they do not like, to his benefit. But this general duty cannot be an absolute duty, because even a society that is in principle just may produce unjust laws and policies, and a man has duties other than his duties to the state."[23]

Though Dworkin acknowledges that differences in "tone" exist among citizens who occupy different political stances, he nevertheless claims that the underlying principle is still the same. In fact, such differences in tone often mask a greater similarity of action. For example, as he claims, "It is not just conservatives who argue that those who break the law [even] out of moral conviction should be prosecuted. The liberal is notoriously opposed to allowing racist school officials to go slow on segregation, even though he acknowledges that those school officials think they have a moral right to do what the law forbids."[24] Both sides, according to Dworkin, are working from a basic presupposition that law is imposed by rulers and that the only two options available to the citizen are either obedience or disobedience. This limitation of possibilities for response often results in a stark and absolutist approach to law and leaves no room for generosity, compromise, or openness to the possible value of a different position: in short, all the virtues that make civic and civil discourse possible. Engagement with law becomes a binary choice: law is either completely valid or has no validity whatsoever, and therefore is either absolutely binding or absolutely not. This binary view also implies that citizens who disagree with a certain law are presented with only two options for response: either with protest and civil disobedience or claiming that the law with which they agree has ultimate authority. Neither response leaves room for considering that the law might be partially correct, might advance valid interests but not be correct in all respects or all contexts, or might be better refined without being overturned. Thus reception and interpretation are also key tools for understanding a law's meaning.

Looking beyond theory, sociological factors have also contributed to the popularity of this view of law. Expansive claims of executive legal authority to act lawfully, even when contradicting established law, have arisen in a political discourse that is driven by fear of terror and uncertainty and have exacerbated impulses toward autocracy and the understanding of law as only what is imposed by the sovereign from the top down. Giorgio Agamben builds upon his analysis of Schmitt's theory of the state of exception to argue that throughout the twentieth and twenty-first centuries, in the United States more and more power has been placed in the hands of the executive branch as a result of the New Deal, World War II, and the War on Terror.[25] Agamben argues that in the face of fear and insecurity, this state of exception—giving the ruler the freedom to act outside the law—has become the norm.

John Milbank presents a similar argument. For Milbank, liberal democracy always has the potential to slide into despotism. Emphasis upon majority opinion alone, rather than on a commitment to some extrinsic truth, leads government open to manipulation through popular opinion, especially through fear. "Thus increasingly, a specifically liberal politics ... revolves around a supposed guarding against alien elements: the terrorist, the refugee, the person of another race, the foreigner, the criminal. Populism seems more and more to be an inevitable drift of unqualified liberal democracy. A purported defense of the latter is itself deployed to justify the suspending of democratic decision-making and civil liberties."[26]

Robin Lovin expresses similar concerns about the decline of democracy in the face of terror, noting that the emphasis on terror and policing have shrunk the topics of discussion allowed in the public square and thus also have shrunk the possibilities of the terms of democratic decision-making: "If security and stability are the criteria of public reason, then who we want to be is our own private concern. We are free to aspire to whatever we wish, but we should not expect that to make a difference in the public discussion."[27] This limitation of public discourse solidifies the shift to the view of law as command, rather than as consensus produced by public deliberation and dialogical engagement. The conviction that protection from potential terrorist threats provides a justification for autocratic violations or rejections of international law and established due process became apparent in the justifications made both by the Trump and Obama administrations in their respective targeted assassinations of the Iranian general Qassem Soleimani and American citizen Anwar al-Awlaki.

Alongside the rising fear stemming from the War on Terror, sociologists have tracked a decline of trust in and respect for institutions. A vast body of sociological literature, including most notably Robert Bellah's *Habits of the Heart* and Robert Putnam's *Bowling Alone*, have tracked the drift away from a sense of allegiance to and connection with the institutions that once formed the framework of American public life.[28] The 2020 Edelmen Trust Barometer report shows a continuing lack of trust in institutions across the globe.[29] Public trust in the American legal system, one of the institutions evaluated, has suffered this same apparent decline.[30] Furthermore, along with this sociological development, academic studies and political changes have revealed the legal system's failures to adequately protect the rights of the poor and ethnic minorities, making it much more difficult to believe claims that the law and legal system are governed by an independent standard of justice rather than simply serving as the vehicle to convey the commands of the party in power.[31] This is especially true at the national level, where decisions from the US Supreme Court are viewed as increasingly partisan. In an important caveat, however, studies show that public confidence and trust in state court systems has improved over the last five years, likely because state courts are viewed as more responsive and more fair to the local communities over which they preside.[32] People who experience this loss of trust are especially prone to seeking out some type of powerful savior figure whom they believe will bring change and improvement from above, instead of believing that change and justice can be achieved by working through existing institutions such as the legal system. However, the popular perception of state and local courts being fairer to the communities they serve indicates at least some sense that smaller communities might still be able to engage with some parts of the legal system to make laws more just and able to advance the common good.

While numerous political theologians have successfully jettisoned many of the pernicious elements of complete sovereign authority and helpfully have critiqued the overbroad assumptions of certain aspects of political liberalism, they also have failed to provide a vision of how Christians can work to improve the legal system from within. Rather, they remain dependent upon the view of law as imposed from above alone and therefore something to be resisted from without rather than transformed from below.

Approaches to Law in Contemporary Political Theology

Broadly speaking, while contemporary political theologians may differ radically in their approaches, politics, and understanding of legal justice, they generally are united when they consider the formation of law. Specifically, they share the assumption that civil law exists only as it is imposed by the sovereign from the top down. This does not mean that law is considered automatically good or authoritative. The Augustinian claim that an "unjust law is no law" perdures through all flavors of Christian political theology. However, the general focus has remained on questions of the law's validity and the replacement of unjust laws using political processes outside the legal system itself, rather than on developing the idea of what constitutes "just lawmaking." This approach relegates citizen engagement with law itself to a second- or third-order question and leads to a large-scale neglect of discussion of the Christian's engagement with law in much of contemporary political theology.[33] In other words, law is often assumed to lack its own intrinsic validity and purpose and is viewed merely as an instrument used to enforce the will of the authority, not as an authority in itself. While at times the only possible response to unjust laws may be civil disobedience, given the corruption of our political and legal system and the aggregation of lawmaking authority to an unchecked executive, it is even more important for Christians to recover as many strategies as possible that permit constructive engagement with the law and provide ways to challenge politically imposed injustice and work to oppose autocratic and authoritarian government.

In order to better outline the contours of this lacuna, three different schools of contemporary political theology are considered here, and Suárez's theological jurisprudence can add to each. As an "Augustinian Thomist," Suárez's thinking can contribute to and supplement developments within both the Augustinian discourse in political theology and the Thomist concept of nature, virtue, and law from below.[34] Specifically, Suárez's insights related to the connection to law from below and the role of the virtuous citizen in shaping that law, developed from Thomistic thought, can enrich contemporary Augustinian political theology's concerns about abuses of authority and the role of the virtuous citizen who is bound to the commonwealth by "common objects of love."

Suárez's Ignatian concept of the engagement of the Church with the world also provides a helpful correction to the approach of the so-called ecclesial theologians. Since the Ignatian view of the relationship between the Church and the culture does not share Karl Barth's concerns with the Church's sublimation into the world, it does provide a path forward for the Church to engage the world without the fear of ecclesial identity being lost. Specifically, Suárez's view of the formation of law through political action from below provides a mode of Christian engagement in the political sphere that preserves the unique role of the Christian community and centers ethics within it, without abandoning the political.

A retrieval of Suárez can also move past some of the limitations that mark classical liberalism, specifically as articulated in the thought of John Locke, the progenitor of classical liberalism. Unlike the other schools under consideration here, Suárez and Locke are genealogically connected through the work of the "judicious" Richard Hooker. However, as has been fairly extensively explored in critiques of classical liberalism, the focus on the social contract and the rights of the individual can often lead to a neglect of any understanding of the common good and a view of justice that is only procedural rather than substantive. Yet the retrieval of Suárez's thought has the potential to supplement Locke's thought in a way that might provide significant potential for an enhancement of classical liberal thought.

The Augustinian Approach

Saint Augustine's political theology has proved an especially fertile source of reflection in political theology throughout the twentieth and twenty-first centuries. Many contemporary theologians have found Augustine's insights into the limits of power and sovereignty, the danger of power's corruption, and the redeeming power of love when confronting the political problems of modernity. As Eric Gregory has traced in his analysis of Augustinianism, the result of Augustine's rejection of the Eusebian correlation between the empire of Constantine and the empire of God leads to a rejection "of earthly political communities as a vehicle of salvation."[35] This rejection does not require a corresponding rejection of the earthly polis, but rather offers a dialectical approach in which "Christians [are] to be pilgrims on the earth, resident aliens, leaving this world's political struggles opaque to the kingdom of charity—yet, and this is an important yet, always trying to discern (the often surprising) Christ-like events of humanization in the world. The contingent fortunes or misfortunes of any particular historical political community [are] no longer tied immediately to the economy of salvation."[36] Gregory identifies a number of different "types" that share in this tradition. For the purposes needed here, two related but distinct approaches and some paradigmatic representatives are considered. This very brief analysis highlights both the insights gained from each tradition and the limitations imposed by the fact that any retrieval of Augustine is necessarily somewhat limited by Augustine's own concerns and preoccupations. Augustine, writing in the time of the Roman Empire, did not focus on the role of Christians as individual citizens so questions of citizens' roles in the formation of law are not a priority in his thought nor generally ones that should be engaged in a retrieval of his approach.

Christian Realism

The first type, Christian realism, is distinguished by its rejection of all forms of political idealism, which seek to conflate the eschatological reality of the Kingdom of God with the realities of political life in the fallen world in which we now live. This realism is the acknowledgment of the reality of sin in the world and its penetration of every earthly institution and the heart of every individual.[37] Because we can never escape sin in our social lives and within ourselves, all of our endeavors to enact the good are corruptible. Thus, each action carries the seeds of its destruction and involves, at best, some form of moral compromise. Reinhold Niebuhr, one of the most prominent proponents of Christian realism, describes Augustine's insight regarding the failure of human political endeavors. The earthly city is "bound to destroy itself since its principle of 'self-love in contempt of god' prompted it to rebellion against God. . . . The very weakness of the earthly city is man's self-worship. . . . Augustine saw the tragic aspect of human history very clearly. With the prophets he regarded human pride as the root of human injustice."[38] Because of this omnipresence of sin, the possible is always permeated by the tragic.

The Christian realist's limited view of political power does not preclude the awareness that political power may be utilized to some good ends. Most importantly, political power correctly deployed protects the community by placing a check on the sinful impulses of the citizens. However, attempts to use this power as a remedy for sin are always morally fraught and flawed. Even at its best, "political power . . . rests upon the ability to use and manipulate other forms of social power for the particular purpose of organizing and dominating the community."[39] Political power is not oriented in and of itself to the supernatural good of the individual (although individuals engaged in politics may orient their own actions, which are not morally neutral because they occur in the political sphere, toward supernatural.)[40]

The goal of political power is not the achievement of civic love but rather the achievement of some form of procedural justice, or "the equilibrium between competing forces that allows that peace to become relatively stable and durable."[41] In Niebuhr's terms, stability is found in an "equilibrium of power and vitalities so that weakness does not invite enslavement by the strong." This creates "an approximation of brotherhood within the limits of conditions imposed by human selfishness."[42] This equilibrium is only an approximation because stability also always creates the possibilities of conflict, even when preserving justice by "preventing[ing] domination and enslavement." In order to control this tension, there must be a center that can "arbitrate conflicts from a more impartial perspective than is available . . . it must coerce submission to the social process by superior power."[43]

The Christian realist does not deny that in some sense government is of "divine ordinance," insofar as it expresses majesty that "embodies and expresses both the authority and power of the total community over all its members, and the principles of order and justice as such against the peril of anarchy."[44] However, in relation to the procedural functioning of the government, or anything that steps beyond its basic protective function, the Christian realist does not necessarily acknowledge any natural good in government. Rather, the exercise of political power is just the best way to maintain limited stability and order. Government is only "a principle of order and its power prevents anarchy but its power is not identical with divine power."[45] Augustine "sees the social life of man as constantly threatened either by conflict between contending forces, held in an uneasy equilibrium, or by the tyranny of the dominant power."[46] The Christian realist therefore acknowledges the tentative balance of the contending powers in the political world and the inevitability of tragedy, yet strives for limited justice as the most practicable solution that can be achieved this side of the eschaton.

Civic Augustinianism

We turn now to the second type, democratic or civic Augustinianism. In many contemporary Augustinian retrievals, the democratic process has stood as the most important tool available for mediating the dangers of untrammeled sovereign authority. Although indebted to Niebuhr, more recent Augustinian thinkers have moved toward a more positive reading of potential use of civic power and life in civil society. Specifically, much of this discourse has focused on retrieving a concept of civic love as a way by which citizens can mitigate the impact of totalizing political power.

Jean Bethke Elshtain, for example, recovers the importance of the domestic sphere, the domus of Augustine's politics. She traces how, in the domestic sphere, Augustine finds the roots of political order based on shared loves: "A righteous domestic order is a *civitas* in miniature ruled by love, compassion, and authority in the person of Christian parents. It offers membership in the society of the faithful during their sojourn on this earth, or one form of membership, at any rate. The church is another body of friends."[47] This emphasis on the household and the Church as the paradigm for civic power provides a counterbalance to the view that all political power is necessarily completely tied to dominion. Augustine reminds us there are other forms of power: forms that are generative, not controlling—and that are exemplified most fully in "God's power to generate a world that he then so loved 'he gave his only begotten Son' to save a fitful and frail humanity."[48]

However, Elshtain retains the concerns of the realist, acknowledging the potential abuse of power in every sphere. The difference between the domus and the polis is not a difference of absolute kind, but rather a difference of quantity of power: "The temptations of arbitrary power and excess grow greater the greater the power there is to be had.... Absolute mastery, or the urgency to acquire it, severs human beings from one another, often violently."[49] Power in the earthly city is always "marked" or "stained" by sin, but this does not mean it inevitably leads to domination or requires a necessary rejection of the common good. But it does require an acknowledgement of earthly limitations: "This peace is attained fitfully in the *altera civiatas* in its earthly pilgrimage; haphazardly, at best, in all earthly cities; and in its full richness only in the city of God when the time of pressing for the human race in temporality comes to an end."[50] Elshtain's focus on the domus's role in the polis also opens up new horizons as to what types of actions can contribute to the good of broader society. "Just as the household is a component part that contributes to the completeness of the whole, so our work in small ways and about small things, contributes to the overall harshness or decency of any social order."[51] Though Elshtain does not explicate exactly how this shift affects the law, it is clear that she envisions a connection between the lived reality of the communal pursuit of the good within households, affecting to some degree the lived reality in the political sphere and not simply the opposite top-down effect of the political upon the personal.

Oliver O'Donovan adheres to the Christian realist's concern with the misuse of authority when he diagnoses the malaise of late-modern political thought as springing out of the early modern placement of all authority into the hands of the representative government, a setting of "positively legislated rationality" against "a desire for freedom to assert right[s] prior to and equal to the unequal constitution of men."[52] However, O'Donovan also shares the civic Augustinian's emphasis on virtue when he proposes a return to the understanding of the importance of the role of judgment on the part of the civil lawmaker.[53] It is worth noting that O'Donovan's view of the legislator still contains much more emphasis on the top-down nature of the ruler's authority.[54] He argues that the only possible response to this "positively legislated rationality" is to place opposite and equal power in the hand of the courts in order to check the legislator. This response has also proved inadequate, since "neither we nor our courts have proved capable of forming a clear idea of what it is to recognize a claim of natural right without erecting the courts as counter-legislature, an equal and opposite imitation, and so precipitating the crisis over sovereignty."[55]

Bringing together two Augustinian themes, then, O'Donovan's description of the capacity of judgment is tied into the community's capacity to be joined by shared objects of love. O'Donovan has focused on how the identification of objects of love can create "organized community.... By sharing a common view of the good, we become a 'multitude' no longer but a 'people,' capable of common action, susceptible to common suffering."[56] Despite our deep disagreements about the use of power, the existence and identification of these common objects of love "'generate common self-understanding.'"[57] O'Donovan specifically identifies the person of the elected representative as a concrete sign of the reality of our common objects of love, "a love that would without a concrete object, be too diffuse to sustain.... Here a society envisages its capacity to act together as a whole through the actions of one person."[58] Although recognizing the limitations of the representative and all those exercising judgment, O'Donovan arguably also sees a possibility for hopeful communal engagement and promotion of the common good in a citizen's engagement with law.

Turning to a final example, Eric Gregory emphasizes the importance of the earthly city for Augustine as "one forum where [the citizen] develops his love of God and neighbor."[59] Rather than seeing the *saeculum* as the forum within which the concerns of the Church are absent, Gregory argues that Augustine understood the saeculum as the place in which Christians are able to develop the virtues appropriate to citizens. He places this claim within the context of Augustine's concern with "responding to the allegations that Christ's teaching and preaching must be incompatible with the ethics of citizenship" (Ep. 136, 29).[60] Gregory translates this Augustinian concern into the need to address the contemporary challenges of ensuring that the "ethics of citizenship today [contain] renewed invocation of the social role of citizens in its relevant moral dimension."[61] This virtue-oriented approach is grounded in the Christian realist approach, in that the Augustinian virtue ethicist eschews "grand solutions." However, going beyond the Christian realists, the virtue ethicist has hope that love can translate into good actions in the present age, rather than being simply deferred to the eschaton.[62]

To achieve this potential transformation by love, Gregory argues that "Augustinians should stand with Thomists in holding that right dispositions are necessary for moral discernment ... and cultivating the desire to do justice in this world."[63] In addition, drawing on Augustine's description of the saeculum as a place where both the City of God and the City of Man can work together to achieve some limited goods, the virtue ethicist does not believe that virtues that are developed in the public *ethic* of the pilgrim citizen contain only a supernatural orientation and are intended simply for use in the realm of the earthly city. Rather, because the Christian citizen is always a pilgrim, *en via* to the heavenly kingdom, all the goods gathered along the road are useful for transforming the pilgrim in a manner appropriate to her ultimate orientation. The dispositions cultivated serve both the earthly city and the heavenly goal. As Gregory writes, "This account resists both pure constructivism and Thomist theologies which can defend natural goods apart from the context of their use. This view lies at the heart of Augustine's account of the two loves that form two cities. Love is not simply determinant of an individual's life. It is the key to understanding world history itself."[64] For Gregory, one of the exemplars of this approach, which he describes elsewhere as Augustinian Thomism, is Martin Luther King Jr. For example, in his "Letter from Birmingham Jail," King describes how the power of love, as expressed in nonviolent protest, can transform civil society. He takes to task white moderate ministers of the gospel because their failure to exemplify self-sacrificial love in the public square has demonstrated a failure of personal disposition to a love modeled on the love of Jesus Christ.[65]

Augustine and the Saeculum

Alongside these Augustinian concerns with power, in the saeculum there runs another strand of analysis related to the relationship between church and state. Robert A. Markus provides one of the classical definitions, arguing that Augustine's saeculum constitutes the "intermediate place in which was situated the *res publica*.... This was the *saeculum*—not a third City between the earthly and the heavenly, but their mixed, 'inextricably intertwined' state in this temporal life."[66] This area, Markus argues, becomes a morally neutral place that exerts equal claims upon both the pagan and the Christian and cannot be divinized by either. The saeculum therefore possesses its own autonomy—belonging to neither the sacred nor the demonic.[67] This neutral sphere creates space for people to make use of the same goods, although for radically different ultimate ends.[68] The justice achieved in this sphere will always be limited, since it is not, of itself, based on true piety. However, this does not mean that an imperfect justice is not possible to a limited degree.

This reading of Augustine's interpretation of the saeculum as a place that cannot be transformed by grace is not accepted without demur. For example, Rowan Williams has argued, contra Markus, that one could also read Augustine's work in Book XIX of *City of God*—when taken in dialogue with his proceeding works—not as a repudiation of the public realm or an atomistic view but rather an argument for the "redefinition of the public itself, designed to show that it is life outside the Christian community, which fails to be truly public, authentically political."[69] In Williams's reading, the contrast is not between "public and private, church and world," but rather between "political virtue and political vice." In many ways these ecclesial theologians are seeking to provide counternarratives to the thesis of both Williams and Markus in their description of the saeculum. We will return repeatedly to this inquiry into the ultimate uses and ends of the saeculum, especially as they relate to the question of how Christians should understand and engage with civil law.

Suárez as Augustinian Thomist

Suárez shares many of the concerns of the Augustinian tradition. In fact, as one of the prominent Augustinian scholars of his day, Suárez drew upon Augustine to inform much of his political theology. He shares a concern about the dangers of pride and the effects of power upon the ruler as well as the Augustinian concept of the importance of the household and then the local community as the bedrock of the civic order. Like Augustine he considers the ends of the earthly commonwealth not to be directly the instantiation of the Kingdom of God, but rather the development of civic virtue, peace, justice, and the common good, which can be achieved under the limiting sinful conditions of this world and may point eventually to the redemption of all the world.

Faced with the rise of authoritarian political power, Suárez shares some of the realists' anxiety and concern about the misuse of power when it is held by the ruler without limits. Suárez, unlike his scholastic predecessors and even earlier scholars at Salamanca, was confronted with a new reality of totalizing and secularized state power, which increased across his lifetime. Theory and practice of absolutist beliefs were not all uniform but, as J. P. Sommerville writes, they did share one common conviction: "They did all look to the prince as the supreme maker and interpreter of human laws (at least in temporal matters), and they held that the prince could not be deposed by the church or by his subjects."[70] Along with an acceptance of this theory was a conviction that without a strong sovereign, a state or community could not survive. In 1621 Englishman Robert Bolton would write, "Take Soveraignty from the face of the earth . . . and you turne it into a Cockpit. Men would become cut-throats and Canibals one unto another. . . . We should have a very hell upon earth, and the face of it covered with blood, as it was once with water."[71] To prevent catastrophe, an absolute ruler was categorically necessary to enable people to achieve the civic goods of peace and stability; any limitations, whether from Church or people, impede the ruler's abilities to achieve these ends.[72] These theories became reality across Europe as traditional government branches that gave voice to the people (or at least to the aristocracy) lost their influence or ceased to convene at all.[73] Suárez was constantly challenged to answer the practical and theoretical impact of the political changes of his time. His theory of law was required to challenge the departure from the traditional Christian understanding of political rule developed from Augustine on through the Middle Ages. However, in order to avoid vanquishing into utopian thinking, it also needed to take seriously the new realities of increased monarchical power. The reality of this power was not simply theoretical for Suárez but also personal. Alongside the threats to his life caused by book burnings, he also experienced personal loss when Jesuit students who had returned to England as missionaries were swept up in the purges following the failed Gunpowder Plot.[74]

In addition, like many contemporary Augustinians, Suárez has a high view of the importance of formation and an orientation toward love of the citizen. Suárez argues for a natural view of political power and a greater potential to orientation to the good—both natural and supernatural. Suárez asks many of the questions and shares the concerns of the Augustinians vis-à-vis totalizing power from above needing to be restrained and seeking solutions in the life of the community. He answers these with resources drawn from the Thomist tradition.

This is not surprising, given that all of Suárez's moral, legal, and political commentaries are treatises expounding on the *Summa Theologiae* of Thomas Aquinas. Whereas Augustinians consider political power as a limited remedy for sin, Thomists tend to have a more positive read on the potentiality of political power. Specifically, they argue for the naturalness of political power, its ability to promote the common good, and even, in some iterations, the sacramental nature of the body politic itself.

For example, Jacques Maritain, in his retrieval of Aquinas, explicitly writes that "the common good of the body politic demands a network of authority and power in political society, and therefore a special agency endowed with uppermost power, for the sake of justice and law. The State is that uppermost agency. But the state is neither a whole nor a subject of right, or a person. . . . This supreme authority is received by the State *from the body politic*. . . . God alone is sovereign."[75] In addition, the Thomistic focus also views political power as entrusted by God's plan for the people. While this does not present democracy as the only acceptable political structure, it does identify the people as those who are entrusted with power by God. The state is conditionally entrusted with this power in order to promote justice and the common good, "to defend and protect the people, their rights, and the improvement of their lives against the selfishness and particularism of privileged groups and classes."[76] Importantly, there is a real, although limited, vision of what the state might achieve, and it is not necessarily tainted by tragedy.

Laws in the Thomist tradition are not only therefore a source of restraint upon sinner but in fact a positive tool to promote justice and the common good. The ruler's lawmaking authority is limited. Since he or she rules according to God's power and, having received in trust the use of this power from the people, rulers are first limited by the natural law. In addition, the granting of power that gives laws their authority is always conditional on laws that actually advance the common good. Rulers are given authority only vicariously—and with limits: "They really hold a right to command and to be obeyed. . . . They are accountable to the people [and] their management has to be supervised and controlled. . . . united with the people in their very essence of deputies for them."[77] With this entrustment to the people comes a great responsibility and duty of the people: to be formed in virtue in order to properly exercise and respond to the civic need. Maritain argues that "to rule in communion with the people means on one hand educating and awakening the people in the very process of governing them."[78] Laws in the Thomist tradition not only restrain evil; they form the people for virtue, making them more capable of following the law.

Because some power remains with the people, there is also a continuing awareness that reception of laws is equally as important as their promulgation. John Finnis writes: "Government (governing, governance) by law means, equally concretely, that these practical propositions conceived in the minds of those responsible for ruling must be assented to by the ruled and adopted into their own minds as reasons for action. . . . The subjects of the law share (willingly or unwillingly) in at least the conclusion of the ruler's practical thinking and in the plan which the rulers propose . . . as a plan for promoting and/or protecting the common good."[79] Therefore, in a Thomistic reading of political theology, the people too have a sort of active participation in the law-making task that goes beyond representation. Finnis describes this type of communal lawmaking responsibility as being "in some respects a joint enterprise, a kind of co-ordination of the acts of the governed amongst themselves by co-ordination of each with the directives given by their rulers."[80]

This communal discourse around law contributes to the nature of the common good that the law might attain. The common good is understood as "a complex good attainable only if the state's rulers, its families, and its individual citizens all perform their proper, specialized, and stratified roles and responsibility."[81] True, responsibility for defining and protecting the common good is not just the government's, since there are certain things beyond the government's potential to legislate. But it is necessary for the government to seek to promote the common good through wise and just laws for all the other potential aspects of the common good to be obtained.

In *Law's Virtues*, Cathleen Kaveny critiques the negative views of law she describes as predominating in certain strands of legal theory and much contemporary engagement with law. Her primary concern is with the view of law as "police officer" rather than "pedagogue of virtue."[82] Under this view, law's only civic function is to serve as a coercive enforcement of certain minimal moral standards necessary to keep people from harm. Freedom must be prized above all else, and laws are only necessary to make as much of that freedom as is possible for as many people as is possible. However, as Kaveny points out, this view makes what she terms "forward-looking autonomy" the only good that law can achieve and fails to see the importance of our embeddedness in communities and social structures as goods of human nature alongside autonomy. Retrieving Aquinas's notion of law as teacher, by contrast, presents a view of law that promotes human flourishing within relational communities and prevents both harm and needless restrictions on individual autonomy. This goal of law is not simply to remedy single acts of injustice, but to promote flourishing among the whole community by contributing to the promotion of the cardinal virtues, thus combining autonomy and solidarity.[83] Through her analysis of how law restores and promotes right relationships, Kaveny considers the role of law in promoting the common good. She provides a convincing rationale for the restoration of the link between morality and law, which legal positivism and the law-as-police-officer approach had sought to sever.

In *Ministers of the Law: A Natural Law Theory of Legal Authority*, Jean Porter also brings the resources of Aquinas's theology of law and his scholastic contemporaries into dialogue with the claims of contemporary legal philosophers. Porter is concerned that the law is not viewed as an instrumental good, but rather "is itself a constitutive element of the common good, an integral component of the flourishing of any community, and correlatively, one of the greatest goods that men and women can share."[84] As the work's title indicates, Porter's primary focus is to describe civil law's authority and grounding in natural law. Her primary focus is the relationship between the sovereign state and the law. However, drawing upon Aquinas and Gratian, Porter insists that the actions of the people, specifically through the development of custom, provide a crucial and mediating link between the natural law and the positive civil law. The people's actions always have the potential to reflexively reform the positive law.[85] Porter's analysis of custom draws upon the thought of Gratian and Aquinas. I highlight her work here to demonstrate the existence of a different tradition running alongside the more dominant narrative of law as imposed only from above in political theology focused only on the role of the rulers. Porter's arguments, many of which deal with increased claims of state authority in response to the War on Terror, highlight the necessity of retrieving an alternative tradition for the present day.

Although not explicitly in the Thomistic tradition, at this point it is worth mentioning Vincent Lloyd's exploration of Black natural law, which also captures an understanding of the possibility of law being shaped from below and shares some thematic similarities to Thomistic thought, and, arguably, at least through Martin Luther King, a genealogical connection to the Thomistic tradition. In *Black Natural Law*, Lloyd draws upon the natural law theology of King and examines the life and thought of four crucial figures who helped develop what Lloyd identifies as the Black natural law tradition leading up to King. Philosophical engagement with natural law was crucial for challenging a system that was so corrupt that change from the outside was the only possible option. However, according to Lloyd, Black natural law lost its power and culture coherence when the legal system was changed just enough to change the lived experiences of Blacks in white culture from "de jure segregation into de facto segregation."[86] This shift, Lloyd argues, has weakened the power of Black natural law to provide crucial "forms of cultural criticism rooted in the black religious tradition." While the Black natural law tradition by necessity operated as critique from outside the legal system imposed from above, Lloyd argues that its power arose from the community "in black living rooms, kitchens, barber shops, and beauty parlors."[87] In this awareness of the possibility of law arising from within the community, he draws close to the awareness of law germinated from below than any of the authors mentioned here, although he does not explicitly make this argument. When discussing questions of equity, this approach—nonviolent protest—is especially complementary to Suárez's theory of law from below.

Considering this key element of Thomistic political thought, Suárez's work should be understood as contributing to the developing tradition of Thomistic political theology. However, it is important to understand that his rendition of the Thomistic tradition was shaped both by the development of Spanish Thomism in the School of Salamanca and his own Jesuit formation. Drawing upon this tradition, he expands on the Thomistic tradition and provides an important resource related to an even more robust understanding of the ways in which citizens receive and transform the law, which then can be retrieved to enhance the discourse of Augustinian Thomism today.

Ecclesial Christian Ethics

In contrast to the Augustinian and Thomistic streams of political reflection, contemporary theologians have developed an additional approach derived from the Barthian proclamation of the radicalness of the Incarnation and questioning of the moral valence of the natural. So-called ecclesial theologians argue for a reassertion of the primacy of the Church as a center for ethical reflection. Robin Lovin categorizes two types of theological responses that have developed from this limited view of law in contemporary political theology. Some theologians, such as ones indebted to the Radical Reformation, including John Howard Yoder, Stanley Hauerwas, and Christians involved in the Catholic Worker Movement, believe that "the distinction between the church and the world is drawn so sharply that Christian identity is defined wholly by the church and Christians have no role in the world."[88]

Karl Barth provides a classical description of how this ecclesial centering grows out of a commitment to the primacy of the spiritual knowledge of the Church, over the natural knowledge. In his short essays on political theology, he describes the role of the Church first.

> The church must remain the church. It must remain the inner circle of the kingdom of Christ. The Christian community has a task of which the civil community can never relieve it and which it can never pursue in the forms peculiar to the civil community. It would not redound to the welfare of the civil community if the Christian community were to be absorbed by it and were therefore to neglect the special task which it has received a categorial order to undertake. It proclaims the rule of Jesus Christ and the hope of the Kingdom of God.[89]

The task of the civil community is limited: it exists simply "to provide for the external and provisional delimitation and protection of human life."[90] This does not mean it is outside of God's providential plan, since it is still "based on particular divine ordinance ... [and] belongs to the Kingdom of God."[91] However, the civil community is neither independent nor conflated with the Church. Rather the state should be understood "as an allegory, as a correspondence and an analogue to the Kingdom of God which the Church preaches and believes in." The state exists in a concentric circle around the Church, with information flowing *out* of the inner circle to illumine the state, but nothing flowing back inward from the state, culture, or community to the Church. The state

> forms the outer circle within which the church, with the mystery of its faith and gospel, is the inner circle, [and] since it shares a common center with the church, it is inevitable that, although its presuppositions and its tasks are its own and different, it is nevertheless capable of reflecting indirectly the truth and reality which constitute

the Christian community.... Its justice and even its very existence as a reflected image of the Christian truth and reality cannot be given once and for all and as a matter of course but are, on the contrary, exposed to the utmost danger; it will always be questionable whether and how far it will fulfill its just purpose. To be saved from degeneration and decay it needs to be reminded of the righteousness which is a reflection of Christ's truth.[92]

The role of Christians is to provide a witness analogous to Christ's Incarnation, bringing the gospel out of the Church into the state, which might transform the state into its allegorical form. On its own "the state is ignorant of the mystery of the Kingdom of God, the mystery of its own center, and it is indifferent to the faith and gospel of the Christian community. As a civil community it can only draw from the porous wells of the so-called natural law."[93] The civil community does not have its own integrity nor its own insights that might inform the form or presentation of the Church's teaching. Rather, "it depends on ultimate words and insights existing elsewhere."[94]

Following Barth's view of one-way knowledge flowing from the Church out to the state, a number of theologians have added an emphasis upon the role of the Church as nonviolent witness, growing out of the Anabaptist tradition. Stanley Hauerwas has articulated this approach, drawing upon both Barth and John Howard Yoder, in his Gifford lectures "With the Grain of the Universe." In his book of the same name, Hauerwas describes a focus upon the view that "what God is doing is being done primarily through the framework of society as a whole and not through the Christian community [as] the presumption that lies behind the Constantinian accommodation of the church in the world." His concern remains with what he views as the flawed Christian realist accommodation, which "attempt(s) to make Christianity necessary, to make the church at home in the world, in a manner that witness is no longer required."[95]

While accusations have at times (justly) been leveled at ecclesial political theologians for promoting a sectarian withdrawal from the sphere of the political, this accusation is by no means always true. Perhaps a more accurate reading, especially as the tradition has developed, is that the approach of the ecclesial theologian is characterized by the conviction, following Barth, that "the primary social location for ethical discernment will be the church."[96] As D. Stephen Long has helpfully distinguished, rather than viewing Augustinian and ecclesial theologians as opposed, a more accurate and charitable read is that "the differences between the ecclesial and Augustinian approaches are best understood as differences within a common tradition that inherits

Augustine's two cities and his critiques of the politics of perfection, bringing them into the multiple concerns of late modern political life. The difference between them is the emphasis upon which the two poles of the relationship between the two cities is placed—is ethics an ecclesial or national project? Must we choose between them?"[97]

However, even with a recent and more positive form of ecclesial political theology as a working platform, the importance of law itself seems to disappear. We can see this approach, for example, in William Cavanaugh's *Theopolitical Imagination*, where he helpfully argues for a transformation of the Christian imagination beyond civil politics so that it can expand beyond "a narrow focus on one political form supervised by the state."[98] When Cavanaugh discusses law he does not consider working to change the law to be one of those potential forums for expansion. Rather, he focuses only upon the Hobbesian view of law in which the concept of law is replaced "as something 'made' or legislated by the state rather than 'disclosed' from its divine source through the workings of custom and tradition."[99] Cavanaugh appears to assume that this understanding of law has been foreclosed in modernity and cannot be reclaimed.

Robin Lovin similarly identifies a second important group of political theologians, who are influenced by social theories such as Marxism or critical theory and who argue that the Christian's calling is not withdrawal from the system but rather rejection and unmasking of the system. By "disenchant(ing) the claim of political authority" they seek to demonstrate that "politics is nothing more than the exercise of power in pursuit of self-interest."[100] For both groups, political authority (the primary point of consideration), and thus the authority of the law (considered as a secondary corollary), is reduced to an "instrumental good whose purposes can only be rendered coherent in light of God's saving work, so that self-contained systems of meaning proclaimed by various modern ideologies all become unbelievable."[101] While both Cavanaugh's and the critical theorist's approaches provide useful theological defenses against totalitarian or authoritarian exceptionalist claims of government, they leave no role for "a theological understanding of ordinary, unexceptional democratic politics that would be recognizable to those who participate in that kind of government, and whether this theology provides any encouragement to Christians for that kind of participation."[102]

The critical theorist often uses as a model the activist or resister, who seeks to promote justice within the political system by changing law from the outside. Kyle Lambelet identifies two important variations of this second approach of resistance and activism—the natural law/higher law accounts and the messianic.[103] Lambelet identifies Vincent Lloyd's *Black Natural Law* as an exemplar of the natural law approach and Ted Smith's *Weird John Brown* as representing the messianic approach. In Smith's analysis of Brown's violent raid on Harper's Ferry, he raises important questions regarding how and whether divine violence, such as that promulgated by Brown, can "break the hold of some particular ethical system and then invite but not determine responses that include ethical deliberation."[104] While potentially crucial at times, this inbreaking of violence can nevertheless only occur outside the law. In contrast, the Black natural law tradition, as mentioned previously, has the potential to bridge the work of changing law from the outside but within the system.

While appropriate and powerful in their context, all of these political theologies relegate citizen engagement with law to second- or third-order questions, leading to a large-scale neglect of discussion of Christian engagement with law in and of itself in much of contemporary political theology.[105] Law is assumed to lack an inherent validity and purpose and is viewed merely as an instrument of authority, not as an authority in itself. While at times the only possible response to unjust laws may be civil disobedience, especially given the corruption of our country's political and legal systems and the increasing aggregation of lawmaking authority to an unchecked executive, it is important for Christians to recover as many strategies as possible that permit constructive engagement with the law, provide ways for Christians to challenge politically imposed injustice, and work to oppose autocracy and authoritarian government.

Suárez as a Jesuit Ecclesial Theologian

Francisco Suárez shares many of the ecclesial theologian's concerns about the importance and value of the Church and Christian witness.[106] There are several important similarities between the Jesuit and Barthian approaches. First, like Barth, Jesuit political theology places a high value on "obedience to secular authority."[107] Second, Jesuits also share the view of the relationship between the Church and the world as being concentric circles. The Jesuit fourth vow of obedience to the pope for the purpose of mission demonstrates the centrality of the Church and Jesuit service to the Church to inform the Jesuit charism.[108]

However, as Bergoglio describes in his discussion of the Jesuit martyrs in Paraguay, whereas Barth's concentric circles assume a one-way information flow, the Ignatian concentric circles perceive information flowing both ways. This greater degree of mutuality is also based on a high theology of the Incarnation, which the Jesuits share with Barth. When this understanding of the transformative power of the Incarnation within nature is combined with the strong Jesuit incorporation of Thomistic natural law, a political theology becomes much more receptive to a positive view of the information flow between the spheres, without reducing the priority of the Church and the gospel.

This Ignatian approach is not simply a relic of a possible synergistic relationship between the Church and the state in Christendom. The fourth vow in the *Constitutions* explicitly names the Jesuit commitment to mission among those outside of Europe. In Suárez's corpus he specifically considers political engagement with people outside of Roman Catholic Christendom, specifically in England, the New World, and even among pagans within Christendom. He avoids many of the concerns about the Church being coopted by the world. He is not concerned about what type of government Christians could live under, but rather in advancing robust theological claims about how God's gift of political power works in the world.

In his engagement with Barth, Hans Urs von Balthasar describes the escape from the "dead end" of Barth's rejection of the natural while still being "as radically Christocentric as Barth."[109] He writes that the "Incarnation demands that there be a relatively solid content of meaning that cannot be totally robbed of its substance when we provisionally abstract from our supernatural goal."[110] This approach is possible because "it is not Christ who is in the world but the world is in Christ."[111] This existence in Christ extends even into the realm of the political. Balthasar traces this understanding of "Christ, the ground of creation" through the writings of Suárez himself, who he argues combines the different Thomist and Scotist understandings of the reason for the creation by "stressing the unity of the *de facto* historical world with God's plan for it, which is its very foundation."[112]

This high Ignatian theology of the Incarnation results in a rich incarnational view of the role of the people. It is no accident that almost all the examples of Suárez' legal theory in action to be examined include a defined role for the Church or the Christian community. Given the Church's special awareness of Christ's redemptive actions in the world, the Church is especially well-equipped to address modern political realities and challenges. Pope Francis has specifically described the importance of the Incarnation for carrying out works of justice: "Dear friends, in promoting these values and this way of living—as we know—we often find ourselves going against the grain, yet let us always remember that we are not alone. God has drawn near to us. Not merely in words, but by his very presence: in Jesus, God became incarnate. With Jesus, who became our brother, we recognize in every man a brother, in every woman a sister."[113]

Classical Liberalism

In closing this brief survey, consider one additional approach to political theology, which is perhaps most closely linked to Suárez in content and contemporaneity: the liberalism of John Locke, especially as influenced by the "judicious" Richard Hooker. Locke describes his reliance upon the ideas of Hooker for some of his foundational ideas; Hooker, in turn, developed a reading of Aquinas that, if not directly derived from Suárez, developed contemporaneously along parallel lines.[114]

In his second treatise Locke explicitly grounds his theory on Hooker's claim that humans are naturally ordered to seek communion in "some politick Society."[115] Locke's innovation is to add to the move from the state of nature to membership in this commonwealth an explicit concept of consent. As John Rawls argues, in Locke's consideration of the social contract he sought to "limit the form of a legitimate regime to exclude royal absolutism" and instead pointed to a reality of political sovereignty that can be based on "the consent of free and equal and reasonable and rational persons, starting from the state of nature regarded as a state of equal political jurisdiction, all being, as it were, equally sovereign over themselves."[116]

Locke can be presented as a political theologian because his political theory is not areligious, as some have argued. Rather, his concept of the social contract is based on a view of the natural law as an outside authoritative moral source legislated by God from which can be derived certain natural rights that inform the idea of the social contract. For example, these rights cannot be surrendered absolutely, making the claims of the absolutist monarch invalid. The fiduciary power granted at the time of the social contract is held in trust by the ruler. By the power of the people's consent, it passes—to a limited degree—to the ruler. It can return to the people if the contract is breached by the ruler's tyranny, that is, if the people's rights are violated.

While Locke upholds in strong terms the rights of individuals against the mandates of rulers (even considering rebellion and tyrannicide), his view of the communal good is, in contrast, impoverished in comparison to the Thomistic tradition that he receives. The goal of law, he argues, is limited: to "preserve the members of that Society in their Lives, Liberties, and Possession."[117] Locke fails to present any theory of the good of the community that goes beyond a protection and delineation of the rights of the individual.

Late-twentieth-century political theologians and ethicists have at times articulated an increasing skepticism regarding classical liberal Lockean rights claims. These critiques cover a wide range of concerns, voiced by theologians and philosophers of widely disparate perspectives, including a critique of the rights discourse as an unfortunate product of the Enlightenment's emphasis on reason and the individual. In *After Virtue,* Alasdair MacIntyre famously equates belief in human rights to belief in "witches and unicorns."[118] Like witches and unicorns, theories of rights rely on myths—in this case the illusion of a universally accessible human reason. Hauerwas has presented a more communitarian critique, arguing that the basic presuppositions of rights regulate relationships between strangers—but also fail to recognize the bonds of community and shared common goods that are necessary for any community to thrive.[119] Nigel Biggar, a prominent proponent of just war, has expressed concerns about the limitations and even the viability of a rights language, as well as the possibility for a rights language to be appropriated as a shield for ideological discourse.[120]

Critiques of a rights discourse have also developed out of theological projects of radical critique. For example, liberationist theologians of the 1970s and 1980s challenged the rights discourse. Many, such as Juan Segundo, drew upon Marxist skepticism regarding a rights discourse to challenge the use of rights language by the United States under the Carter administration, which they argued was simply a façade to justify supporting the concerns of the elites under "the logic of imperialism."[121] Drawing upon both communitarian and radical critiques, Serene J. Khader has argued that some Western-centric rights discourses can both drive imperialist motives of rescue and white salvation and ignore the kinship and community networks that are essential for the lives and flourishing of women living in the majority world.[122]

Even with these concerns, Christians should not want to abandon all freedom of individual action and protection of conscience for individuals. The claims of human dignity and freedom inherent in creation, and the responsibility that each individual has to prepare to stand before the judgment of God, remain strong and compelling theological claims. Christian theologians have been articulating a qualified support of rights language for centuries. For example, since the work of Jacques Maritain following World War II, emphasis on rights language has become a staple of Catholic Social Thought.[123] Since then Catholic social teaching has retained a more positive view of the rights discourse. For example, Pope John XXIII, in *Pacem in Terris,* argues that protecting the long list of the rights possessed across a person's lifetime is necessary for upholding human dignity.[124] Rights language has continued to be held as significantly valuable for resisting the state's abuses of power in contemporary philosophical discourse as well, although with different emphasis on the importance of a theological grounding for natural rights.[125]

Suárez's understanding of the formation of law within the political community in order to promote the common good while still protecting freedom of individual action contains key distinctions that seem to have fallen out of this chain of discourse in Locke's work. For Suárez, it is specifically this commitment to the individual that in part justifies the authority of the sovereign, not just the community, in enacting laws. The sovereign, standing above and apart, is able to protect the one or the few from the many, to ensure that individual disagreements or concerns are not lost in the noise and rush of communal action. However, this protection of individual freedom is not opposed to the common good by good law but rather actually advances the common good, since the individual, even the one who does not appear to belong to the communal group, is still a part of the community and must be protected as far as possible. This idea can be developed scripturally out of the call to the Israelites in Leviticus 19: to work for the good of the alien among them, not just the good of themselves, their families, their tribes, or even other Israelites. Rather, God's command is that "The alien who resides with you shall be to you as the citizen among you; you shall love the alien as yourself, for you were aliens in the land of Egypt: I am the LORD your God" (Lev. 19:34).

In the face of the danger of the liberal overemphasis on the individual's freedom to self-determination, some theorists have turned instead to overemphasizing the importance of the common good as the determining factors for law's content. This approach has its own roots in the Christian tradition. Augustine's understanding that the earthly and the heavenly cities hold goods in common, which they must work together to develop and advance, provides an important example of the development of this theological concept. Even in Augustine we can see that the notion of the common good includes material needs but also goes beyond that to include nonmaterial goods such as peace and tranquility, and even some form of direction to civic virtue.[126]

In his analysis of the common good, David Hollenbach traces the intellectual history of this "skepticism about the possibility of theoretical knowledge of the social good." As he writes, "any notion of the common and its good became suspect over the past few decades—and from opposite conceptual angles. On the one hand, movements for the liberation of divergent identities, within their singular contexts, and on the other, the philosophical challenges to any substantive identity, any totalizing oneness, both pressed the question: *whose* common, *whose* good?"[127] Hollenbach argues that the danger that accompanies this disintegration in the belief of a true common good is that if individual interests alone are the standard for measurement, then the only driving force behind claims of social good are ultimately motivated by self-interest.[128] It is this very commitment to self-interest that has been alleged against many of the religious liberty claims that have dominated the political landscape of the United States over the last few decades. Rightly or wrongly, these claims are often perceived to be motivated by the self-interests of the particular claimant, rather than a broad concern to protect religious expression as a matter of the social good. In considering similar situations, Hollenbach diagnoses a potential cultural malaise. "When a loss of confidence in the ability to know the shape of a good society is combined with the modern impulse to control, action becomes a matter of me controlling you on my terms, of us controlling them on our terms . . . this can lead to the reduction of all practical undertakings in society and the polis to matters of power and will. This undercuts the very possibility of an intellectually defensible normative vision of a good society."[129] This is the same danger Robin Lovin diagnoses in his concerns about the limitations of aspirational discourse in the public square.[130]

The danger, as Hollenbach astutely identifies, is that if we are unable to cognitively and socially grasp the social good, then rights talk quickly becomes merely an instrument of power and control. In order to resolve this intellectual difficulty, we need to find a way to avoid saying that all goods are perceived and received in the same way. This concept of the common good should *enable* individual rights or the rights of the minority, not repress them. In Suárez's theory of law—as received and discerned from above rather than simply imposed from above—contemporary readers can find a process of discernment that leaves room for the complexities and cultural contingencies of the common good without surrendering all of the shared elements of the common good, all the while also affirming that there are goods that we pursue in common and that bind us together in pursuit of some form of common goal and in civic unity.

Conclusion

By tracing a brief outline of both the serious concerns and some deficiencies as they have been raised by various other theological schools, we are now prepared to retrieve the theories of law from below as articulated by Suárez. These helpful conceptual tools will allow consideration of some of these deficiencies. Ironically enough, many of the solutions Suárez has provided have actually in other contexts been perceived as part of his own contributions to the problems of modernity. These critiques are further explored in chapter 3. For example, whereas Suárez shares the commitments of the Augustinians to the careful analysis of power imposed from above as possibly abusive, he also has been accused of being a voluntarist. Whereas a healthy integration of the ethics in the public sphere and ecclesial sphere draw upon Jesuit political theology, he has been accused of voiding the public square of all ecclesial content. Many of these same points will be considered but from a different angle, with a focus specifically on how each of the identified angles of Suárezian thought are exemplified in the specific tools of popular action that he identifies as key for citizen engagement with law: custom, equity, and interpretation.

Notes

1. Jorge Mario Bergoglio, SJ, "Proyección cultural y evangelizadora de los mártires rioplatenses," in Jorge Mario Bergoglio, SJ, ed., *Reflexiones en esperanza* (Romana Editorial: Madrid, 2013): 194. For further arguments for the influence of Suárez on Pope Francis, see Thomas R. Rourke, "Pope Francis: The Historical-Theological Roots and Development of His Social Thought," *Journal of Catholic Social Thought* 13, no. 2 (2016): 285–309.
2. Bergoglio, 195–96.
3. The standard and most comprehensive biography of Suárez is Raoul de Scorraille, *François Suárez de la Compagnie de Jesus*, 2 vols. (Paris: Leithielleux, 1911).
4. For a more complete list and chronology of Suárez's corpus of theological writings, see Robert Fastiggi, "Francisco Suárez as Dogmatic Theologian," in *A Companion to Francisco Suárez*, ed. Victor Salas (Leiden, The Netherlands: Brill, 2014), 149–54.
5. Raoul Scorraille, *François Suárez*, 1:156, quoted in Daniel Schwartz, "Introduction," in *Interpreting Suárez: Critical Essays*, ed. Daniel Schwartz (Cambridge, UK: Cambridge University Press, 2012), 2.
6. Schwartz, 3–4; Fastiggi and Salas, "Introduction," in *A Companion to Francisco Suárez*, ed. Victor Salas (Leiden, The Netherlands: Brill, 2014), 4–5, 19–20.
7. Schwartz, "Introduction," 2–4.
8. José Casanova, "The Jesuits through the Prism of Globalization, Globalization through a Jesuit Prism," in *The Jesuits and Globalization: Historical Legacies and Contemporary Challenges*, ed. Thomas Banchoff and José Casanova (Washington, DC: Georgetown University Press, 2016), 263–65.
9. Robert Maryks, *The Jesuit Order as a Synagogue of Jews* (Leiden, The Netherlands: Brill, 2010), 107.
10. For further discussion of the development of the distinct style of Thomistic moral theology oriented to political critique in the School of Salamanca, see David Lantigua, "Aquinas and the Emergence of Moral Theology during the Spanish Renaissance" in *The Oxford Handbook of the Reception of Aquinas* ed. by Matthew Levering and Marcus Plested (Oxford: Oxford University Press, 2021). I have written elsewhere on the relationship between Suárez's work on natural law and the theories of Soto, Vitoria, and Bartolomé de las Casas. See "Natural Law and Cultural Difference: Innovations in Spanish Scholasticism," in *Innovation in Early Modern Catholicism*, ed. Ulrich L. Lehner (London: Routledge, 2021).

11. There is extensive literature examining Suárez's contributions to arguments for religious freedom. For example, see Robert Fastiggi, "Francisco Suárez: Religious Freedom and International Law," in *Francisco Suárez: Jesuits and Complexity of Modernity*, ed. Robert Aleksander Maryks and Juan Antonio Senent de Frutos (Leiden, The Netherlands: Brill, 2019), 113–27; Aaron Pidel, SJ, "Francisco Suárez on Religion and Religous Pluralism," in *Francisco Suárez: Jesuits and the Complexities of Modernity*, ed. Robert Aleksander Maryks and Juan Antonio Senent de Frutos (Leiden, The Netherlands: Brill, 2019) 128–53; and Jerome C. Foss, "Francisco Suárez and the Religious Basis for Toleration," *Perspectives on Political Science* 42, no. 2 (2013): 94–102.
12. I elaborate further about Suárez's theological arguments for women's ability to hold political power, and his departure from Aquinas in this regard, in "Sharers in the Divine Image: Francisco Suárez and the Justification of Female Political Authority," *Political Theology* 19, no. 4 (2018): 331–48.
13. Joseph Henry Fichter, *Man of Spain: Francisco Suárez* (New York: Macmillan, 1940), 282–83.
14. Suárez quote from August 28, 1603, in J. A. de Aldama, SJ, "Un Parecer de Suárez sobre un Estatuto de La Orden Militar de Alcántara," *Archivo Teológico Granadino* 11 (1948): 284–85. In making this argument I am indebted to Elizabeth Terry-Roisin, "Two Types of Nobility: Francisco Suárez's parecer in Support of Morisco Nobleman Don Pedro de Granada Venegas's Application to the Order of Alcántara," presentation at conference "Francisco Suárez: Jesuits and the Conflict of Modernity," Sevilla, Spain, June 1–2, 2018).
15. Aldama, "Un Parecer de Suárez sobre," 278.
16. Maryks, *The Jesuit Order*, 104.
17. Raoul Scorraille, *François Suárez*, 1:307, quoted in Daniel Schwartz, in *Interpreting Suárez: Critical Essays*, ed. Daniel Schwartz (Cambridge, UK: Cambridge University Press, 2012), 5.
18. Maryks, *The Jesuit Order*, 108.
19. Henriette Peters, *Mary Ward: A World in Contemplation* (Leominster, UK: Gracewing, 1994), 156.
20. Michael Hollerich, "Carl Schmitt," in *The Blackwell Companion to Political Theology*, ed. Peter Manley Scott and William T. Cavanaugh (Oxford, UK: Blackwell, 2004), 116.
21. Giorgio Agamben, *State of Exception*, trans. Kevin Attell (Chicago: University of Chicago Press, 2005), 1.
22. Ronald Dworkin, *Taking Rights Seriously* (Cambridge, MA: Harvard University Press, 1978), 186.
23. Dworkin, 187.
24. Dworkin, 187.
25. Agamben, *State of Exception*, 1.
26. John Milbank, *The Future of Love: Essays in Political Theology* (Eugene, OR: Cascade, 2009), 244.
27. Robin Lovin, "Public Reason and the Future of Theological Ethics: Indications from the American Experience," *Studies in Christian Ethics* 25, no. 2 (2012): 138.
28. See Robert N. Bellah et al., *Habits of the Heart: Individualism and Commitment in American Life* (Los Angeles: University of California Press, 2007). See also Robert D. Putnam, *Bowling Alone: The Collapse and Revival of American Community* (New York: Touchstone, 2001).

29. Edelman Trust Barometer 2020, January 19, 2020, accessed at https://www.edelman.com/trustbarometer, 23.
30. See Benjamin H. Barton, "American (Dis)Trust of the Judiciary," Institute for the Advancement of the American Legal System, 2019, https://iaals.du.edu/blog/public-trust-and-confidence-legal-system-way-forward. I am indebted to Charles Matthews for this helpful insight regarding the significance of loss of public trust in law as an institution.
31. See, e.g., William J. Stuntz, *The Collapse of American Criminal Justice* (Cambridge, MA: Belknap Press of Harvard University Press, 2011).
32. National Center for State Courts, "2018 State of the State Courts–Survey Analysis," 2–3, https://www.ncsc.org/2018survey.
33. For a further example of the neglect of this question, see *Eerdmans Reader in Contemporary Political Theology*, *The Cambridge Companion to Political Theology*, or *Brill's Companion to Political Theology*, none of which have a single article discussing law and theology.
34. I am indebted to Eric Gregory and Joseph Clair for the articulation of this concept, and to Eric Gregory for several helpful conversations developing it further. See Eric Gregory and Joseph Clair, "Augustinianisms and Thomisms," in *The Cambridge Companion to Christian Political Theology*, ed. Craig Hovey and Elizabeth Phillips (Cambridge, UK: Cambridge University Press, 2015), 176–95.
35. Eric Gregory, *Politics and the Order of Love* (Chicago: University of Chicago Press, 2008), 78.
36. Gregory, 78.
37. Reinhold Niebuhr, *The Nature and Destiny of Man*, vol. 2 (Louisville, KY: Westminster John Knox, 1996), 245. For a discussion of the development of Christian realism as a reaction to the idealism of the social gospel movement arising after World War I, see Robin Lovin, *Christian Realism and the New Realities* (Cambridge: Cambridge University Press, 2008), 66.
38. Reinhold Niebuhr, *Beyond Tragedy* (New York: Charles Scribner's Sons, 1965), 120.
39. Niebuhr, *The Nature and Destiny of Man*, 263.
40. For a further discussion of the natural/nonnatural divide between Augustinians and Thomists, see Gregory and Clair, "Augustinianisms and Thomisms," 177–79.
41. Lovin, *Christian Realism*, 67.
42. Niebuhr, *The Nature and Destiny of Man*, 265.
43. Niebuhr, 266.
44. Niebuhr, 267.
45. Niebuhr, 269.
46. Niebuhr, 273.
47. Jean Bethke Elshtain, *Augustine and the Limits of Politics* (South Bend, IN: University of Notre Dame Press, 1996), 40.
48. Elshtain, 94.
49. Elshtain, 40.
50. Elshtain, 94.
51. Elshtain, 97.
52. Oliver O'Donovan, "Government as Judgment," in *Bonds of Imperfection*, ed. Oliver O'Donovan and Joan Lockwood O'Donovan (Grand Rapids, MI: William B. Eerdmans, 2004), 213.
53. See, e.g., Oliver O'Donovan, *Ways of Judgment* (Grands Rapids, MI: Eerdmans, 2005).

54. See Charles Mathewes, *A Theology of Public Life* (Cambridge: Cambridge University Press, 2007), 184–87.
55. O'Donovan, 197.
56. Oliver O'Donovan, *Common Objects of Love* (Grand Rapids, MI: Eerdmans, 2002), 21–22.
57. O'Donovan, 20.
58. O'Donovan, 29.
59. Eric Gregory, *Politics and the Order of Love: an Augustinian Ethic of Democratic Citizenship* (Chicago: University of Chicago Press, 2010), 55.
60. Gregory, 59–60.
61. Gregory, 60.
62. Gregory, 95.
63. Gregory, 130.
64. Gregory, 260.
65. Martin Luther King Jr., "Letter from Birmingham City Jail," in *A Testament of Hope*, ed. James M. Washington (New York: Harper One, 1986), 289–302.
66. Robert A. Markus, *Christianity and the Secular* (Notre Dame, IN: University of Notre Dame Press, 2006), 39.
67. Markus, 37.
68. Markus, 45.
69. Rowan Williams, "Politics and the Soul: A Reading of the City of God," *Milltown Studies* 19/20 (1987): 58.
70. J. P. Sommerville, "Absolutism and Revolution in the Seventeenth Century," in *The Cambridge History of Political Thought, 1450–1700*, ed. James H. Burns (Cambridge: Cambridge University Press, 1991), 348.
71. Sommerville, 350–51.
72. Sommerville, 354.
73. Sommerville, 347–48.
74. Suárez explicitly defends the actions of one of these students, Henry Garnet, SJ, in maintaining the seal of the confessional, in the *Defensio* challenging James I's requirement of an oath of supremacy. See Francisco Suárez, *Defensio Fidei Catholicoe* VI, ix.
75. Jacques Maritain, *Man and the State* (Washington, DC: Catholic University of America Press, 1951), 23–24.
76. Maritain, 126.
77. Maritain, 136.
78. Maritain, 137.
79. John Finnis, *Aquinas: Moral, Political and Legal Theory* (Oxford: Oxford University Press, 1998), 256–57.
80. Finnis, 257.
81. Finnis, 238.
82. Cathleen Kaveny, *Law's Virtues: Fostering Autonomy and Solidarity in American Society* (Washington, DC: Georgetown University Press, 2012), 19.
83. Kaveny, 33.
84. Jean Porter, *Ministers of the Law: A Natural Law Theory of Legal Authority* (Grand Rapids, MI: Eerdmans, 2010), 288.
85. Porter, 254–55.
86. Vincent Lloyd, *Black Natural Law* (Oxford: Oxford University Press, 2016), 119.

87. Lloyd, 119, citing bell hooks, *Yearning: Race, Gender and Cultural Politics* (Boston: South End Press, 1990), 4.
88. Robin Lovin, "The Future of Political Theology: From Crisis to Pluralism," in *Political Theology for a Plural Age*, ed. Michael John Kessler (Oxford: Oxford University Press, 2013), 183. For a further discussion of what he refers to as "non-revolutionary Christian anarchy" and its connection with the Catholic Worker Movement, see Craig Hovey, "Liberalism and Democracy," in *The Cambridge Companion to Political Theology*, ed. Craig Hovey and Elizabeth Phillips (Cambridge: Cambridge University Press, 2015), 213–15.
89. Karl Barth, *Community, State, and Church* (Eugene, OR: Wipf and Stock, 2004), 157.
90. Barth, 158.
91. Barth, 169.
92. Barth, 169–70.
93. Barth, 169–70.
94. Barth, 158.
95. Stanley Hauerwas, *With the Grain of the Universe: The Church's Witness and Natural Theology* (Grand Rapids: Brazos Press, 2001), 221–22.
96. D. Stephen Long, *Augustinian and Ecclesial Christian Ethics* (Washington, DC: Lexington Books–Fortress Academic, 2018), 154.
97. Long, 156.
98. William Cavanaugh, *Theopolitical Imagination* (London: T. & T. Clark, 2002), 94.
99. Cavanaugh, 73.
100. Lovin, "The Future of Political Theology," 183.
101. Lovin, 183.
102. Lovin, 184.
103. Kyle Lambelet, "Lovers of God's Law: The Politics of Higher Law and the Ethics of Civil Disobedience," *Political Theology* 19, no. 7 (2018): 601.
104. Ted A. Smith, *Weird John Brown: Divine Violence and the Limit of Ethics* (Stanford, CA: Stanford University Press, 2014), 176.
105. For a further example of the neglect of this question, see *Eerdmans Reader in Contemporary Political Theology; The Cambridge Companion to Political Theology; or Brill's Companion to Political Theology*, none of which have a single article discussing law and theology.
106. Harro Höpfl has argued there is not some unified Jesuit political theology that extends beyond general Thomist concerns. *Jesuit Political Thought: The Society of Jesus and the State, c. 1540–1630* (Ideas in Context Series 70) (Cambridge: Cambridge University Press, 2008). This point is not uncontested. See, e.g., Dominque Bertrand, SJ, *La politique de saint Ignace* (Paris: Cerf, 1985).
107. Höpfl, *Jesuit Political Thought*, 53.
108. *The Constitutions of the Society of Jesus* (St. Louis, MO: The Institute of Jesuit Sources, 1996), 529.
109. Hans Urs von Balthasar, *The Theology of Karl Barth*, trans. by Edward T. Oakes (San Francisco: Ignatius Press, 1992), 362.
110. Von Balthasar, 362.
111. Von Balthasar, 329.
112. Von Balthasar, 327.
113. Pope Francis, "Address of His Holiness Pope Francis to Participants in the International Convention of the Centesimus Annus Pro Pontifice Foundation," October, 23, 2021,

https://www.vatican.va/content/francesco/en/speeches/2021/october/documents/20211023-fondazione-centesimus-annus.html.
114. Alexander S. Rosenthal, *Crown Under Law: Richard Hooker, John Locke and the Ascent of Modern Constitutionalism* (Plymouth, UK: Lexington, 2008), chap. 1.
115. John Locke, *Two Treatises of Government*, ed. Peter Laslett (Cambridge: Cambridge University Press, 2009), 277.
116. John Rawls, *Lectures on the History of Political Philosophy*, ed. Samuel Freeman (Cambridge, MA: Belknap Press, 2008), 107.
117. Locke, *Two Treatises of Government*, 171.
118. Alasdair MacIntyre, *After Virtue* (London: Gerald Duckworth, 1981), 67.
119. Stanley Hauerwas, *Suffering Presence: Theological Reflections on Medicine, the Mentally Handicapped, and the Church* (Notre Dame, IN: University of Notre Dame Press, 1986), 130.
120. Nigel Biggar, *What's Wrong with Rights?* (Oxford: Oxford University Press, 2020). I have addressed Biggar's claims regarding rights in "Are Rights Really So Wrong?," *Anglican Theological Review* 103, no. 4 (Fall 2020): 416–22.
121. Mark Engler, "Towards the 'Rights of the Poor': Human Rights in Liberation Theology," *Journal of Religious Ethics* 28, no. 3 (2000): 343–46.
122. Serene J. Khader, *Decolonizing Universalism: A Transnational Feminist Ethic* (Oxford: Oxford University Press, 2018), 21, 40.
123. David Little, "Law, Religion, and Human Rights: Skeptical Responses in the Early Twenty-First Century," *Journal of Law and Religion* 31, no. 3 (2016): 354–66.
124. Pope John XXIII, *Pacem in Terris* (1963), §11–13.
125. See, e.g., David Little, *Essays on Religion and Human Rights* (Cambridge: Cambridge University Press, 2015), 25–56. See also Nicholas Wolterstorff, *Justice: Rights and Wrongs* (Princeton, NJ: Princeton University Press, 2010): 239–361.
126. Saint Augustine, *City of God*, trans. Marcus Dods (New York: Modern Library, 2000), XIX.17, 696.
127. David Hollenbach, *The Common Good and Christian Ethics* (Cambridge: Cambridge University Press, 2002), 58.
128. Hollenbach, 58.
129. Hollenbach, 58.
130. Robin Lovin, "Public Reason and the Future of Theological Ethics: Indications from the American Experience," *Studies in Christian Ethics* 25, no. 2 (2012), 134–40.

2

Law as Activity

SUÁREZ'S THEORY OF LAW FROM BELOW

The political theology of Francisco Suárez challenges absolutism in its recognition that law is not only a coercive measure imposed from above but also is a communal rule and standard that exists in a constant state of development and constructive dialogue between ruler and citizen. Contrary to the popular perceptions of our own day and of his, Suárez argues that valid law is not necessarily an instrument of domination or merely a tool to restrain sin. Rather, law is the result of a dialogical process of discernment by the community that can constructively advance the common good and promote justice.

This theory of law being developed from the ground up extends to protection of the individual conscience and of the discernment of minority communities without sacrificing a vision of the common good that transcends the particular. Suárez developed his insights regarding law's final end as the advancement of the common good in order to challenge the contemporary legal theories of his day, which are surprisingly similar to our own. An examination of the theological and philosophical groundings for Suárez's understanding that law develops through the dialectical engagement between the ruler and the people, especially the foundational role of the people in mediating God's legislative authority to the ruler, their role in discerning the natural law, and their power as manifested through reception of the ruler's laws, indicate ways in which Suárez's theological jurisprudence might be relevant to our contemporary context.

Suárez's Intellectual Opponents

In his *De Legibus* and *Defensio*, Suárez presents both an abstract theory and actionable practices he believes are capable of challenging the dominant legal discourse and political systems of his day.[1] While these views do not map exactly upon most contemporary understandings of law, they are similar enough to provide an intellectual framing for examining how Suárez's theory of law might be appropriate in our contemporary context.

The first view is represented by Martin Luther who, according to Suárez, holds that just men are "exempt from the yoke of law."[2] Suárez bases this claim upon Luther's famous statements regarding the freedom of the Christian. For example, in one of his sermons, Luther defines Christian liberty as "the just man being free before God of having the duty to obey the law, so that all works are indifferent to him, so to speak, neither commanded nor prohibited."[3] In this category Suárez also includes the long-running heresy of which he believes Luther is a part. This heresy, he argues, claims that Christians, because they have been justified and have no lord but Christ, are therefore not subject to the laws imposed by rulers or courts (that is, civil laws) with which they disagree.[4] The core belief of this heresy, according to Suárez, is the conviction that the freedom that comes from justification by faith in Christ also frees the justified person from the authority of civil and even natural laws.[5] Civil laws must still exist, but their only purpose is to restrain the sinner; Christians have no compelling interest in engaging with laws or working to change or improve them, since the value of civil law is so limited. Suárez argues that this attitude results in both an association of law with sin and a rejection of engagement with civil laws in favor of individual discernment of divine commands.

Suárez is equally concerned about those who claim too much authority for civil laws and executives. He divides this type into two distinct varieties: the first is represented by the divine absolutist, specifically James I; the second is comprised of the secular absolutists, the Machiavellians. Both types identify the authority of the lawmaker as absolute and unbounded: either by the authority of the Church (James I) or by the requirements of morality (Machiavelli). Both types also reject the authority of the people in lawmaking. In addition, the divine absolutist claims that the ruler has the divinely granted authority to proclaim the content of the divine and natural law to the people by making civil law, which then cannot be challenged.[6]

Suárez set himself in opposition to the divine right theorists and their totalizing view of executive lawmaking authority, especially as expressed by King James.[7] In James work of political theology, *The Trew Law of Free Monarchies*, written when he was still only James VI of Scotland, he argues that the ruler can make authoritative laws because he possesses a direct grant of God's divine lawmaking authority. James explicitly contrasts his claims of the sovereignty of a ruler with both "Calvinist anti-monarchical views as well as

Roman Catholic claims of papal supremacy."[8] He worries that both groups attempt to set the divine and natural law against the positive law imposed by the ruler and in doing so disregard what he considers to be the actual definition of law: the imposition of the will of the ruler. According to James, monarchical law's authority is buttressed by divine and natural law. Since God, the creator and king, has given rulers the absolute authority to make laws that carry out His will, any claims of natural law and common law that contradict the ruler's authority cannot be inspired by God and therefore are not true law. When advancing this theory to Parliament in 1610, James grounded it in one of the classic proof texts for absolutist theory, Psalms 82:6, which states that rulers are more than God's lieutenants but are called gods themselves because they share in divine authority.[9] Although the will of the ruler should generally conform to reason, God's special grant of lawmaking authority means that the ruler (just like God) may act at times in ways that seem contrary to reason. Even when the ruler's civil laws appear to contradict reason or the natural law, they are just as valid as God's laws and should be obeyed by his subjects in all circumstances.[10]

One of James's favored court preachers, the Anglican bishop Lancelot Andrewes, provided a more elegant theological articulation of the same view of law. In one of his court sermons preached on November 5, 1610 (the anniversary of the Gunpowder Plot of 1605), Andrewes explicitly associates obedience to Christ as King with obedience to James as ruler. Both are cornerstones upon whom "our future salvation . . . and our present prosperetie depend; upon obedience to Christ and then upon obedience to the King sent in his name, James I."[11] For Andrewes there is no potential conflict of obedience; rather, obedience to one is, by definition, obedience to the other.

In a later sermon Andrewes explicitly associates the absolute ruler with Christ the King because of their common anointing by the Holy Spirit. This anointing, he reminds his hearers, is one which can never be "forfeited . . . drie up or be wiped off."[12] The anointing remains efficacious and authoritative, even if the ruler is a pagan or a heretic. It grants the unconditional right to rule, even if, as Andrewes (perhaps ruefully) acknowledges, the ruler does not possess the gift of governing well.[13] Regardless of the ruler's gift or state of divine grace, Andrewes's text of "Touch not mine Anointed" (I Chronicles 16:22) protects the ruler, his government, and all associated with him from any type of rebellion or resistance on the part of his subjects. The rule of the king, in fact, at least in England, should be perceived as a gift and provision from God intended to endure even to the *eschaton*.[14]

Thomas Hobbes would later articulate this new absolutism in a more secular key. Although not a direct contemporary of Suárez, Hobbes articulates the same problematic approach to absolute power that concerned Suárez with James's political theory. In his political theology in *Leviathan* and *De Cive*, Hobbes is concerned to ground law only in the command of the sovereign, believing that this alone will preserve peace and stability. Being governed by one ruler's will means more to Hobbes than just allowing one person to make the law. Rather, it means that all other wills must be completely subordinated to the ruler's, to the extent that the ruler becomes the animating force behind the deployment of all of the subjects' resources, whether financial or physical. This "over-mind" is necessary to ensure that the strengths and gifts of all persons can be appropriately deployed for the common good.

The empowering of this single will calls not only for the surrender of the subjects' resources; it also demands the surrender of reason. Rather than the individual seeking to evaluate the law, the royal lawmaker alone determines what is good and evil: "Legitimate kings therefore make the things they command just, by commanding them, and those which they forbid, unjust, by forbidding them. But private men, while they assume to themselves the knowledge of good and evil, desire to be even as kings, which cannot be with the safety of the common weale."[15] Adam and Eve fell because they desired to have the knowledge of good and evil themselves, rather than simply acceding to the sovereign's command. The same thing can happen to citizens who critique or evaluate the edicts of the sovereign too much. Thus the law is associated not with the reason of the individual or the trained artificial reason of the common law, but only with the reason of the sovereign. The citizen does not have the ability to determine whether the ruler's will actually reflects God's will in making the laws, since "the measure of Good and Evil actions is the civil law" and not something that can be determined by the individual citizen.[16] For Hobbes the ruler's power is the exact mirror of God's power: total, absolute, and unable to be questioned. The reason it is obligatory is because the ruler's assumption of power protects people from the dangers of unrestrained passion. Obligation under the law is a "renunciation of rights" rather than a protection of rights.[17]

In a similar secular vein, the Machiavellian rejects any claim that law has moral content because this would limit the law's purposes: to conserve the state and promote its aggrandizement. Since there is no moral limit on the ruler's ability to make laws, there are no potential grounds for the people to contribute to or challenge them.[18] As Machiavelli writes in *The Prince*: "Nobody who attends to the laws of virtue or submits to them, can be the true king or secure in his throne."[19] Law, therefore, functions only as an instrument of domination according to both groups.

Although the parallels are not exact, the similarities between these approaches and the contemporary understanding of law described in chapter 1 are striking. Like some contemporary political theologians, Luther failed to see the investment that Christians have in engaging with law to make it more just and more capable of promoting the good of the community. However, James I's royal absolutism and modern turns to governmental autocracy share the assumption that law at best exists to restrain sin and at worst exists as an instrument of domination. Both are skeptical of law's ability to obtain a truly common good that goes beyond individual self-interest.[20] Rather, they always ask, "Whose common, whose good?"[21] David Hollenbach identifies this view of law as domination as contributing to a skepticism about the possibility of any type of institutional or societal contribution to the common good: "When a loss of confidence in the ability to know the shape of a good society is combined with the modern impulse to control, action becomes a matter of me controlling you on my terms, of us controlling them on our terms.... This can lead to the reduction of all practical undertakings in society and the polis to matters of power and will. This undercuts the very possibility of an intellectually defensible normative vision of a good society."[22] In addition, because both accept the assumption that law is only imposed from the top down, they lack a vision as to how it is possible for ordinary people to engage in practices to make law more just from the bottom up.

Suárez's Solution: Law in Augustine's Two Cities

Suárez contrasts these problematic approaches with the Christian understanding of civil law as articulated by Saint Augustine. According to Suárez, Augustine defines law as a necessary connection between the earthly City of Man and the heavenly City of God.[23] This connection does not burden the heavenly city but is actually a crucial gift to the Christian citizen during her time of pilgrimage. Just civil laws that protect peace and advance the common good are necessary for sustaining the mortal lives of the citizens of both the heavenly and earthly cities. Laws can therefore unify all people as they work together to achieve these limited natural goods.[24] Although earthly laws can never institute the full peace of being at rest in the presence of God, such laws are capable of contributing to the peace of the earthly city if they are based, however imperfectly, in divine peace and justice. Without true concord and laws that enact true justice, the earthly city cannot achieve even the natural good. Therefore, the two cities should be understood to be united in seeking common goals for the common good, even though the inhabitants of the heavenly city are always aware that the laws can only instantiate limited and temporal goods that are never sufficient for the fullness of human flourishing.

These limitations do not, however, rob civil laws of their inherent moral significance. Supernatural fulfilment does not abolish the natural order or natural goods, but rather perfects them.[25] Because they contribute to natural goods, the laws of the earthly city do not exist outside of God's control or plan. Rather, God has ordained both the existence of human laws and the rulers necessary to create and administer those laws in order to protect the natural goods of civil peace and justice.[26] Therefore, obedience to legitimate earthly laws that advance justice and peace is not contrary to the redemptive activity of Christ but has the potential to be conformed to it.[27]

Suárez's connection of the natural good of civil laws to the supernatural end of the City of God is not an endorsement of rulers like James I, who claim to hold supernatural lawmaking authority. For rulers to claim the type of spiritual authority that James I does is to exceed their jurisdiction.[28] Even worse is for the ruler to claim that he can make valid laws that are contrary to the natural law. "Neither the law of the emperor or of the king is able to have validity before the law of God, as St. Augustine certainly concludes. Since therefore the natural law is the law of God . . . the civil law is not able to prevail against it."[29] Rulers also do not possess the totality of lawmaking ability. Rather, Suárez's understanding of the common loves that bind together the citizens of the earthly kingdom leads to the demand for room for these same citizens to shape the law that governs them from below, as well as receiving it from above.

In opposing the other theories prevalent at the time, Suárez explains how a rule of law that inevitably curtails freedom can also serve the common good. He demands that laws must be just in every way, while also realizing that not all justice can be achieved through the civil law. His aim is to show how civil laws are essential to achieving the natural good in society but do not constitute the whole of that good, nor are sufficient for grace and salvation. He seeks to ground laws in the nature and power of the subjects, without diminishing the lawmaking authority of the ruler or the importance of the rule of law. He upholds the authority of the laws of the earthly kingdom as instituted by the governing authority, while also maintaining the idea that law's intrinsic requirement of justice cannot silence the voices or remove the power of individuals or the community who have the on-the-ground insight to make laws more just.

Suárez's appropriation of Augustine depends upon several key suppositions about the nature of the human person and how it is deformed by sin.

Suárez follows Augustine in primarily understanding evil as privation. Evil "lacks of what things ought to have ... what things ought to have is dictated by their nature ... such as blindness in man."[30] Sinful acts are those morally evil acts "contrary to the nature of the agent" though they originate in the free will of the agent.[31] Thus we see that sin impedes a person's ability to achieve the perfection of her nature and is willingly chosen. But what is this perfection?

Suárez's theological anthropology became a subject of controversy in the last century, when Henri de Lubac argued that Suárez's understanding of pure nature, as described in *De Gratia*, provided too low of a theological anthropology. He writes that Suárez argues that "by virtue of his creation man is therefore made for an essentially natural beatitude. If we suppose that in fact he is called to some higher end, strictly speaking this could only be superadded."[32] Suárez himself, at least in *De Legibus*, does claim human nature should be understood as "two-fold": one part of pure nature (*puram naturam*) and one part of nature infused by grace (*naturam gratiae desuper homini infusae*).[33] This twofold nature is governed by two different aspects of the natural law: that which directs humans in respect to their nature and that which directs them in respect to their nature when it has been infused by grace.[34] However, Suárez does not, at least in *De Legibus*, present the idea of pure nature as something that can exist on its own or attain a purely natural end. Rather, he argues that no purely natural end has ever existed: "Humans never lacked in any moment the supernatural divine law, without whose assistance they would not have been able to attain the supernatural happiness."[35] Thus, pure nature stands in as a theoretical concept to assist with understanding how humans are formed for happiness, but it is never meant to have any normative significance in assessing human nature—because humans are always in some relationship to God's law and God's grace. As Victor Salas convincingly argues, Suárez's use of the concept of pure nature is not intended to give undue significance to human nature, but rather to illuminate even more the work of grace.

> For Suárez and his Salamancan confreres, while "pure nature" might be merely a theoretical possibility, it retains its own metaphysical structure even if already enveloped within the theological economy of grace. The claim that grace builds on nature without destroying it only highlights and calls attention to the intelligible structures upon which the *additum* of grace supervenes and, in a fallen context, redeems.[36]

Considering de Lubac's concern that Suárez views the end of man as purely natural, Salas provides a further helpful distinction. In line with Suárez's commitment to emphasizing grace as strongly as possible (surely a riposte to the claims of Luther and Calvin that Catholics understand salvation as accomplished by merit), he distinguishes between a natural appetite for the beatific vision and an "obediential potency." If we possess a natural appetite, we also possess a natural potency for the beatific vision, which makes salvation possible apart from grace. Laws and human actions can conduce toward the achievement of the natural perfection but cannot on their own orient us to the supernatural good. On the other hand, humans do possess an "obediential potency" for the beatific vision, which depends on God's grace for activation, not our own works. Our own actions in avoiding sin and pursuing the good can cooperate with grace to achieve the full perfection of our supernatural as well as natural ends.[37] Civil law is intended to orient humans first to achieving natural perfection and then may, with God's grace, contribute to formation for supernatural ends as well.

Law's Final Cause: The Common Good

The first question Suárez must answer to support this theory is to explain law's final cause: Why is law crucial for the preservation of an earthly peace and to advance the common good? Each of the theories he opposes claims the opposite: that law's only purpose is the exercise of top-down dominion—not advancement of the common good. For Luther (as Suárez reads him), law is only capable of restraining sin, not of achieving any positive natural goods. Therefore justified Christians are freed from concern or care for the law's content. For the Machiavellians, law's only purpose is as an instrument of power and control in order to maintain the survival of the state. Divine absolutists fail to see law as having any identity outside the command of the ruler—the law accomplishes nothing, only the ruler.

Law and the Common Good in Scripture

Suárez begins with a theological reading of scripture in order to explore why law should be understood as advancing the common good rather than serving as simply a restraint on sin or an instrument of domination. Because humans are created, we are finite, limited, and dependent. Without outside guidance and support, we can never hope to obtain even "simple necessities." We definitely are incapable of structuring our lives in such a way as to "attain the better state" and realize the full potential of our nature.[38] Because of these limitations, positive law should be understood as one of God's good gifts of creation that enable human flourishing, rather than simply a remedial measure to solve the problem of sin or to preserve the state or status quo. The first example of this use of law to promote flourishing occurs in the Book of Genesis, when God seeks to protect Adam and Eve by giving them one simple law to follow in Paradise: Do not eat the fruit of the tree of knowledge.[39]

Although Suárez acknowledges that human political rule (*principatum humanum*) does not originate with nature, he also argues that human-made positive law could have existed even in a state of innocence.[40] He speculates that if Adam, Eve, and their children had continued to live in Paradise, civil law as well as natural and divine law would eventually have been necessary to enable humans to flourish according to their created, finite nature.[41] While the natural law directs humans to live in community, it does not direct the whole community to act together for the common good. This is because it is inherently "more general and only includes determined self-evident moral principles and only extends, at the most, to those which follow necessarily and evidently."[42] Even in a state of innocence, humans, because of our finitude and dependence on others, require direction to assist each person in looking beyond his or her individual needs to determine the good of the community and provide encouragement and incentive to strive for this good as a primary object. Given these limitations, some form of common direction according to reason would have been needed to help each person "focus on the common good, signaling the line of conduct in order to achieve it and obliging compliance."[43] Suárez insists that this type of encouragement, toward relationships that promote the common good and protect "the temporal morality and utility" required for human coexistence, is not the coercive dominion described by Augustine.[44] Rather, when Augustine states that "dominion of one man over another derives from the occasion created by sin," he is speaking of "dominion which corresponds to slavery and conditions of servitude."[45] This hypothetical prelapsarian legal system would not have sprung from sin or disorder, but rather would have provided further direction to flourishing in a way wholly appropriate to the human condition. Of course, in our fallen condition laws do have an additional important role, both to constrain sin and to maintain order and stability in society. However, this limited acknowledgement of restraint is only a baseline description of what laws can achieve for a community. It is not the description of the totality of their contribution.

Does the claim that laws are necessitated by humanity's created nature, not sinfulness, contradict Saint Paul's statement in Romans 7:23 that the law produces death? This statement was, after all, an important text for the Lutherans.[46] Luther, Suárez believes, reads this text as rejecting all forms of law. Suárez argues that this reading contradicts the general discussion of law in scripture, including texts such as Psalms 18:8, which point to the goodness of God's law and the necessity of God's law to make people good, something that Paul also claims in Romans 7:12. Suárez also claims that Paul's statement that the "law 'produces wrath and death'" does not mean that the law is intrinsically and intentionally ordered to this end, but rather that it is because of the human sinful condition, that it becomes the "occasion" of death for humans.[47] Even this deadly effect of law is within God's grace and care for us: "This effect has been permitted by God by special providence in order that the people are able to know their fragility and the necessity of the divine grace and the redemption of Christ."[48] Thus Paul should be understood as saying that the law shows us what is good but, without grace, lacks the force to make us good. This view of law as good is strengthened by Suárez's claims that laws still oblige those whose natures have been transformed by grace. Grace does not abolish the law, but rather gives the ability to keep the law perfectly.[49]

The Content of the Common Good

Looking beyond a scriptural justification for these claims, what does the common good that law advances actually include? Suárez is both expansive and realistic in his description. The common good entails

> the natural happiness [*felicitatem naturalem*] of the perfect or autonomous human community which it governs, and of each of the people who are members of it. This is, certainly, living in peace and justice and with enough goods which are necessary for the maintenance and well-being in the material life, and with the proper customs which are necessary for the social peace, the happiness of the republic, and the adequate conservation of human nature.[50]

This definition covers a large range of topics—from economic to legal to interpersonal engagement—which civil law can appropriately address, thus emphasizing the importance of law for human flourishing in community. By describing the common good as requiring not only peace and justice but also economic benefits that go beyond mere sustenance to actual well-being, Suárez reminds us that law is not simply present to impose order. Rather, it is meant to advance and improve the conditions of human lives.

However, the protection of justice remains the first and most important element of the common good that law can promote. Only just laws are capable of adding to the flourishing of the two cities. Suárez's theory of justice is quite broad. Drawing on Aquinas (I–II q. 96, art. 4), Suárez identifies two different types of justice: justice of subject-matter—that laws "prescribe just things"—and justice of form—that laws are justly enacted. To these he adds what I call justice of expectation: the requirement that laws must be practicable.

When considering justice of subject matter, Suárez distinguishes this more general type of justice from the specific virtue of justice. The general definition for the justice he is considering is simply that the acts mandated must be capable of being executed justly or virtuously.[51] This definition is fairly broad, since it only immediately implicates the limited group of laws that command or prescribe acts contrary to natural or divine law. Justice is also implicated at a more secondary level regarding laws mandating actions which are in themselves either morally indifferent or morally neutral. These actions only become good or evil because of their legal status. It is the law itself that makes the actions, and their ends, good; the goodness being according to "obedience or legal justice."[52] This conversion includes even actions that had some inherent goodness about them. Once promulgated, legislation takes on a binding character, making obeying it essential to righteousness, "even though before they were voluntary and their omission was not bad."[53] In the case of optional actions, the goodness is already inherent, but an obliging force is added. For Suárez the important point is that in each case, contra a legal positivist view, it is not only the command of the superior that makes the action good or bad but also "the end to which that law is directed"—and which is assumed to be something that adds to the citizen's virtue, even if the virtue that is added is only the virtue of obedience or legal justice.[54] Suárez provides an example of this legal transformation in a case study that we will return to several times. In itself, carrying a weapon is a morally neutral action. However, carrying a weapon can become morally good or morally evil, as it is the subject of regulation. Laws prohibiting the carrying of a weapon may not directly increase any specific virtue of the citizen but does contribute to the common good by making the city safer and forming citizens in obedience.

Suárez claims that it is equally important that the mode of the law be just (internal morality of the law) as that the subject matter be just. As with the lawmaker's promotion of the common good, an objective standard is applied to make this determination; a subjective assessment of the lawmaker's intention is not enough.[55] The three requirements of justice of form are: (1) legal—having the common good as the end; (2) commutative—not exceeding the agent's power to legislate; and (3) distributive—not effecting an unjust distribution of burden because of the law.

The final requirement for justice is practicability: the possibility that the law can be performed. Law can only regulate that which can be freely chosen, and since the impossible cannot be chosen, impractical laws remove the requirement to choose between two alternatives. Law must, of its nature, carry binding force, but there is no guilt for not performing what is impossible. Although this perhaps seems the least theological of Suárez's claims, it is clearly addressed to the Lutherans who claim that the fulfillment of divine laws is impossible and thus permit the severing of the link between validity and predictability, which then trickled into their concept of human laws, too. Suárez argues that, although God commands certain things that may be impossible to achieve when we are in our natural state, He provides the gift of grace to make completion of the law possible. Human lawmakers, who cannot give grace, can at least take into account the weakness of human nature when crafting laws, and can thereby ensure that all subjects have an opportunity to participate in obedience. As an example of this, he references the Church's practice under canon law of not requiring the same fasts of children as of adults.[56]

The requirement of practicability also brings in the requirement of law's conformance with custom, assuming custom to be good and virtuous. Since custom is considered even almost second nature, to expect people to obey laws that conflict with custom is unjust and therefore impracticable.[57] Although custom is discussed at greater length in chapter 3, it is important to note how closely it is related to the question of justice.

The Common Good and Concrete Reality

Although Suárez presents a broad vision of the common good, his argument is neither abstract nor idealistic. First, a crucial element of his understanding of the common good is its context-specific nature. There is no universal instantiation of the common good. Rather, the common good has different expressions, "at the time and place involved, and with respect to the people and community in question."[58] Trying to enforce certain concepts of the common good that apply in one community onto a different community that is not morally prepared shows a failure to realize that every law must be intended for a specific community and take account of the community's vices and virtues. Legislating moral actions that are impracticable for one community both diminishes the power of the rule of law and fails to make citizens more virtuous, since they gain nothing from laws that they are incapable of obeying.

Second, Suárez measures law's attainment of the common good from the objective standard of law's concrete achievement, not from the subjective standards of the lawgiver's intentions. "In this sense the essential factor... is the end of the act and not the intention of he who acts. The reason is evidence, because, even in the case that the legislator promulgating the law is moved by hate or some other perverse end, if in spite of this the law in itself will yield the common good, this is enough that it may be valid."[59] Since, unlike God, we cannot know whether the lawmaker is truly good and loving, and since, also unlike God, we cannot see into the hearts of men to know their intentions, we can only look at how the law, as it is given, tends toward or strays from the common good.[60] Thus we are moved away from a subjective appraisal of the inner state of the lawmaker to a more realistic and objective standard, that the "common good must be sought in the law itself and not in the extrinsic intention of the lawgiver."[61] This distinction is important for examining Suárez's theory of communal engagement with interpretation of statutes.

Third, taking account of the common good results in a continual struggle between the demands of proper content and a recognition of the pragmatic difficulties of legislating the common good in a sinful and complex world. In order to advance the common good, law must be both necessary and useful. Drawing explicitly on Aquinas (I–II q. 95, art. 3), Suárez connects necessity with the removal of evil and utility with the promotion of the good, with both essential for the common good. Incorporating both of these aspects into law is no simple task. Rather, there must be a high awareness of the intersectional nature of all lawmaking and the global impact of any single decision. One should take care lest the removal of one bad law leads to another worse to follow, or if in seeking to improve the law, one actually makes the situation worse for the community or gets in the way of something better.[62]

Fourth, the common good requires a commitment to ensuring that the good of the community and of the individual are noncompetitive. The concept of the common good requires commonality: the whole community should benefit. This requirement of commonality leads to a generality requirement that although each subject is obliged as an individual, laws must be given generally—for the whole community—to be considered valid laws.[63] This generality requirement is one of the key elements that distinguishes laws, strictly speaking, from commands. Commands are given to individuals, while laws are given to and for the community. Since laws bind the community, they are appropriately perpetual (which is not possible if given for an individual rather than a community) and public (since they must be promulgated to the whole community).[64]

Suárez's focus on generality, however, is not collectivist and does not ignore the importance of the well-being of each individual who comprises the community. While laws address the community, reception of and response to the law remains the responsibility of the individual. His description of the generality requirement acknowledges the fact that inappropriately framed laws may disadvantage private individuals, even as they benefit the community. The generality requirement ensures that laws are framed to focus only on the common good ("in absolute form") of the entire perfect community.[65] Even so, the generality requirement does not preclude the protection of private individuals who may be harmed. The lawmaker "must have in mind two things: one, that the particular damages may not be such that they overcome the benefits of the others; and the other, that if necessary, dispensations or exceptions are added."[66] This protection may even be at times morally obligatory. The attempt to balance the obligation to protect the individual while promoting the common good is one of the factors that separates Suárez's eudemonism from utilitarianism. While he does emphasize law's general and communal aspects, he is always seeking opportunities to ensure that justice is promoted both for the community and the individual (who is not a factor in the utilitarian calculus).[67] As much as possible, therefore, laws that uphold the common good will not be in competition with the good of the individual.

Who Can Make Law?

The next question Suárez must answer is whether law's efficient cause is capable of achieving law's final goal of advancing the common good. In this discussion of the final cause, Suárez makes his most important contribution by explaining how laws that promote the common good depend upon two efficient actors operating dialectically: the ruler and the subject. The complexity of an emerging nation-states requires the presence of a lawmaker to provide direction to the community. However, the laws promulgated by the lawmaker are simply a first step in law's actual development. The responses of the subjects to the laws are equally important in determining law's final content. Suárez emphasizes the importance of the subject's role from the beginning of *De Legibus*. Rather than taking the traditional approach of considering the lawmaker first, he starts by analyzing the nature and the importance of the subject's lawmaking ability. His consideration of the subject first is crucial because, as he quotes Aristotle, "The laws should be adapted to the commonwealth [*republicam*], and not the commonwealth to the laws."[68]

Rather than a ruler receiving a direct divine grant, lawmaking power is given immediately to the community by "God, as the author of nature."[69] God gives this lawmaking power to the perfect community as part of the natural order because laws are necessary for both survival and flourishing. This granting occurs anytime a community, extending beyond the family and household, comes together to provide one another the support or mutual aid required for preserving life and promoting welfare. "Community" should not be understood as simply a loose collection of people, but rather as individuals who have realized their needs for one another and therefore seek to be a group "united as a true body politic."[70]

Because of God's provision through the natural order, when these disparate households unite "into one political body through one bond of fellowship and for the purpose of aiding one another in the attainment of a single political end," they form something greater than themselves: a community that is capable of functioning as a single "mystical body [*corpus mysticum*]."[71] Just as an individual body is capable of ordering itself toward action, the mystical body of the commonwealth spontaneously and immediately possesses the power to order itself toward action as well.[72]

> In the same way that the man, from the fact only of being created and having use of reason, has power over himself and over his faculties and members for his use and is for this reason naturally free—or perhaps, that he is not a slave but ruler of his own actions—in this way also the political body of the people, by the fact alone of being formed in its own peculiar way, has the power and government of itself and, therefore, has power and a peculiar dominion over its own members.[73]

There are several crucial points in Suárez's distinction, which set his legal theory apart from other early modern theories. First, this union is not some Lockean democracy to which every citizen must consciously consent. Rather, Suárez argues, the lawmaking ability arises from the nature of the mystical body, without humans necessarily intending to generate this ability for themselves. To explain this involuntary ability, Suárez continues the free will analogy. Although the original power in question comes from God, it is mediated through parents (for the individual) and through the community (for the lawgiver). In the same way that parents may desire the sexual union but not necessarily the child produced, the community may not desire to produce lawmaking power but are joined through a desire for the other benefits produced by uniting into political union. The power to make law, therefore, is not produced by human planning, but "arises from God as its primary and principal author. This clearly seems to be the meaning of St. Paul . . . and this power is part of the nature of things and—whether of character physical or moral—is good without more, of great value and very necessary for the correct habituation [*consuetudinem*] of human nature."[74] The power given by God is not given as some special grant or act distinct from creation. Just like other natural powers, it is given "as a characteristic property resulting from nature, just as the bestowal of the form involves the bestowal of that which is consequent upon the form."[75] Like the parents, the members of the community do not consent to the result, although they do consent both to joining in the perfect community and then in determining subsequently how the community's power should be allocated.[76] This understanding of the mystical grant of lawmaking power both removes the problems of locating the beginning of a state in one mythical moment of consent and provides a richly theological understanding of the state's origin without arguing that the state must be theocratic.

Although the power to make laws is immediately granted to the community, in most situations it would be unwieldy and impracticable for the community to continue to wield the power corporately.[77] Rather, like any actual person, the mystical body also needs a head, which can provide the guidance through law to bind the community together and to direct it toward its proper ends.[78] The head is never imposed. Rather, the community determines who will serve as the head (which does not have to be an individual, and can also be a representative assembly) and how much power it will cede to the ruler.[79] The crucial part of Suárez's description of this transmission of power is that the community can never surrender all of its power to the ruler. Exactly what does this mean for the people? Crucially, that they retain some basic lawmaking power even following the appointment of a ruler.

And what do these limitations mean for the ruler? The grant of ruling power is not the direct grant of the plentitude of God's power that absolutists envision. Once the power has been surrendered, the ruler does rule as vicar of God and subjects are bound by divine and natural law to obey her—but only according to the terms of the grant, which includes both limitations on powers and limitations on the ends. "Because those who exercise this power in the human community are ministers of God, they are not able to do otherwise than administer the power that they have received from God. Therefore, God is not only the principal author but also the exclusive author of this power."[80] The people can give no more power than they have, so they cannot authorize a sovereign to make laws that ignore justice and the common good or that contradict natural law. Often they give far less than that, both in democracies and in limited monarchies.[81]

The ruler should not understand himself as a second David or Saul, who is explicitly anointed by God's prophet to rule. Rather, the specific goods appropriate to a specific perfect community both justify and limit the lawmaking power.[82] Thus, although the power is "in an absolute sense an effect of the natural law, its concretization in a specific and certain form of power and government depends upon free human choice."[83] Therefore the power to make laws should be considered to contain a "quasi-moral property," like title and ownership rights, which can be changed by human will even though they derive from nature.[84]

In a certain way the power to make laws is a form of dominion, but a power very different from the dominion that other contemporary political theorists imagine. Rather, it is a form of dominion "that calls, not for slavery to a despot, but rather for submission to civil order. Therefore it is a dominion of jurisdiction."[85] Dominion of jurisdiction is completely opposed to the dominion of the tyrant or absolute ruler. Monica Viera explains the distinction between the ruler's and the tyrant's dominion by distinguishing between the king's control over his power versus his control over his kingdom.

> Because whatever power he is transferred, it is always literally given to him, the king acquires true *dominium* over this power and cannot be deprived of it, unless he lapses into tyranny. In stressing this, Suárez seems close to equating two concepts clearly distinguished in Roman law, *dominium* (a private right of ownership) and *imperium* (an objective function of public law). But he is perfectly aware of the distinction, which he puts to good use when denying the king the right to alienate his kingdom. So although the king is to use the transferred sovereign power as its proper *dominus*, he must also bear in mind that he *has* his powers in virtue of his *public office*, to which is attached the duty to rule politically (for the sake of the common good), not despotically (selfishly, and contrary to the natural principles of morality).[86]

The tyrant rules like the pater familias, only able to issue commands, not laws. The true lawmaker rules by making laws that advance the community's ends, not frustrating or limiting them. If the ruler does not use the power appropriately to achieve the ends of the common good for which the power was entrusted to him, the power returns to the community.

There are internal limits as well as external limits upon the ruler's use of this power. Although the ruler's exercise of this lawmaking power has some similarities with God's lawmaking, the processes are not identical. The differences indicate further limits on the ruler's power. While each stage of lawmaking is completed perfectly in God, there is no guarantee that each occurs perfectly within the human lawgiver. Some rulers lack the will to advance the common good or fail to use prudence when issuing laws. If it is clear that the will to advance the common good is missing, then the resulting legislation fails to qualify as a law and remains a command only. However, if it is prudent enactment that is lacking, then whether a command qualifies as law will vary depending on each circumstance, since law may prudently govern in some situations and not in others. These issues are discussed in more detail later. For now it suffices to simply note that the lawmaker may fail in either foundational desire or prudent enactment.

Equally important are Suárez's claims that understanding laws as the static product of the will alone equates law only with the moment of the lawmaker's promulgation. The much more interesting component of Suárez's theory of law, identified by Pauline Westerman, is that for Suárez obligation may begin in the will of the lawmaker, in the production of the legal sign, but it is far from the final word as to what the law really is. Rather than seeing laws as rules, she suggests that Suárez anticipates Lon Fuller in understanding law as an activity:

> This tendency to understand law as a set of rules, conceived as things, as entities, was eloquently criticized by [Lon] Fuller, who wrote: "It is truly astounding to what an extent there runs through modern thinking in legal philosophy the assumption that law is like a piece of inert matter—it is there or not there." ... According to Fuller, law should not be seen as a system of hierarchically ordered rules, but essentially as an activity.... The definition of law as an activity enables Fuller to assert that there is a point, a purpose to that activity, and that we should be able to develop criteria in order to assess whether that activity has been successful or not in achieving that purpose."[87]

Thus, understanding law as an activity explains Suárez's description of law as the product of a constant dynamic interplay between a lawmaker's will and intellect and the community's will and intellect. The moment of producing an obligating sign—law's promulgation—occurs in the will. However, to focus only on that one point is to misunderstand the whole of civil law and its operation and development as coming from above and below. This is why understanding the community's role is as important as understanding the lawmaker's. As Westerman writes, "Suárez sees very clearly that law cannot be understood as the direct outcome of the immediate intents and purposes of the legislators. Law starts to lead a life of its own, so to speak. That is why he asserts 'but this good and virtuous behavior on the part of the legislator who makes a given law is not necessary to the validity of the law. For a prince may conduct himself wickedly and unjustly when he makes the law, while the law that he makes may nevertheless be just and good, and also valid.'"[88] It is this distinction of law from the ruler's will and understanding of law as the active interchange between the lawmaker and the people that provides the structure of law, which creates space for understanding law as constructive dialogue.[89]

Discernment of the Natural Law

As noted earlier, Suárez follows Aquinas and Augustine in claiming that lawmakers do not have the authority to make binding civil laws that contradict the natural law. However, a lawmaker also depends on the people to determine the natural law and to ensure that laws do not contradict it.

In order to understand this relationship, it is first important to understand Suárez's theory of natural law. Suárez grounds his understanding of natural law in Aquinas's claim that "all who are steered by divine providence participate in some form of eternal law."[90] Drawing on I–II q. 91, art. 2, Suárez writes: "Man participates by the light of reason in the eternal law, which dictates what must be done or left undone. The light [of reason] then is the natural law; which is nothing other than a certain natural participation in the eternal law."[91] Natural law should be considered only in the most strict sense: as it exists in the human mind, not as the term "law" is applied analogically to nonrational beings. In this sense he distinguishes between natural law and natural instinct, which humans share with lower animal forms. Since instinct does not depend on freedom, it cannot be truly law. Natural law is only possible within rational creatures, since law must first exist in the intellect of the subject before it is applied through the will. As a property of the intellect, natural law, strictly speaking, can be understood as referring only to the discernment between good and evil undertaken by the reason.[92]

However, natural law can also be described, less strictly, as a habit.[93] Natural law is different from conscience because it determines what should be done as "a rule in general terms," whereas conscience is "a practical dictate in a particular case. For this reason, it is better understood as an application of the law to a particular action."[94] Natural law is the type of law most related to the human subject, because it is the form of law that dwells by nature within the human mind.[95]

Only certain parts of the natural law are immediately accessible by human reason. Suárez discusses three types of norms that are recognized by natural reason:

1. "Primary and general principles of morality": such as "one must do good and shun evil."[96]
2. More particular or specific principles that are "*per se nota* by their very terminology." For example, "justice must be observed" and "one must worship God."
3. Conclusions that are "derived with an evident inference out of natural principles and which cannot be known save through rational reflection."[97] The best example of this third category are the commands of the Decalogue.

Laws of the first two categories are understood by all rational humans.[98] No one, Suárez argues, can be in ignorance of at least "the primary and most universal principles. They are known absolutely in their simple enunciation and in such conformance and, so to speak, so adjusted to the natural inclination of the reason and the will that there does not exist the possibility of turning away from them."[99] However, the third category is not universally accessible. Rather, within this group are various gradations of accessibility: some are recognized easily, some with much more difficulty. Some of the conclusions are manifest and others are much more difficult to discern.

Therefore, at this third level, differences in discernment of the natural law inevitably varies between people and between nations. Under this three-part model, the general first- and second-level principles must inevitably form the basis of any legal system oriented to the common good (debts should be paid, prices should be just). Yet the existence of these uniformly accessible precepts does not mean that every legal system will look the same.

In fact, none of these natural law precepts can fully determine the content of the civil law. While natural law in its substance is unified, the knowledge and application of the third category of the natural law is never complete or full. In other words, when considered as "the intellectual understanding itself," the natural law is the same in all places and for all times. Even so, within the third category there is always a gradation of understanding and access to the natural law, depending on the lawmaker's and the people's own virtues, culture, and capacities.

The role of the human lawmaker is to take these precepts and determine, with prudence, exactly how they should be applied and expanded in the manner most appropriate for a given context and people. "In this way, all good acts are made concrete in particular by the reason and the criteria of men."[100] Thus, just as human sovereignty is grounded in God's sovereignty, civil law is grounded in natural law but must be mediated by human reason and judgments. Actual lawmaking is really an exercise in discernment at the third level of the natural law.[101] The question, therefore, becomes generally not whether civil laws are perfect but to what degree of perfection and helpfulness they may obtain and how reason can improve them. "In reality, there are able to be many different forms, more or less perfect, of moral specification including those acts which are commanded in a general mode of the divine or natural law, and the human law is not able to establish pre-emptively any form of moral specification."[102] This analogous connection calls for a humility in knowing what civil law can govern and achieve, since the civil law never can and never should appropriate the whole of natural law.

This differentiation of natural law into different categories explains how civil law's obliging force differs from that of the natural law. The general principle that law must be obeyed falls into the second category of natural law: one that is accessible to all humans.[103] The binding authority of civil law in this sense does not reside therefore in the ruler's authority to issue the law, but is due to the natural law, albeit remotely.[104] The ruler's will can establish laws, but this fact is not what actually makes law binding. Furthermore, while the general precept that laws should be obeyed is imposed by natural law, the fact that each specific civil law is always issued by the lawmaker means that its binding authority directly rests on the lawmaker's will. The fact that its obliging force depends on a human lawmaker means that civil law always "binds less proximately" than natural or eternal law.[105] This less-proximate binding serves as a limit on the power of the civil ruler, just as the claim that obedience to the ruler is based on natural law serves as a limit on the autonomy of the subject.

It is true that, to a certain degree, natural law exists more fully in the intellect of the lawmaker who makes the law, since the power to make the laws comes from God and is granted to the lawmaker. The fact that human lawmakers have a more proximate connection to the eternal law in a certain sense means that subjects, when analyzing and critiquing laws, should display epistemic humility in setting their own opinions of the demands of the natural and eternal law against the civil laws. The determination by a ruler that a civil law is in accord with natural law provides a prima facie reason to obey. Subjects must also be careful to acknowledge that the primary way in which humans have access to the divine law is usually not through direct access, as law exists in itself, but rather through signs and effects given by God, which include the just laws that are created by human government. "Even as secondary causes uncover the primary cause and creatures show the Creator, so do temporal laws which are participants in the eternal law, reveal the source from which they flow."[106] Therefore, instead of being negative or an impediment, civil law is actually conductive in a certain sense to the knowledge of God. Understanding that civil law is generally derived from the natural law through an act of the imperfect lawmaker's judgment always means that the lawmaker cannot assume that any civil law perfectly corresponds to the natural law.

Additionally, understanding natural law as a capacity for judgment explains why there are large areas of human existence that come under the jurisdiction of the civil law without being directly informed by the natural law. First, permissive natural law leaves many questions related to human flourishing open, to be determined by humans based on context.[107] Certain things may be therefore permitted or permissible under natural law but changed by civil law. The most obvious example of this is nakedness, which was permitted to humans in a state of innocence. After the fall, given the exigencies of fallen human nature, it became necessary that humans should wear some sort of clothes.[108] Another more complex example of this relates to property ownership. Before the fall, all goods were held in common. Several theologians therefore use the change to private property ownership to justify a claim that natural law had changed to allow property ownership. Suárez claims that the form that property ownership takes is left open by permissive natural law, with different precepts coming into effect at different times. There is no necessary connection between common ownership and the state of innocence, since an unfallen society might divide property and a fallen one might theoretically practice common property ownership. Therefore, when we see specific division of property in a fallen state, this does not mean it was prescribed by natural law, but rather that the natural law "has been adapted to the state and condition of humanity."[109] There are certain precepts relating to justice and the care of the poor that govern all property ownership, at all times and in all places, but the applicability of other precepts may vary.

Second, in certain situations natural law will govern, but only after affirmative human actions trigger natural law's authority. For example, once humans decide to make a contract, the natural law comes into effect to govern the requirements of fulfilling a contract. Since precepts of the natural law "depend for their perceptive binding force upon the prior consent of human will," they may also be modified or dispensed with by human will. For example, a superior who had received a vow may release the person who made it or a party in a contract may agree to excuse the other party's performance.[110] The natural law precept that vows must be kept would still govern, but the recipient of the promise has the ability to nullify the vow's binding force.

Finally, and most important for theories of communal engagement with law: although human law cannot change natural law, it may change circumstances so that "it may produce such a change in the object of the natural law, that the obligation of the natural law may vary also."[111] This also does not mean the natural law itself changes, but rather that different precepts begin to apply.[112] This flexibility within the natural law also means that different civil laws are in operation at different times. In fact, this "is convenient and frequently necessary for men, in accordance with the various changes of estate which befall them."[113] This facet of the natural law explains why civil laws, although they must not mandate actions that contradict natural law, always fail to require all the content of natural law. For example, "The civil law is not able to prohibit all the vices contrary to the virtue, such as may be the simple fornication which is not scandalous and does not damage the community in other ways."[114] Another important limit on what civil law can prohibit is the state of the community, particularly its habitual vices and virtues.[115] To draw on one of Suárez's favorite examples, the moral condition of a community may lead to regulations pertaining to carrying arms in public appropriate at some times and pernicious at others, without either regulation contradicting the natural law's support of self-defense.

While permissive natural law leaves a large scope for civil laws to regulate, this does not mean that the natural law precepts do not apply in some way to all civil laws, even if they do not directly inform its content. Rather, the natural law still requires that all laws must be general, instituted for the common good, and just. Suárez describes how some theologians have used arguments relating to the permissibility of private property ownership to justify the attempt by absolute monarchs to usurp property rights within their realms. These arguments ignore the fact that while permissive natural law may allow for certain changes to be made, natural law never permits changes that go against the requirements of peace and justice for the entire community.[116]

In considering the importance of natural law and convention, Suárez works to ensure that civil law is always appropriate to the subject, both by considering the objective standards of God's law as revealed through the natural law and through taking into account the importance of convention to shape how people understand and receive this law. Both components are equally important for a law to be valid. In addition, building upon Suárez's understanding of law as developed through a dialectical engagement between ruler and subject, both the ruler and the community are essential in determining that laws accord with natural law and with justice. A ruler, who may be better educated and ideally, although sadly not always, more virtuous, may possess a broader perspective in determining how the first two levels of precepts of the natural law are applied in the laws of the specific community. However, it is the people in the community, whose lived experience and engagement with convention will shape those laws, who determine whether they are most appropriate for each individual community. In a similar fashion, a ruler is responsible for ensuring that laws are enacted according to extrinsic standards of justice but it is the people who are best able to determine the objective standards of justice by which a law is judged, as well as being able to speak to a law's practicability.

In summary, certain judgments derived from natural law must be incorporated into any system of civil law for it to be valid as law. Since at certain levels of clarity natural law is not universally understood, it is derived by reflection and varies based on application to different circumstances. This mediated nature of natural law means that parts of the natural law can never directly be translated to civil law by the lawmaker. Since civil law is by definition "proximately" established by humans, the conversion process is always to some degree "temporal and imperfect," since it is formed by fallible humans for a specific moment in time. The ruler depends upon the people for assistance in discerning the instantiations of the natural law in each context and must work with them in shaping law that is appropriate to each specific situation.

This understanding of the relationship between natural and civil law challenges the assumptions of Lutherans, royal absolutists, and Machiavellians. Royal absolutists categorically cannot claim that no one except rulers has access to natural law. According to King James, God, the Creator and King, has bestowed on monarchs the absolute authority to make laws that carry out His will, so any claims of natural law and common law that contradict this authority cannot be inspired by God and are therefore not true law. Although the will of the ruler should generally conform to reason, God's special grant of lawmaking authority means that the ruler (just like God) may act at times in ways that seem contrary to reason. Even if civil laws appear to contradict reason or natural law, these laws are just as valid as God's laws and should be obeyed by the ruler's subjects in all circumstances.[117] To the contrary, Suárez argues that true natural law is understood to different degrees by different people. But, since natural law is the same thing as the human capacity for righteous judgment, to reserve to rulers alone this ability to assess denies the very humanity of a ruler's subjects. Subjects have not just the power, but at times the obligation, to correct the ruler's misappropriation of the natural law.

On the other hand, although he does say that one of the ways the eternal and natural laws can be understood is through the civil laws, Suárez also wants to avoid the claims of the Lutherans that the only thing civil law can be for Christians is a restatement of the divine natural law.[118] This would limit civil law to matters that the natural and eternal laws already cover and ignore the fact that civil law also regulates neutral issues for the benefit of the common good in each societal context, and possibly that a given regulation is supported by permissive natural law.[119] The other approach would be to say that the natural law provides the material but does so only in a generic mode and that it is the human law itself that makes the generic natural law concrete in each human context and setting. This would raise the important question of understanding the righteous way to make natural law concrete. While Suárez finds this probable in some situations, he finds it insufficient: "The human law does not always suppose a natural or divine law precept over the same act which it orders but that, at the most, it supposes the general principles. For example, that the crimes should be punished, that the prices of things should be just, and other principles in this style."[120] The reality is that there are many different ways and forms, each more or less morally perfect, to make concrete the acts that are required by natural and divine law, and it is impossible to say preemptively which form of concretization is right for which time.[121]

Suárez also denies Machiavelli's claim that to ground laws in natural law is to make it impossible for the state to succeed.[122] The claim that conforming to the natural law limits a state's ability to exist completely misunderstands that it is the natural law that indicates what is necessary for the peace and well-being of the state.[123] In fact, since the natural law creates a capacity for judgment, all rulers making laws with the right will of advancing the state's good are in some way utilizing the natural law. To try to pretend that moral content must be removed from the law completely misunderstands the nature of law itself and how we understand what actually constitutes the state's well-being and peace.

Critical Reception: The Community's Lawmaking Role

In considering both the subject and the lawgiver, as well as the limits on and contents of the subject matter of law, Suárez performs a careful balancing act. Law must obligate morally but cannot be totalizing. Law must not violate natural or divine law, but is not coextensive with natural law in every way. Law makes humans into good citizens, but not good persons as such. Law advances the common good and justice, but cannot create an abstractly ideal society. Rather, law must always legislate in a way appropriate for each unique cultural and political context. The lawgiver must possess actual power, but that power comes from the people on its most basic and foundational level and therefore can be limited by the people.

Within this careful edifice, this constant seeking for the mean, Suárez creates space for citizens to engage and challenge unjust laws in a way that does not deny the rule and authority of laws. Although he never specifically deals with resistance to unjust laws (as opposed to his treatment of tyrannicide), his analysis of the reception of laws and approaches to unjust laws in general acknowledges the complexity of delineating laws as unjust and opens a space for creative engagement with them.

In creating this space, he sets one boundary as the law that is "with all clarity and without even the least type of doubt" unjust.[124] In this case, subjects are not only not obliged to obey the law but cannot obey it because it is not even law. An unjust law cannot by definition be an actual law since, being unjust, it is not a measure of rectitude but rather "partakes of the name of law by analogy . . . in so far as it prescribes a certain mode of action in relation to a given end."[125] To obey a law that is clearly unjust would be to violate divine law and fall into mortal sin.[126] On the other extreme, a perfectly just law should be kept for reasons of rectitude and should always be obeyed. However, as Suárez is well aware, most laws do not fall neatly into either of these clear-cut categories. It is in determining how to engage with this middle type of law where his theory of law is most useful.

Suárez discusses this complexity most directly in his writings on reception. He finds none of his contemporaries' approaches to the question of the importance of reception by the people to be adequate for addressing this complex question. The first claim, which he describes as the common opinion of the jurists, claims that the acceptance of the people is an indispensable prerequisite for law to have binding authority. The advantage of this view is that it recognizes that the civil magistrates' authority is received from the people. It also recognizes the importance of the common good and acknowledges that the people may at times have a better sense of what actually advances the common good than the magistrate.[127] However, making law's obligation depend wholly on reception eviscerates the power of the sovereign's will to make law.[128] The second claim, advanced by many (although not all) theologians, is that the reception by the people is insignificant for the law to have any authority. While this claim considers popular acceptance to be valuable, since it can lead to firmness of establishment, it holds that a law can be valid on its own and regardless of how the people receive it.[129] While this position has the advantage of acknowledging that the will of the lawmaker is sufficient for law to be binding, in some forms it can ignore the reality that many governments, particularly democracies, do not grant absolute power to the lawmaker and make reception necessary for establishing a law's validity.[130] However, if these limits were not originally put in place at the moment of political unity, Suárez agrees that reception is not necessary for a law's validity: "Although the consent of the people would have been necessary in the construction of the law when the political regime of the state was in some sense a democracy, a similar consent is no longer needed after the power has been transferred to a true ruler."[131] What Suárez grants to the ruler he then promptly limits. This normative rule is subject to a number of exceptions.

If an injustice is unclear, then the presumption is that the subject should give prima facie deference to the judgment of the lawgiver. There are several reasons for this response. First, by the nature of divine grant of lawmaking authority, the lawmaker "is in permanent possession of a superior right."[132] Second, the lawmaker's responsibilities to oversee the common good, along with the resources that accompany her offices, often mean that the lawmaker "is directed by superior counsel and may be moved by general reasons hidden from [her] subjects."[133] Finally, a subject should be motivated by a general concern for the common good and should seek to uphold the general authority of the rule of law wherever possible. If the presumption against the lawgiver is widely disregarded, subjects "would assume an excessive license to disregard the laws, since the latter can hardly be so just that it is impossible for them to be treated as doubtful."[134] But this requirement is only a presumption: the transfer of power to a lawmaker is never total, and is always ultimately dependent on the ruler's use of her power to advance the common good of the community. The conditionality of the grant leaves space for the presumption to always be open to being overcome and never an absolute mandate.

The fact that this presumption is in the lawgiver's favor leads to a second very important criterion for discernment: the nature of law itself requires the subject to be prudent and careful in evaluating most situations involving an apparent, but not clear, injustice. There are two reasons for this. First, as Suárez writes when discussing tyranny, upholding the general rule of law at times may serve the common good better than overturning a single unjust law if such overturning will damage the stability of the government or respect for law.[135] "[Some] government is less bad than lacking completely a just system of . . . political direction."[136] Suárez understands that civil laws serve as a concretization of natural law, but how this concretization is achieved can result in a wide range of laws, especially depending on the cultural context and moral state of each particular nation. Even more important, there is no such thing as one perfect way to concretize the natural law, but rather a broad spectrum of greater or lesser conformity, depending on many different factors and subject to critique and change.

This understanding of civil law as never fully concretizing natural law but rather presenting a range of potential conformity means that Suárez can identify most laws as unjust in part but not descending to the total injustice that justifies complete disregard. Conversely, this also means that laws are rarely so perfectly just that the lawmaker cannot be questioned or challenged, even though the presumption in the lawmaker's favor requires criticism to be approached with respect and prudence.

There may be laws that are not unjust as far as an act mandated but that fail to be "suitable to time and place." One of the requirements for the lawmaker to govern prudently is a proper consideration of circumstance and context when determining which actions should be mandated or forbidden. This determination requires acknowledgment that "a given thing may be regarded as morally impossible at one time, and as easily [accomplished] at another time."[137] A law may therefore be unjust to a certain extent, even if it is not completely unjust.

When applied generally laws may also not be unjust as far as subject matter but still be unjust in relation to a particular subject, unduly burdening her without forcing her to fall into sin. In such a situation, the subject is not obligated to accept the precept as being binding as law because the lawmaker has both exceeded the limits of her power in making a law that is unduly burdensome but also because no one can be forced to accept this type of injustice.[138] However, simply because a type of law does not obligate as law does not mean that a subject should resist it without taking into account other considerations that might indicate obedience, including the benefit to the common good of upholding the authority of law. Laws may not simply be burdensome to an individual without being just, but may also be excessively burdensome to the community. In this case, the community is most likely not bound to accept the law unless compelling external circumstances exist.[139]

It is also possible, Suárez acknowledges, that laws may be just as far as subject matter but still suffer from injustice of mode. In response to the wide variety of possible injustices of mode, the prudent subject will realize that the law may not be morally binding even though other important considerations may compel obedience, "provided he does not cooperate in [any resulting] injustice; for he has the power to cede his own right."[140] This can include an acknowledgment that reasonable minds might differ on the type and degree of injustice and the need to avoid scandal or confusion in the community that might result, causing more damage than a possible injustice of mode. A consideration of all these varieties of injustice shows how difficult it is to determine how to respond to an unjust law in a proper and responsible way. As Suárez writes, determining a proper response requires a great deal of "prudent judgment; and this judgment must be based upon a high degree of certainty."[141]

There may be cases where a law issued is so extreme that the community is not bound to accept it. However, the community should not see this as granting license to disregard all laws, but rather to presume to interpret the sovereign's design as only to advance this law as a trial, not with the intent of making this law absolutely binding.[142] There may also be a situation in which a large part of the community does not comply with the law. For citizens to join in failing to comply would not advance the common good and would significantly penalize those who do comply, as well as create a danger for society at large, resulting in sedition and scandal. A sovereign's response to large-scale resistance should be to retire the law, even though it is not unjust, to avoid greater injury occurring.[143]

When considering the theory of reception, while Suárez seeks to set as an initial parameter that the role of the lawgiver must be accepted, he also provides a great deal of leeway in the community's response to injustice or to inapplicability or lack of enforcement of laws. He makes it clear that the community's freedom to reject a problematic law must always be determined by the preservation of proper order and justice within the community. The obligation falls on both sides (lawgiver and subject) and the range of responses available must be determined using the rubric of the common good, characterized by its furtherance of a well-ordered society.

In considering both the natural law and justice as material causes of law, Suárez ensures that civil law is always appropriate to the subject, both by considering the objective standards of God's law, as revealed through the natural law, and by taking into account the importance of convention to shape how people understand and receive the law. Achieving both components—meeting objective standards and adhering to convention—are equally important for a law to be valid. In addition, according to Suárez's understanding of law as developed through a dialectical engagement between ruler and subject, the actions of the ruler and the community are essential in determining that a law accords with natural law and with justice.

Conclusion

Francisco Suárez's theory of law as developed through dialectical engagement between a ruler and the people ensures that both the role of the lawmaker in issuing law and upholding the rule of law and the role of the people in developing law to make it suitable for each particular community and advance the common good, create a stable and yet flexible approach to civil law. In addition, his consideration of law's ability to advance the common good of all citizens is applicable in our own time and context. This theory of law as activity transforms our understanding, opening space for creative communal engagement with law, shaping and improving the law and making it more just and able to advance the common good without rejecting the law's authority.

Notes

1. As with most typologies, Suárez clearly does not intend *De Legibus* to present a point-by-point challenge to any of these views. There are undoubtedly errors in his presentation of all viewpoints. For example, several of the doctrines that he identifies with Lutheranism seem to have more in common with the radical wing of Reformation activists. In his *Defensio*, a polemical work written in a different style, he does directly address the errors of royal absolutism by challenging James I's own *Apology* (Suárez, *Defensio*, preface, section 1). Suárez's references to Luther's works are fairly limited. He mentions Luther's sermons in *De Legibus* I.xviiiI.2 and Luther's *Babylonian Captivity* in *De Legibus* III.v.3. For an in-depth analysis of Suárez's engagement with Luther, Calvin, and other questions related to grace and free will, see Victor M. Salas, "Francisco Suárez's Encounter with Calvin on Human Freedom," *Perichoresis* 18, no. 6 (2020): 103–18.
2. Suárez, *De Legibus*, I.xviii.2.
3. Suárez, I.xviii.2.
4. Suárez, III.v.2.
5. Suárez, III.v.2, 4.
6. See, for example, Suárez, *Defensio*, III.7.
7. For additional discussion regarding how Suárez's opposition to Luther and King James framed *De Legibus* and influenced his understanding of popular consent, see Wim Decock, "Counter-Reformation Diplomacy Behind Francisco Suárez's Constitutionalist Theory," *Ambiente Jurídico* 11 (2009): 68–92.
8. Harold J. Berman, "Origins of Historical Jurisprudence," *Yale Law Journal* 103 (1993–94): 1667.
9. Berman, 1667.
10. Berman, 1667.
11. Lancelot Andrewes, *Lancelot Andrewes*, ed. Trevor A. Owen (London: Twayne, 1981), 160.
12. Andrewes, 189.
13. Andrewes, 191.
14. Lancelot Andrewes, "Certain Sermons Preached at Sundry Times Upon Several Occasions: Sermon VIII," in *Lancelot Andrewes Works: Sermons, Vol. 5*, ed. J. P. Wilson and James Bliss (Oxford: John Henry Parker, 1843): 169–85.
15. Thomas Hobbes, *De Cive* (New York: Appleton-Century Croft, 1949), 129.
16. Thomas Hobbes, *Leviathan*, ed. by Richard Tuck (Cambridge: Cambridge University Press, 1996), 223.
17. Terence Irwin, *The Development of Ethics, Vol. 2* (Oxford: Oxford University Press, 2007), 35–36.
18. Suárez, *De Legibus*, III.xii.2.

19. Suárez, III.xii.2, quoting Machiavelli, *The Prince*, chap. 18.
20. David Hollenbach, *The Common Good and Christian Ethics* (Cambridge: Cambridge University Press, 2002), 58.
21. Melanie Johnson-DeBaufre, Catherine Keller, and Elias Ortega-Aponte, "Introduction," in *Common Goods: Economy, Ecology and Political Theology*, ed. Melanie Johnson-DeBaufre, Catherine Keller, and Elias Ortega-Aponte (New York: Fordham University Press, 2015), 3.
22. Hollenbach, *The Common Good*, 58.
23. Although today Suárez is considered primarily a Thomist, he was also known in his own day as a respected expositor of Augustine, possibly explained by the resurgence of Augustine studies following the Counsel of Trent and the later condemnation of Michael Baius. Suárez engaged at great length in the controversy following the condemnation and turned to Augustine to challenge Baius's reading. Eleuterio Elorduy, "San Augustin y Suárez: el doctor de la gracia," *Augustinus* 16, no. 61 (1971): 13.
24. Suárez, III.xii.3, quoting Augustine, *City of God*, II.21.
25. Suárez, *De Legibus*, I.iii.17, citing Augustine, *Tractates on the Gospel of John*, VI.1.25.
26. Suárez, *De Legibus*, III.i.1, citing Augustine, *City of God*, XIX.15.
27. Suárez, III.v.12.
28. See Suárez, *Defensio*, IV.viii.3.
29. Suárez, *De Legibus*, III.xii.4, citing Augustine, *Epistolarum classes quator*, no. 105.
30. Jorge J. E. Gracia and Douglas Davis, *The Metaphysics of Good and Evil According to Suárez* (Munich: Verlag, 1989), 35.
31. Gracia and Davis, 49.
32. Henri de Lubac, *Augustinianism and Modern Theology* (New York: Herder, 1969), 177. See also de Lubac's *Surnaturel: Études historique* (Paris: Aubier, 1946).
33. Suárez, *De Legibus*, I.iii.11.
34. Suárez, I.iii.12.
35. Suárez, I.iii.12.
36. Victor Salas, "Suárez and Salamanca: Magister and Locus of Pure Nature," *Disputatio: Philosophical Research Bulletin* 7, no. 8 (2018): 14.
37. Salas, 7–8.
38. Suárez, I.iii.3.
39. Suárez, I.xviii.3.
40. Suárez, III.i.12.
41. Suárez, I.iii.3.
42. Suárez, I.iii.18.
43. Suárez, I.iii.19.
44. Suárez, III.xi.7, III.xi.6. The fact that secular governments regulate sins relating to heresy and blasphemy does not contradict this rule. Rather, it is partly due to a concession on the part of the Church and partly due to legitimate concerns related to the common good, since indulging in heresy and blasphemy can damage the peace of a society. See also III.xi.10.
45. Suárez, III.i.12.
46. Suárez, I.xiii.4.
47. Suárez, I.xiii.5.
48. Suárez, I.xiii.5.
49. Suárez, I.ix.17, I.xviii.9.

50. Suárez, III.xi.7. For a further discussion of the centrality of this definition in Suárez's work, see Paul Pace, SJ, "Francisco Suárez and Justice," *Gregorianum* 93 (2012): 503.
51. Suárez, I.viii.3.
52. Suárez, I.ix.5.
53. Suárez, I.ix.5.
54. Suárez, I.ix.5.
55. Suárez, I.ix.11.
56. Suárez, I.ix.19.
57. Suárez, I.ix.19.
58. Suárez, I.vii.9.
59. Suárez, I.vii.9.
60. Suárez, I.vii.9.
61. Suárez, I.vii.9.
62. Suárez, I.vii.15.
63. Suárez, I.vi.2. Suárez distinguishes between laws issued for the whole community and laws issued for the common good. Here he explicitly distinguishes himself from Aquinas (*Summa* I–II 90, 2), who he believes elides this generality requirement by focusing only on the common good requirement.
64. This concern for the public nature of law is a recurring theme throughout *De Legibus*. See I.ix for Suárez's discussion of the importance of promulgation.
65. Suárez, *De Legibus*, I.vii.14.
66. Suárez, I.vii.14.
67. Suárez, I.vii.14. Annabel Brett provides further discussion of Suárez's attempts to balance the rights of the individual against the authority of the community. Although she claims that Domingo de Soto's emphasis on the spiritual, as opposed to the natural aspects of citizenship, left far more room for individual freedom, she convincingly defends Suárez against claims that he surrenders all freedoms of the individual in his explanation of the surrender of some individual liberties to constitute the city. See Brett, "Individual and Community in the Second Scholastic," in *Philosophy in the Sixteenth and Seventeenth Centuries*, ed. Constance Blackwell and Sachiko Kusukawa (Abingdon, England: Routledge, 1999), 166–68.
68. Suárez, *De Legibus*, I.vii.2.
69. Suárez, III.ii.2.
70. Suárez, III.ii.4.
71. Suárez, III.ii.4.
72. Suárez, III.iii.6.
73. Suárez, III.iii.6.
74. Suárez, III.iii.4.
75. Suárez, III.iii.4.
76. For further discussion see Daniel Schwartz, "Francisco Suárez on Consent and Political Obligation," *Vivarium* 46, no. 1 (2008): 59–81.
77. Suárez, *De Legibus*, III.i.4.
78. Suárez, III.i.4.
79. Suárez, III.iii.7.
80. Suárez, III.iv.4.
81. It is worth noting that this is one way Suárez substantively differs from Hobbes, who expresses no concept of gradation of grants of power. The development of this principle

of "dual sovereignty" based on Aquinas was not unique to Suárez and was characteristic of many theologians of the Spanish scholastic. See Ramon Tapia, "Derecho y poder en el pensamiento juridico español del siglo XVI," *Pensamiento* 54 (1998): 54–55.
82. Suárez, *De Legibus*, III.iv.1. Here Suárez is drawing on Aquinas, *Summa Theologiae*, I–II q. 90, art. 3, ad 2 and I–II q. 97, art. 3, ad 3, where Aquinas writes that the prince has the power to make law and this power was transferred from the community.
83. Suárez, III.iv.1.
84. Suárez, III.iii.7.
85. Suárez, III.i.8.
86. Monica Vieira, "Francisco Suárez and the *Principatus Politicus*," *History of Political Thought* 29, no. 2 (Summer 2008): 289.
87. Pauline C. Westerman, "Suárez and the Formality of Law," in *Politische Metaphysik: Die Entstehung moderner Rechtskonzeptionen in der Spanischen Scholastik*, ed. Matthias Kaufmann and Robert Schnepf (Frankfurt: Lang, 2007), 231.
88. Westerman, 228–29, citing Suárez, *De Legibus*, I.ix.12.
89. Suárez draws an explicit connection here between the intention of the ruler and the intention of the priest carrying out the sacrament. In accordance with the doctrine of "*ex opere operato*," simply because the priest has a bad intention does not invalidate the sacrament, as long as it is not against "its substance." Suárez, *De Legibus*, I.vii.9.
90. Suárez, I.iii.7, quoting Aquinas, *Summa Theologiae*, I–II q. 91, art. 2.
91. Suárez, II.v.10.
92. Suárez, I.iv.5.
93. Suárez, II.v.13.
94. Suárez, II.v.15.
95. Suárez, I.iii.9.
96. Suárez, II.vii.5. Much of the debate concerning Suárez's theory of natural law has revolved around whether or not he presents an independent standard of righteousness apart from God. See, for example, Jerome B. Schneewind, *The Invention of Autonomy* (Cambridge: Cambridge University Press, 1997), 60–61; and Knud Haakonssen, *Natural Law and Moral Philosophy* (Cambridge: Cambridge University Press, 1996), 19–23. While Irwin has offered persuasive arguments contrary to these claims, this debate is not specifically relevant to the argument of the current work. For further discussion, see Irwin, *Development of Ethics*, 2:28–69.
97. Suárez, *De Legibus*, II.vii.5.
98. Suárez, II.viii.3.
99. Suárez, II.viii.6.
100. Suárez, III.xii.15.
101. Paul Pace claims that "Suárez makes a very insightful 'common-sense' affirmation: while all three orders of precepts belong to the natural law, and the first two are practically self-evident, the natural law is put into practice (*exercetur*) more in the third order of immediate conclusions than in the universal principles. Since law is an immediate rule of conduct, the general self-evident principles can be considered laws only to the extent they are applied to concrete situations by other, more proximate principles." Paul Pace, SJ, "Suárez and the Natural Law," in *A Companion to Francisco Suárez*, ed. Victor Salas and Robert Fastiggi (Leiden, The Netherlands: Brill, 2014), 284.
102. Suárez, *De Legibus*, III.xii.15.
103. Suárez, II.ix.12.

104. Suárez, II.iv.9.
105. Suárez, II.iv.10.
106. Suárez, II.iv.9.
107. In understanding and assessing Suárez's concept of "permissive natural law," I am significantly indebted to Brian Tierney's work on the history of permissive natural law generally, and on Suárez in particular. See Brian Tierney, *Liberty and Law* (Washington, DC: Catholic University of America Press, 2014), 193–214.
108. Suárez, *De Legibus*, II.xiv.7. This example is interesting given Suárez's own cultural context, since it leaves room for a wide variety of modesty norms. It is also worth noting that another example Suárez provides is a concept of human liberty. Interpreting this statement might lead one to think that Suárez's claims could be used to support a natural law concept of slavery. His strong concept of the freedom of human will does leave room for individual humans, acting in freedom, to alienate their own liberty. However, he strongly dismisses the claim that permissive natural law justifies slavery as an institution in a later section. See Suárez, *De Legibus*, II.xiv.14–16.
109. Suárez, II.xiv.13.
110. Suárez, II.xiv.11.
111. Suárez, II.xiv.12.
112. Suárez's statement that the precepts of the natural law do not change, but rather apply or not according to specific circumstances, has been criticized as yet another departure from Aquinas. For example, James Gordley writes, "According to Aquinas, secondary precepts of the natural law are changeable, depending on circumstance. According to Suárez, different secondary precepts may apply at different times" (Gordley, *The Jurists: A Critical History* [Oxford: Oxford University Press, 2013], 165–71). Sydney Penner provides a convincing rebuttal to the claim that the difference is as substantial as it has been presented. See "'The Pope and Prince of All the Metaphysicians': Some Recent Works on Suárez," *British Journal for the History of Philosophy* 21, no. 2 (2013): 400–401. See also Pace, "Suárez and the Natural Law": "Confronted with the formidable authority of Aristotle and Aquinas, who admitted that the natural law precepts can change or admit exceptions in *paucioribus*, Suárez argues that this statement is based on an insufficiently rigorous use of the term 'change.' Accordingly, Suárez explains that any relation can change or cease to exist in one of two ways: either through intrinsic change, as when a father is no longer a father because he dies, or through extrinsic change, where the change occurs in the other partner, for instance, when a father is no longer a father because of the death of his son. Intrinsic change is only possible in positive law, since natural law, Suárez insists, can only undergo extrinsic change, i.e., when, through a change that occurs in an object, it no longer falls under the law. Thus, it is not the law that has ceased to oblige, but the object has been removed from under the law's domain" (295).
113. Suárez, *De Legibus*, II.xiv.12.
114. Suárez, III.xii.12. For further discussion of Suárez's concern with the danger of scandal to a community, see Daniel Schwartz, "Scandal and Moral Demandingness in the Late Scholastics," *British Journal for the History of Philosophy* 23, no. 2 (2015): 256–76.
115. Suárez, *De Legibus*, III.xii.12. It is impossible for the law ever to regulate all vices, since to do this would result in perfect humans, something beyond the law's power.
116. Suárez, II.xiv.15.
117. Suárez, II.xiv.15.
118. Suárez, III.xii.13.

119. Suárez, III.xii.13.
120. Suárez, III.xii.15.
121. Suárez, III.xii.15.
122. Suárez, III.xii.5.
123. Suárez, III.xii.15.
124. Suárez, III.xix.11.
125. Suárez, I.i.6.
126. Suárez, I.ix.4.
127. Suárez, III.xix.2.
128. Suárez, III.xix.3.
129. Suárez, III.xix.5.
130. Suárez, III.xix.6.
131. Suárez, III.xix.7.
132. Suárez, I.ix.11. In this analysis he draws on Aquinas, who also provides the standard for certainty in I–II q. 96, art. 4.
133. Suárez, *De Legibus*, I.ix.11.
134. Suárez, I.ix.11.
135. Suárez, III.x.9.
136. Suárez, III.x.9.
137. Suárez, I.ix.19.
138. Suárez, I.ix.16.
139. Suárez, I.ix.16. For further discussion of this form of engagement with law, see chap. 6 regarding equity.
140. Suárez, I.ix.20.
141. Suárez, I.ix.19.
142. Suárez, III.xix.10.
143. Suárez, III.xix.12.

3

Suárez and Modernity

CRITICS AND CONCERNS

Francisco Suárez's engagement with the political and legal questions raised in early modernity makes his theological jurisprudence a compelling and relevant resource for engaging with legal questions of our own time. However, for some contemporary theologians, especially those who craft a "decline to modernity" narrative, it is precisely Suárez's adaptation of scholastic theology to respond to the challenges of his day that makes his work concerning or problematic. We now consider three key critiques often leveled against Suárez related to his perceived abandonment or corruption of the tradition of scholastic theology and philosophy. Although these critiques engage with various parts of Suárez's extensive corpus, especially his metaphysics, in this chapter we will consider critiques related to Suárez's legal philosophy and theological jurisprudence.[1] The first critique is Alasdair MacIntyre's claim that Suárez's method of philosophical engagement is both ahistorical and operates outside of a tradition, in the mode characteristic of the Enlightenment.[2] The second is John Milbank's claim that Suárez's philosophy of law is divorced from theology because of his claim that law can only orient people to natural ends and form them in acquired virtues. Milbank claims that this neglect of the infused virtues and the supernatural last end is the sign of an abandonment of theology and a total secularization of law.[3] Third is that Suárez's departure from Aquinas's legal theory makes him a voluntarist who contributes to absolutist theories of law rather than opposing them. Examining these responses and critiques will demonstrate more clearly how Suárez's work functions as an authentic development of the Thomistic tradition that is intended to address the problems of the modern world and is suitable for retrieval and action today. Rather than seeing Suárez as functioning outside a tradition, we should see his ideas as connected to an important contemporary theological tradition dedicated to practices of justice and the common good.

Suárez's Philosophy: Rejection of History and Tradition?

In *Three Rival Versions* MacIntyre claims that "for Suárez the notion of working within a tradition had clear relevance in theology but not in what he took to be the timeless studies of the philosopher."[4] To this criticism—that Suárez operates outside of a tradition and thus presents an ahistorical Enlightenment approach to philosophy instead of a tradition-based argument—Robert Miner develops a two-stage response. First, he draws on Étienne Gilson to argue that Suárez is, in fact, extremely aware of and sensitive to the tradition, always writing in dialogue with the tradition rather than ignoring or rejecting it. Gilson writes:

> Suárez enjoys such a knowledge of medieval philosophy as to put to shame any modern historian of thought. On each and every question, he seems to know everybody and everything, and to read his book is like attending the Last Judgment of four centuries of Christian speculation by a dispassionate judge, always willing to give everyone a chance, supremely apt at summing up a case and, unfortunately, so anxious not to hurt equity that a moderate verdict is most likely to be considered a true verdict.[5]

Faint praise, in a certain sense, but, as Miner points out, definitely not an evaluation of Suárez that implies that he errs in departing from the tradition too much. Rather, Gilson implies that Suárez may be almost too respectful to tradition in refusing to reject any part of it. This breadth of knowledge is apparent throughout Suárez's literary corpus. While Suárez most often refers to Aristotle and Aquinas, he widely draws on scripture, patristic writers, scholastics, jurists, and even liturgy.[6]

Terence Irwin also argues for Suárez's solid grounding in tradition. Irwin claims that contemporary scholars who levy critiques that Suárez departs from tradition (such as MacIntyre) may simply be neglecting to take into account the presuppositions that underlie Suárez's writing style. Irwin points out that Suárez intended for his entire discussion of natural laws in *De Legibus* to be understood as a commentary on Aquinas's *Prima Secundae*. Because Suárez was so immersed in the genre of Jesuit commentary on the *Summa Theologiae* and assumes the reader's familiarity, he does not always explicitly state that he is taking the rest of the *Secunda Pars* for granted as an assumed background to the discussion.[7] Suárez himself explicitly links his work to the prevailing scholastic and juristic traditions, even when he acknowledges that doing so may actually impede his goals rather than advance them. For example, in Suárez's introduction to *Defense of the Catholic and Apostolic Faith*, he acknowledges that even though it might have been more effective to write in a polemical style, he was unable to cease writing as a scholastic theologian.[8]

Miner reverses MacIntyre's critique. He argues that rather than a rejection of a tradition-based approach, Suárez's work presents a prime exemplar of the type of tradition-based development that MacIntyre supports: "The play between preservation and innovation is no less present in Suárez than it is in Thomas. Far from being antithetical to MacIntyrean 'tradition-constituted enquiry,' Suárez may well be an exemplary case."[9] While MacIntyre is undoubtedly right that there are points at which Suárez innovates or departs from tradition, MacIntyre's own understanding of tradition-based arguments should leave room for exactly these types of departure as a tradition develops and grows. Irwin makes a similar claim in evaluating Suárez's contribution to legal thought and political theology: "These features of Suárez's views about political society are worth attention not because they are new, but because they are familiar from Aristotle and Aquinas. His contribution is to make clear their implications in the face of the questions, objections, and alternative views presented by Aquinas's successors, including Suárez's own contemporaries."[10]

In his approach to appropriating and developing the work of Thomas Aquinas, Suárez is working very much within the tradition of the School of Salamanca. Following on his Dominican predecessors Vitoria and Soto, Suárez engaged in an interpretive project in which the thought of Aquinas was appropriated to make arguments and develop concepts without the expectation of conformance to the complete Thomistic system. "While the *Summa Theologiae* was the source of many discussions, it did not frame them."[11] This "open Thomism" or "eclectic Thomism" made Thomism the centerpiece of reflection but understood Aquinas's work to be an impetus to theological inquiry, not a limit.[12] As David Lantigua writes in considering the goals of the Salamanca School in creating a synthetic development of Aquinas, "a related characteristic of the school was its usage of diverse theological sources, which extrapolated Aquinas' insight about theology's reliance on arguments from multiple authorities to explain holy teaching (*sacra doctrina*), including scripture and church doctors, but also philosophers and poets (ST I.1.8 ad 2)."[13]

This method of reading Aquinas was also incorporated into the Jesuit tradition of education. The *Ratio Studiorum*—the guide to training Jesuits—in fact explicitly calls upon Jesuits to "expressly follow the teachings of St. Thomas in *scholastic theology*."[14] However, along with this high respect, the

Ratio also notes that these professors "are not to consider themselves so restricted to his teaching that they may not depart from him in any single point."[15] In addition, in situations where ambiguity or openness in the *Summa* exists, "it is permitted to choose either side if Catholic scholars are not in agreement."[16] The appropriate attitude of the Jesuit professor regarding Aquinas's philosophy is helpfully summarized: "He should always speak favorably of St. Thomas, following him readily when he should, differing from him with respect and a certain reluctance when he finds him less acceptable."[17]

As a critical and constructive recipient of this tradition, there are of course times when Suárez departs from Aquinas or at least modifies or narrows Aquinas's definitions.[18] He does not shy away from or try to hide these divergences. Rather, he himself at times points them out. He has much less compunction about disagreeing with some of the prominent Thomists of his own day.[19] However, this readiness does not mean that he does not view himself as deeply indebted to Aquinas and as engaging with the Thomistic tradition. He defines himself as writing within the scholastic tradition formed by Aquinas and deferential to his claims.[20] His legal theory is motivated by the conviction that prevailing political and theological controversies have raised questions that Aquinas did not intend to answer, simply because they had not been raised in Aquinas's own time.[21] Suárez claims that the most faithful way to receive the teaching of Aquinas is to take the resources of his teaching and use them to answer new questions and new challenges. It is precisely this mode of engaging with the tradition that makes Suárez so valuable as a bridge between past legal tradition and contemporary political theology.

A corollary claim to this argument, also presented by MacIntyre, is that Suárez departs from tradition by presenting only abstract theories, not actually serving as a pedagogue seeking to change people's lives and actions by his teaching.[22] This claim can be overturned by recognizing that Suárez's work was intended for practical application in his own time. I am not alone in considering this view. Pierre Hadot, for example, in his work cited by Milbank to discredit Suárez's separation of natural and supernatural ends, actually presents Suárez as one of the last exemplars of the scholar whose work is fundamentally pedagogical because Suárez views philosophy as intended to promote spiritual growth.[23] Clear examples of this are seen in Suárez's own work. For example, in *Metaphysics* he attempts to develop a philosophical method that departs from the standard contemporary approach to teaching Aristotle, that is, a method motivated primarily by pedagogical concerns. He writes that he has moved away from the traditional order of teaching derived directly from the order of Aristotle's works because he finds it too disorganized for effectively instructing novice philosophy students.

In *De Legibus* Suárez's legal work is motivated by the same practical concerns. Amid the European upheaval, he sought to provide a comprehensive source for training lawyers, both in civil law and canon law, synthesizing the works that theologians, jurists, and canon lawyers had developed up to that point. He then draws upon this accumulated wisdom to address questions regarding law raised both by new political theories and the new theologies of the Reformation. The result of this effort was the multivolume legal textbook *Of Laws and the Lawgiver* (*De Legibus*). While *De Legibus* was being printed, Suárez was approached by ecclesial authorities, asking him to respond to a theological dispute that had developed between King James I of England and Cardinal Robert Bellarmine. Bellarmine had written in support of a papal bull condemning a loyalty oath that the king was demanding of his Catholic subjects. James, always eager to join in theological debate, had responded, and Suárez was asked to take up the polemical baton.[24] This request resulted in the work *Defense of the Catholic and Apostolic Faith against the Errors of Anglicanism*. Although the polemical nature of the work is undeniable, it was also intended to serve as a practical handbook to guide United Kingdom Catholics in the basics of faithful citizenship under a hostile ruler who was demanding an oath of spiritual supremacy.[25] These resources are still capable of empowering civic engagement with law today.

Is Suárez's Philosophy Divorced from Theology?

John Milbank has been one of the most prominent critics of Suárez on the grounds that Suárez's political and legal philosophy does not offer any theological basis due to Suárez's covert rejection of theological grounding for politics. Milbank grounds this belief in the claim that Suárez's division of natural ends (which can be determined by philosophy) from supernatural ends leads to a system where "the former remains substantially independent of the latter" and results, among other problems, specifically in a secularization of law.[26] One important example of this separation that Milbank identifies is Suárez's claim that the civil laws can develop the acquired virtues only to advance natural ends, which Milbank claims indicates that Suárez rejects the ultimate supernatural end of all creation.[27]

Milbank is not alone in this assumption, but rather continues a longer English tradition of this mode of reading Suárez.[28] One of the prominent earlier exponents of this critique, the English historian John Figgis, extended the critique to all Jesuit writers of the time period. In a series of lectures on Jesuit political theory, he condemned the Jesuits for the secular character of their conception of the civil power. It is a purely human institution for the worldly ends of peace and riches. It might be said that taking the civil State as a separate entity, they accepted a purely utilitarian view of its activity. It is to them non-moral. Its laws have a merely outward sanction; although it is a duty to obey them, in so far as they do not conflict with higher ends. Their idea of the civil power is, in fact, that of Locke and the individualists who regard the State as necessary for certain indispensable ends, but as in itself dangerous if unchecked, and rather evil than good in its activities. The Jesuit view is that the end of the State being purely external, it cannot be in the last resort worthy of high reverence; and must be kept under tutelage, if man is to reach his highest. They separate sharply the civic life of man, which is external and partial, from his religious, which is internal and all-embracing.[29]

Roman Catholic theologians have expressed similar concerns. John Mahoney, in a footnote in his study *The Making of Moral Theology*, implies that the influence exerted by Suárez, Bellarmine, and their contemporaries was responsible for the Church withdrawing too much from the world, and their reading of Augustine resulted in too much of a separation of the Christian view of law from a secular understanding. "What had been the 'two cities' of Augustine, the city of God and the city of men, gave a spur to Counter-Reformation theologians such as Bellarmine, and to the papacy opposed to the political dissolution of the nineteenth century, to develop a theology of the Roman Catholic Church as a distinct society fully self-sufficient to achieve its own purposes."[30]

These readings of Suárez ignore both his own description of the relationship between theology and philosophy and the deep theological convictions that inform his Jesuit understanding of ecclesiology, politics, and virtue development. Countering the claim that Suárez's work is not theological, Suárez very clearly defines the priority of theology over philosophy in the prologue to his work on metaphysics. "In the present work I am doing philosophy in such a way as to keep always in mind that our philosophy should be Christian and a servant to divine theology. I have kept this aim in view, not only in discussing the questions but all the more in choosing my views or opinions, inclining toward those which seem to comport better with piety and revealed doctrine."[31] Given Suárez's own stated goals and his reputation in his own day as the "most excellent and pious doctor," how then did this disconnect arise between Suárez's stated project of having philosophy serve theology and later readings of his work as rejecting theology? Several factors have contributed to this misreading of Suárez, including ignorance of Suárez's theological writings, confusion regarding the relationship between acquired and infused virtues and natural and supernatural ends, and a lack of consideration of the Jesuit privileging of the Church's role in the world.

Suárez's Legal Theory in Theological Dialogue

This complaint of philosophy divorced from theology ignores Suárez's works on moral theology and sacramental theology, which he viewed as integrally related to his legal philosophy. In a recent article Tobias Schaffner traces this neglect of the broader Suárezian corpus and corresponding limited reading of Suárez's legal theory to a tradition of reading the work of scholastic theologians through one specific view of the development of moral theology. That lens reads the alleged legalism of the manuals back onto scholastic and early modern authors and focuses, therefore, only on their legal works.[32] Schaffner points out that this same legalistic approach characterized much Thomistic scholarship until the 1960s, at which point scholars began to focus more on the theological grounding of Aquinas's theory of law.[33] Schaffner argues that a broader recovery of Suárez's theological work, especially on the virtues, grace, and Christian eudemonism, would result in a reappraisal of Suárez's legal theory as well.[34] Terence Irwin's claim, that Suárez's legal theory is intended to be read as an extended commentary upon the *Secunda Pars,* complements Schaffner's theory by demonstrating the theological content that Suárez assumed was incorporated into any reading of his legal treatise.

While Irwin and Schaffner's claim is accurate, there is also enough theological content in *De Legibus* alone to establish Suárez's work as thoroughly theological. Near the beginning of *De Legibus* Suárez explains why theologians should engage with questions of law. Theological concern is appropriate because the foundation of law implicates a basic question of theology: eternal law, which should be understood specifically as law as it exists in God Himself, or "law by essence [*lex per essentiam*]."[35] All other forms of law, both human and divine, participate in this law to some degree. Every law "derives in some sense from the eternal law ... 'because there is no authority [*potestas*] but from God'" (Romans 13:1).[36] To attempt to make a civil law that contradicts God's law would both violate the intrinsic character of law and exceed the jurisdiction of the human lawgiver, whose jurisdiction does not extend to contradicting God's ultimate authority. However, insofar as eternal law exists in God, it is impossible for humans to access it. Rather, we can only understand "law by participation."[37]

There are four different forms of law by participation. The first two, and the ones that most closely correspond to eternal law, are the law of reason as revealed by nature (natural law) and the law of grace and faith (positive law, given through scripture and the Church).[38] The other two are the law of the people (*ius gentium*) and civil law, considered generally. In addition, law is manifested in three different forms. First it most certainly exists "in an act of the mind and in this way it requires only the judgment of the intellect and not the act of the will, since this is necessary for the observance and execution of the law not for its existence."[39] Second, it exists in the sign (*signum*) or external manifestation (*materia exterior*) that the lawgiver decides.[40] Finally, it exists in subjects' understanding.[41] To understand how positive law exists in subjects' understandings, Suárez argues, depends upon understanding how God's law impacts the subjects' consciences and then, analogously, their reasoning:

> In this same vein are the words of John of Damascus: "The law of God, upon arriving to us, illumines our minds, attracts us to itself and forces our consciences and for this reason we call it the law of our minds." The same thing happens, excepting the distance with the positive laws. Once promulgated, they are applied to each one by means of the judgement of reason, in the sense of which in virtue of the law that which before was not necessary is determined to be necessary and in this form that dictated is then converted into a type of law existing within the subject.[42]

Thus, even to begin to engage in philosophical or legal reasoning for the Christian requires a theological understanding of who God is and how God reveals the eternal law in order to understand the limits, contents, and goals of civil law. The following chapters contain a further exploration of the theological underpinnings of Suárez's legal thought—especially as he relates sacramental theology, moral theology, and scriptural interpretation to theological jurisprudence.

Separation of Natural and Supernatural Ends

Henri de Lubac raises concerns about Suárez's identification of the two different ends for humans and the different ways humans are oriented to those ends. This distinction is crucial for Suárez's theory of civil law. While "human nature is ordered to supernatural happiness as its ultimate end," this ordering does not mean that all natural powers are ordered in the same way or are directed by the same instruments. Suárez illustrates this point by drawing a comparison to the virtues. While the infused virtues are ordered to the end of supernatural happiness through their "intrinsic form of being," the acquired virtues are ordered that way only in "virtue of a relation or an external imperative."[43] The natural powers are ordered in the same way. Political power "is able to be ordered so much to the supernatural happiness as its ultimate end in virtue of an extrinsic relationship . . . with relation to God it is true that all the good—including the natural—that he has given to humans he has given with a view to the supernatural happiness, and in this sense also the political power is given with a view of this end." However, the relationship to this end, because it is not intrinsic, is not something that humans can perceive by the natural light of reason alone; it can be perceived only through supernatural knowledge. "Therefore, if we keep only to the state of pure nature, the civil law is not able to order itself to the supernatural end, not even in this sense."[44]

Suárez does not argue that saying civil law can only direct to a natural happiness denies the existence and primacy of a supernatural happiness, just as saying that it can only direct to the development of the cardinal virtues does not deny the existence of the infused virtues. Rather, he is simply arguing for an appropriately limited view of human power, in line with what he considers to be the Augustinian and Thomistic traditions that civil laws are intended to advance the shared common good of the two cities. Much of the theological reflection grounding Suárez's philosophy of law is grounded in Suárez's analogical reasoning between the figure of the human lawgiver and the divine lawgiver. The fact that Suárez often highlights the dissimilarities between God as lawgiver and humans as lawgivers can make Suárez's work appear nontheological. However, for Suárez, always operating in the traditional Jesuit mode of engagement, such a distinction is actually motivated by deep theological convictions regarding the limits of any analogy between human action and God's authority.[45] These differences crucially include differences in God's power and jurisdiction from humans and results in a limitation of the power of the civil lawgiver when opposed to God, and even when opposed to the power of the Church.

But what about Christian legislators? Surely, aided by the light of faith, they can pass laws that direct to supernatural ends? This is, in fact, part of the claim made by King James in presenting himself both as spiritual and temporal head of England and the Church of England.[46] Christian legislators may have supernatural ends in mind when passing a law, but they can accomplish little as far as obliging citizens to supernatural ends, since neither the objects nor the acts regulated by civil law are directed to spiritual ends.[47] Christian rulers are not given any greater power than pagan rulers in making civil laws, so they have no higher or greater jurisdiction.[48] to promote supernatural ends. However, this can only be done through legislative counsels, which provide good advice and helpful direction to supernatural ends.[49] Rather than limiting the usefulness of Suárez's theory of law, this rejection of theocracy makes Suárez's theory of law more rather than less important to retrieve for our context.

To expect civil lawmakers to comprehend divine things in order to provide proper direction toward them, without the special guidance of the Holy Spirit granted to the Church, expects far too much of them.[50] Suárez argues that the power to make civil laws is derived from the perfect community for the common benefit of that community, which is obtained by promoting peace and justice. God does not grant lawmakers special powers to direct citizens toward divine ends along with the communal grant of authority to direct toward natural ends. Such power expects far too much of citizens in demanding that they obey civil laws directed toward supernatural ends rather than natural ends achieved by their natural abilities. The ability to obey civil laws depends upon the cultivation of the acquired virtues, not the infused virtues. Only the grace of the Holy Spirit, not human lawgivers, can provide the infused virtues. To expect citizens to obey supernatural laws without this infusion is impracticable, and therefore unjust. "The spiritual good or the happiness in this life is a disposition ordered in itself to the ultimate supernatural happiness of the future life or, rather, a certain initiation of that. Thus the power which is not ordered of itself to direct people to that happiness is not able to direct to the spiritual end of this life."[51] Suárez follows this theory of the hierarchy, although not separation, of human happiness in the order in which he presents his theories of law. Because natural happiness is more accessible, Suárez begins by focusing on civil law (book 3) and then moves on to canon law (book 4).[52]

The emphasis on the power of civil law as distinct from the law of the Church, which authors such as Figgis and Milbank read as a rejection of theological authority and a move toward secularization, can arguably also be read as the result of Suárez's Jesuit concern to make sure that the authority of the reigning Christ is not confused with temporal authority, whether of pope or king. Suárez seeks to exalt Christ and extend the reign of God, rather than reject theology. To focus solely on the Church's temporal power, specifically that of the pope, is to run the risk of ignoring the more important spiritual power that Christ gave St. Peter: the keys of the kingdom of heaven.[53]

In addition, as part of his Jesuit charism, Suárez was also influenced by the concept that the natural provides a guide to the supernatural. Laws can be instrumental in directing people toward a growth in virtue but cannot force them to attain supernatural virtues without the aid of the Holy Spirit. Murphy describes Suárez's view of the Jesuit vocation as "that of one standing at the door of the Church looking out toward those who are still in the square outside rather than toward those who are already taking part in the ritual within."[54] For Suárez, civil laws can serve the same function: they can bring people to the church door, but only an encounter with the grace of the living Christ can actually bring them into the Church itself.

Although it is of course possible for this extrinsic perspective to be developed into a classical liberal approach, where the religious is completely excluded from the public square and civil law is detached from any connection to divine revelation (a concern often raised regarding Suárez's potential connection to Locke), Suárez's system does not intrinsically require this approach. Rather, it envisions a substantive role for the importance of scriptural, liturgical, and moral theology in informing how citizens understand and develop law from below.

Acquired and Infused Virtues

Milbank's critique of Suárez as being un-theological also addresses Suárez's claim that civil laws can only promote the development of the acquired virtues. This critique stems from a mistaken assumption that a focus on acquired virtues is inherently not theological. In his analysis of how the cardinal and the theological virtues were understood in the Middle Ages, István Pieter Bejczy writes that modern theologians often err in assuming that questions associated with the cardinal virtues are "philosophical" rather than theological. Although the cardinal virtues relate to natural ends on earth and the common good of the individual and the community, while the theological are directed to achieving supernatural ends and the salvation of souls, "generally speaking, the cardinal and theological virtues bear on two different but complementary dimensions of human existence, one natural, the other supernatural; the theological virtues make us *frui* eternity while the cardinal virtues govern the *uti* of temporal affairs, as several authors repeat after Philip the Chancellor."[55]

This same emphasis on the different but complementary roles of the acquired and infused virtues appears in Suárez. According to Suárez, civil laws enhance human flourishing by developing virtue, even if the virtues developed are limited to the virtues of good citizenship. The only way to make good citizens is to make good people. Being a good citizen does not require goodness in every area, since there are only certain areas of the human life that directly relate to life in the polis. However, within this limit, civil laws can regulate all acquired virtues, not simply virtues related to justice. This is because all acquired virtues are needed for the peace and well-being of a community, just as they are in the life of the individual.

Justice will appear commonly, since relationships between people—which civil laws are intended to regulate—often involve questions about what it means to give others their due. But temperance can be inculcated, for example, in laws prohibiting waste of food or resources (an instance of Suárez expressing one type of environmental concern). And laws relating to the defense of the homeland can promote fortitude. Although laws cannot directly regulate prudence, since all the other moral virtues only operate after prudence has established standards of rectitude and morality, prudence informs both the making of and obedience to all laws.[56] Although law can regulate each of the virtues, this does not mean it regulates each and every act of all virtues. For example, civil law cannot order virginity or forbid adultery, since neither of these directly affect the common good and virginity, at least, is not within the grasp of many people.[57] Civil law cannot even prohibit simple injustices, such as milder forms of deception in sales, when a seller lets a buyer pay more than the item is worth. The reason is that none of these vices cause sufficient scandal to damage the whole community. Additionally, it is unreasonable to expect perfection in every area, since perfection is beyond the grasp of anyone not empowered by grace.

Suárez is clear that a focus upon the development of cardinal virtues alone as the proper effect of civil law is not a rejection of the infused virtues. Rather, his argument is based on an explication and development of Aquinas's claim in I–II q. 90, art. 2, that "the law makes good absolutely or a relative form (*secundum quid*)."[58] How does Aquinas intend the use of the word "relatively"? By one reading it would be possible to understand "relatively" as meaning that law does not make a person good in a moral sense, where "good" is understood as accomplishment and proficiency in skill within some chosen field of human science or art. This is clearly the type of relative "good" that Aquinas means when he says that if robbers obey the laws of robbery, they are "good robbers."[59] However, this cannot be what Aquinas means by relatively here, since civil laws, by definition, do regulate moral matters and, as demonstrated by experience, can make good citizens. "The reason, in the beginning, is that the end of the community consists in a true political happiness, which without (*honestis*) honorable customs is not possible. By laws, however, the citizens are steered to this happiness, and for this reason it is necessary that these laws should extend in themselves to the moral good, that is to say the absolute good (*bonum simpliciter*)."[60] Thus, this is not the sense of relative good that Aquinas intends to apply to civil laws.[61]

In contrast, Suárez argues that when Aquinas says that civil laws can only make a person "relatively" good, he is concerned with how a person is only "relatively" good when she has developed only one virtue, rather than all the virtues.[62] A person may have developed the public virtues required to be a good citizen without also being a good person, so her status should only be understood as "relatively good."[63] The only way in which a person can be absolutely good is by cultivating the virtues required both for being a good person and being a good citizen. In making this argument, Suárez draws upon the traditional Thomistic understanding of the unity of the virtues. In I–II q. 65, arts. 1 and 2, Aquinas identifies two different kinds of perfection. First, in article 1 he describes the acquired virtues as perfected when they are connected to the other moral virtues through prudence. In article 2 he uses the word "perfect" to describe an analogous connection of the other infused virtues through charity. This second type of perfection is the truly (absolutely) perfect kind, since it directs to the supernatural end, while the "perfect" possession of acquired virtue is only relatively perfect, as it directs to natural ends.[64]

Suárez himself points out that this limited understanding of the end of civil law is opposed to the arguments of some theologians who claim civil law can guide humans to true interior happiness and salvation.[65] These theologians, he claims, are subscribing to a "novel" view in which they conflate civil law and canon law, rather than realizing that canon law exists separate from civil law to provide spiritual direction under the authority of the Church.[66] Canon law can provide guidance for developing the virtues appropriate for a good individual, but it does not provide everything necessary to guide a person to the virtues of becoming a good citizen:

> This affirmation is applicable to whatever law in particular, since it does not order to all which is good, but only to a single practice, excepting the law of charity, which completes all virtues. In this way, each law makes the person good only in part (so to speak) ... in this sense they make good in a relative mode, and in the conjunction of the laws they make good in the plain sense.[67]

This distinction, between ends and virtues, also helps make Suárez's theory of law useful in today's diverse and pluralistic society. Without entering too much into a discussion of the role of the Church in the public square, it is worth noting that Suárez, following Aquinas and Augustine, gives Christian citizens the tools to talk about law's ends in a way that does not ignore or contradict their supernatural significance but, by focusing on the law's natural ends, is readily accessible to other citizens who do not share Christian beliefs. Discussing what natural happiness means and how laws can help citizens develop the civic virtues creates plenty of space for aspirational discourse in which Christians and non-Christians can engage together. This does not mean Christians should abandon the supernatural insights granted them by the light of faith and of the Church's teachings, but rather that, as they seek common ground to work for common goods, they can use their supernatural insights to define these goods better and more clearly for all people, knowing that the achievement of even limited natural goods are ultimately related to God's good plan as well.

Is Suárez a Voluntarist?

The third critique to consider are claims that Suárez departed from Aquinas's legal theory in a way that in fact contributed to absolutism rather than challenged it. The earlier work that provided the foundation for the recent restatements of this criticism is *The Natural Moral Law according to St Thomas and Suárez* by Walter Farrell, OP. Farrell's work has influenced some of the more prominent critics of Suárez, including Germaine Grisez, John Finnis, and William Daniel.[68] Farrell begins his treatment of Suárez by writing that "Suárez is the chief opponent of the Thomistic teaching within the church, and his notion is quite directly opposed to that of the Thomists."[69] The reason for this opposition, Farrell argues, is that Suárez identifies the law as essentially "an act of the will." Farrell does acknowledge that Suárez presents this act of the will as being preceded by "counsel and judgement on the part of the intellect."[70] Additionally, he notes that this order, in which will succeeds intellect, only exists in the human legislator since Suárez also acknowledges that "in God there is no succession."[71] However, this does not affect his final conclusion that Suárez falls into voluntarism. The accusation of voluntarism also usually leads to portrayals of Suárez's theory of law as purely penal, where law's only motivating force is to produce sanctions.[72] This entire school of criticism seems to associate Suárez's legal theory with the exclusively voluntaristic approach of Thomas Hobbes or at least John Austin. This critique must be considered on two fronts: the obliging nature of law on the subject and the functioning of the lawgiver.

To begin, Suárez is clear from the beginning of *De Legibus* that his definition of law does depart from Aquinas's definition by stating: "Law is the ordinance of reason to the common good, promulgated by the one who has care of the community."[73] At first it may seem surprising that he begins by departing (at least to a degree) from Aquinas on such a foundational claim, especially after having referenced Aquinas's authority as a justification for why a theologian can study law.[74] It is not that Suárez thinks Aquinas is wrong, but rather that Aquinas's definition is too broad. The contemporary challenges to a Thomistic understanding of law call for more specific definitions and explanations to answer questions that Aquinas was never asked.

Suárez's concern here is not with Aquinas's reliance on reason, nor a critique that those who view him as a voluntarist might expect. In fact, as he points out, Aquinas's emphasis on reason does not limit law to understanding (*intellectus*) or the will (*voluntatis*), but he demonstrates that the ordinance is given in both: "That which proceeds from the will is able to be of the reason, maybe because the will is a rational power, maybe, at the least, because it must be directed by right reason, especially when speaking of the granting of a law."[75] Rather, Aquinas's definition is too broad because it does not distinguish law from counsel or petition. Suárez is concerned that this definition gives too much credence to the claims of those who admit that a counsel is a class of law, rather than a view of law as simply precept. This distinction is important because, unlike Aquinas, he was forced to confront the challenges of the Reformers who conflated evangelical counsels with precepts.[76] Because Suárez strictly emphasizes the role of law as precept, it can appear as though he is only interested in presenting a very rigorous and formalist view of law.[77] However, if we consider his argument fully, it becomes clear that his goal for using this claim is to save the non-obliging nature of counsel.

Suárez addresses the Reformers' conflation of counsel and law by challenging those who argue that even Aquinas places evangelical counsel under the law (*legis*) of grace. In this case, he points out that Aquinas uses law very broadly, to include all the dispositions (*dispositionem*) that the legislator provides to guide his subjects, including not only precepts but counsels over the more perfect things, as we see in civil law, canon law, and, most importantly, in the Gospels.[78] In this sense the counsels "form part of the law of grace in that they are approved and established by it."[79] However, to read these counsels as obligatory for all leads to a far too strict and unreasonable understanding of God's requirements for Christians. In fact, it can lead to exactly the type of rebellion that Suárez believes characterizes followers of Luther: they condemn the counsels because they fail to grasp the difference between a counsel and a precept and believe that because the counsels are impossible to achieve by those acting without God's grace, they should be disowned completely. "For this reason and in defense of the evangelical counsels, we condemn the heretics who censure the poverty and the chastity as contrary to nature."[80]

Precept, counsel, and petition (*pracepetum, consilium, et petition*) are the same in the sense that they are the means by which one person "is ordered or directed to action by the reason of the other. In this sense, it should be said of them that they are an ordinance of reason."[81] However, they differ both in source and in obliging power. Counsel should be understood as taking place between equals or between one who is superior in wisdom, not power, and one who is inferior. Counsel directives, in addition, are not promulgated, in the sense that the promulgation means "the end of establishing an obligation [*ordinem ad obligationem inducendam*]."[82] Suárez believes that he must limit Aquinas's definition to avoid this confusion. Rather than simply saying an "ordinance of reason," he specifies which type of ordinance of reason to use in order to arrive at the definition that "law is a general, just, and stable precept, sufficiently promulgated."[83]

An integral part of this reading of law implies obligation, since the key distinction between counsels and laws is that laws morally oblige but counsels do not. Suárez begins by differentiating obligation from absolute necessity (*necessitatem simpliciter*).[84] Absolute necessity is understood as the force that compels irrational and inanimate creatures to act, through inclination or natural instinct. Things that lack reason may metaphorically be described as obeying law, but this is not, strictly speaking, true. Reason is required for obedience to true moral obligation, which animals lack.[85] In these situations, the term "law" may be applied metaphorically while not carrying its full proper meaning.[86]

Suárez seeks to avoid the identification of law with the instinctual urges of animals, for example, separating the act of a robber holding a gun to somebody's head or a master physically coercing obedience from a slave.[87] He claims that the term law (*lex*), strictly understood, can be applied only to that which pertains to "moral conduct [*actuum moralium*]."[88] Law, therefore (as opposed to command or coercion) gains its authoritative power through moral obligation, not through physical coercion, since it is appropriate to the nature of free rational beings that they should be morally obliged rather than physically coerced. Physical coercion nullifies freedom, but moral obligation upholds freedom since it operates through the power of choice.

Under this logic, Suárez identifies only one type of potential subject for law: the free rational being.[89] When considering the subject of laws, Suárez focuses on one type of free rational agent only: humans, not angelic beings.[90] This limitation of subject matter is determined by his work's very practical pedagogical and polemical goals. Because humans are rational, they are not simply directed by instinct alone, like other animals. In addition to instinct, they can also understand and recognize commands. More important, they can discern whether a command is appropriately given by someone who possesses actual authority. Because of this capacity, laws should be understood as existing in one form in the intellect of the subject, when the subject exercises a judgment of reason that acknowledges that a law has been properly issued.[91] The effect of making this judgment is that even an act that is "not necessary *per se* is judged necessary by virtue of the law. And in this form that judgment is converted into law in the subject herself."[92] Suárez plays with the traditional etymologies of *lex* to make this point. While Aquinas's derivation of *lex* from *ligandum* highlights law's obliging force, the derivation of *lex* from *legendum* asserted by Saint Isidore (the famous jurist) leads to subjects reading the law both from law books and from within their own reason.[93]

In addition to making this intellectual judgment, which makes law exist within the intellect, free humans possess free will, which enables them to choose whether or not to obey. Thus although law exists in the intellect of the subject, laws are obeyed through an act of the will.[94] The involvement of human free will gives law its moral nature. The will is appropriate for this type of choice, since laws do not create habits or potencies, but rather move subjects proximately to actions, which are determined by the will.[95] Each subject therefore receives and obeys law as an individual. It is this combination of will and intellect in the subject that Suárez believes makes law morally obliging, rather than coercive.

It is true that laws can be physically coercive in the sense that breaking them may be followed with punishment. However, punishment is described by Suárez as an "accessory to" rather than of the actual substance of law. Punishment may assist in achieving law's end of making men good, but it follows upon a breach of law, rather than constituting part of law itself, and it may be detached from law, depending upon circumstances.[96] The proof of this separation lies in the fact that while civil laws bind clergy, they are not necessarily subject to punishment in civil courts.[97]

The notion of an obligation-imposing precept implies a relationship of superior and inferior.[98] The sovereign in the case of natural and divine law is clear: God. God, the Creator, Sustainer, and Redeemer of the universe, has obliging power over us and the authority to issue supreme commands.[99] Therefore, when humans hear God's commands and understand that they come from God, there is no room for intellectual judgment as to their validity (although these laws can obviously be disobeyed by the act of the will). The discussion of why humans might have obliging power over others is much more complicated and problematic. As Suárez writes, "humans are by nature free and are not submitted to anybody other than their creator."[100] Because of this complication, there is also much more room for intellectual judgment as to the obliging nature of the laws.

Suárez has been critiqued both by John Finnis and others for his emphasis on law's obliging force. They have read this claim as Suárez seeking to impose a moral obligation through law without any warrant beyond the sheer force of brute will.[101] As noted earlier, it is clear that this is exactly the opposite of Suárez's view of law, which is intended to highlight the moral aspects of legal obligation, not the coercive. Terence Irwin has convincingly challenged this critique through a careful close reading of Suárez's use of the word *obligatum*. Obligation, as distinct from duty (*debitum*), implies the command of a superior.

Irwin's analysis establishes that Suárez's theory on *obligatum* is a description of the action of the lawmaker only: "The features of obligation belong to an act of moral binding. Hence, moral moving means 'morally setting in motion' not 'morally being moved.'"[102] This obliging action places the law within the subject's intellect. It does not physically compel or coerce the subject's action. The subject has the moral responsibility to evaluate whether the command is morally obliging and then must act accordingly. This is why the subject's intellect and will are both important for the law's final phase of existence within the subject. Irwin claims that part of the confusion around Suárez's theory results from a failure to distinguish the general understanding of duty (*debitum*) from *obligatum*. Duties may still impose an action (obligation in the broad sense) but not in the same manner as the moral obligation imposed by a superior.[103]

Conclusion

Through the correct understanding of Suárez's theory of law's obliging force, it is again possible to see how Suárez both emphasizes the importance of the lawgiver to make law obliging and places responsibility on the subject to properly evaluate the law and then act in accordance with that determination of moral obligation. Rather than restricting freedom, this theory of obligation emphasizes and upholds it.

In examining the role of the human lawgiver, Suárez is attempting to negotiate between two dangers. He seeks to derive some positive support for the lawgiver's authority from God's own creative act of making law, thereby strengthening his claims of law's goodness and obliging force. But he is also anxious to avoid falling into a trap of equating the human lawgiver with the divine lawgiver and human law with divine law, both of which would give civil law too much force. The statement that kings are "ministers of God" is not simply a statement of their power. It is a statement of the limitation on how that power is intended to function.[104] Thus, in one verse Suárez finds warrant both for the importance of the lawmaker's authority (coming from God) and the limitations that this warrant for authority places on it (the power must meet the ends for which God intends it). In order to achieve this difficult balance, he first explains how God's act of lawgiving is the analogical model of human lawgiving and then differentiates God's power and authority from that of the human lawgiver.

While it is true that human rulers were not present before the fall, and thus did not originate with creation, this does not mean their existence is contrary to the natural law. Rather, Suárez's concept of permissive natural law means that they are perfectly reasonable developments out of natural law. There is nothing about nature that precludes the existence of people who provide directives for the common good, even in a state of innocence. Suárez explicitly rejects the idea that this power is given through the family unit. There is some form of power in the family unit, by which the master of the household commands the hierarchy of those who are under him and who "are not united as principal members for the composition of one political body, but only exist as inferior members as destined for the use of the master, and to the extent that they are, in some sense, under his dominion."[105] Suárez defines this power as a power of dominion, in which different types of command are given to different people and can be enforced by coercion rather than through moral obligation (in the way that parents may at times physically force their child to act).[106] This means that the ruler is not a second Adam who, because of his role as head of a family, has assumed patriarchal authority over a kingdom as well.[107] This is the opposite from the claim advanced by the absolutist, who believes that the power comes from God directly to the ruler. Suárez writes that there is no grounding either in natural reason or scripture to back up this claim. While Adam may have had domestic power over his children, there is no indication that this power continued after the fall (in fact, given the familial chaos in the chapters of Genesis post-fall, it seems likely that it did not).[108]

Beginning with the figure of God as the ultimate and paradigmatic Lawgiver (as well as the source of all lawgiving authority) means that law must be understood as always good, gift, and grace-filled. Divine law (both natural and positive) is good for us because it shows us what is necessary for salvation, but it also provides the direction for purely natural flourishing. Understanding how God the Lawgiver gives laws to free rational humans provides the exemplar of how human lawgivers should give laws. It also demonstrates how, as free rational creatures, human lawgivers are able to authoritatively will obliging laws into existence in an analogous manner to God's willing.

The similarity between God and the human lawgiver lies in the analogous mental structure of lawgiving required to promulgate a law as opposed to issuing a simple command. For Suárez, lawgiving requires both the intellect and the will of the lawgiver. He posits that both properly oriented intellect and will are required faculties. In order to create valid law, the lawmaker must possess a will that focuses on "the intention of the common good and good governments of the subjects."[109] Only then can the lawmaker conceptualize the law in the intellect or understand which of the myriad possibilities of various laws can be considered just and likely to promote the common good.[110] All eternal laws, therefore, are "conceived in the mind of God from eternity."[111] This same type of intellectual requirement for human lawgivers is justified in Proverbs 8:15, where Wisdom proclaims, "By me kings reign, and lawgivers decree just things."[112] This act of judgment within the intellect is crucial for ensuring that law is prudent, rationally enacted, and appropriately directed. Prudence functions the same way in making political judgments as it functions in enabling each individual to make private judgments for personal welfare: "These two acts constitute in the human a discursive and stair-stepping process. In God, on the contrary, we understand them as a simple and perfect act in the order of reason."[113]

Once the law has been conceived in the mind of the lawgiver, then the lawgiver's intellect must ratify and actualize the judgment of prudence in the will. This final act of the will is that by which the lawmaker "agrees, decides, and desires that his subjects shall be obedient to that which his intellect has judged expedient."[114] This act of the will, which transforms judgment into law, is one of the key distinctions between law and coercion or counsel. This act of will also enables Suárez to distinguish between the physical coercion of the robber and the morally binding obligation of law. When the superior wills to create a law, she wills to create a moral effect in the subject, which obliges the subject's action or restraint. Thus the object of the will is not directly the physical action (again, this would result in physical coercion rather than obligation), but is actually designed to create a moral obligation.[114] In this emphasis on moral obligation, rather than on physical coercion, Suárez is attempting to steer away from the course he believes is advocated by the Machiavellians, who want to strip law of all moral content in order to make it purely coercive. Suárez ensures that law is never described as an act of pure will and always springs from a prudent intellect. On the other hand, as will be discussed in more detail later, he is also seeking to avoid the claims of the Lutherans, who have rejected the theological distinction between counsel and precept.

It is on this point, regarding the importance of the lawmaker's will, that Suárez has been described and at times condemned as a voluntarist.[116] In assessing the justice of this claim, there are several relevant points to be considered. First, Suárez's emphasis on the obliging will never implies that it displaces reason. Rather, he is clear in saying that both are necessary, at different stages, in order for correct lawmaking to take place. The intellect is the "root" of law, since it is a "judgment that precedes, directs and, so to speak, regulates the will."[117] However, it is the will that imposes obligation and is key to Suárez's definition of law as obliging precept. Thus, while Suárez does eventually decide on the primary definition of law as will, since it is "better understood and upheld," he does not want this primacy to result in an abandonment of the identification of law with reason. Rather, he sees the identification of will and intellect as inextricably intertwined. Therefore, Suárez writes, although he has identified law with will, it is just as reasonable to define law as it exists in the lawgiver as an act of the intellect, since it is through the intellect that the lawgiver dictates the external law and it is in the lawgiver's intellect that it is "written."[118]

Notes

1. I am indebted to Robert Miner for his identification of the first two critiques and literature review of the claimants. See Robert Miner, "Suárez as a Founder of Modernity: Reflections on a *Topos* in Recent Historiography," *History of Philosophy Quarterly* 18, no. 1 (January 2001): 17–36: 20. See also Richard Cross, "Duns Scotus and Suárez at the Origins of Modernity," in *Deconstructing Radical Orthodoxy*, ed. Wayne J. Hankley and Douglas Hedley (Farnham, UK: Ashgate, 2005), 85–102.
2. Alasdair MacIntyre, *Three Rival Versions* (Notre Dame, IN: University of Notre Dame Press, 1990), 73–74.
3. Miner, "Suárez as a Founder of Modernity," 23.
4. MacIntyre, *Three Rival Versions*, 73–74.
5. Miner, "Suárez as a Founder of Modernity," 22.
6. For an illustration of this influence, in Suárez's philosophical work, *Disputationes*, Aristotle is cited 1,735 times, followed by Aquinas, who is cited 1,008 times, Scotus 363 times, and Augustine 334 times. See John Doyle, "Francisco Suárez: His Life, His Works, His Doctrine," in *Collected Studies on Francisco Suárez, SJ (1548–1614)*, ed. Victor Salas (Leuven, Belgium: Leuven University Press, 2010), 7.
7. Terence Irwin, *The Development of Ethics, Vol. 2* (Oxford: Oxford University Press, 2007), 2. Suárez's uncle and predecessor in the Jesuit Order, Cardinal Francisco de Toledo, wrote one of the first Jesuit commentaries on the *Summa*. See Bernhard Knorn, SJ, "Theological Renewal after the Council of Trent? The Case of Jesuit Commentaries on the *Summa Theologiae*," *Theological Studies* 79, no. 1 (2018): 112–14.
8. See Francisco Suárez, SJ, *Defense of the Catholic and Apostolic Faith*, trans. Peter L.P. Simpson (New York: Lucairos Occasio, 2012), 35.
9. Miner, "Suárez as a Founder of Modernity," 24.
10. Irwin, *Development of Ethics*, 2:31.

11. Lidia Lanza, "The Commentary Tradition on the *Summa Theologiae*," in *Summistae: The Commentary Tradition on Thomas Aquinas' Summa Theologiae from the Fifteenth to Seventeenth Centuries*, ed. Lidia Lanza and Marco Toste (Leuven, Belgium: Leuven University Press, 2021), 11.
12. Juan Belda Plans, *La Escuela de Salamanca y la Renovacion de la Teologia en el Siglo XVI*, Vol. 63 (Madrid: Biblioteca de Autores Cristianos, 2000), 211–12.
13. David Lantigua, "Aquinas and the Emergence of Moral Theology during the Spanish Renaissance," in *The Oxford Handbook of the Reception of Aquinas*, ed. Matthew Levering and Marcus Plested (Oxford: Oxford University Press, 2021), 176.
14. *The Jesuit Ratio Studiorum of 1559*, 33, trans. Allen P. Farrell, SJ, accessed March 3, 2023, https://academics.lmu.edu/media/lmuacademics/centerforteachingexcellence/documents/ratio1599.pdf.
15. *Jesuit Ratio Studiorum of 1559*, 33.
16. *Jesuit Ratio Studiorum of 1559*, 34.
17. *Jesuit Ratio Studiorum of 1559*, 40–41.
18. For example, Suárez explicitly departs from Aquinas on the doctrine of the Immaculate Conception in order to advance a theory more in line with Catholic teaching today. See, for example, Robert Fastiggi and Victor Salas, "Francisco Suárez, the Man and His Work," in *A Companion to Francisco Suárez*, ed. Robert Fastiggi and Victor Salas (Leiden, The Netherlands: Brill, 2015), 7.
19. In one letter Suárez rejects the claims of those who say he is departing from the teaching of Aquinas to present new doctrine and those who are speaking against him, he argues, are the ones actually departing from Aquinas and presenting the claims of their own teachers as a certain rule. They condemn those who depart or add from their teachers (not Aquinas) as introducing "a new and dangerous idea." Cited in Ramón Camacho, "Francisco Suárez, teólogo y filósofo de la imaginación y la libertad," *Revista de Filosofía* 25, no. 58 (2008) : 79–101.
20. Camacho, "Francisco Suárez."
21. Irwin, *Development of Ethics*, 2:29–30.
22. John Milbank, *Beyond Secular Order* (Hoboken, NJ: John Wiley & Sons, 2014), 27.
23. Pierre Hadot, *What Is Ancient Philosophy?* (Cambridge, MA: Harvard University Press, 2002), 255.
24. Fastiggi and Salas, "Francisco Suárez," 21–22.
25. See Suárez, *Defense*, VI.8 for a discussion of how faithful Catholics under pressure could proceed to take a heretical oath.
26. John Milbank, *Beyond Secular Order* (Hoboken, NJ: Wiley-Blackwell, 2013), 34.
27. Milbank, 27.
28. For a full genealogy of this view, see Tobias Schaffner, "Is Francisco Suárez a Natural Law Ethicist?," in *The Concept of Law (lex) in the Moral and Political Thought of the School of Salamanca*, ed. Kirstin Bunge et al. (Leiden: Brill, 2016), 154–55.
29. John N. Figgis, *Studies of Political Thought: From Gerson to Grotius, 1414–1625* (Cambridge: Cambridge University Press, 1907), 204.
30. John Mahoney, *The Making of Moral Theology: A Study of the Roman Catholic Tradition* (Cambridge: Clarendon, 1989), 224n1.
31. Francisco Suárez, Preface to *Disputationes Metaphysicae*, quoted in the translator's introduction to Francisco Suárez, *On Creation, Conservation, and Concurrence: Metaphysical Disputations 20–22*, trans. Alfred Freddoso (South Bend, IN: St. Augustine's Press, 2002), iv.

32. Schaffner, "Is Francisco Suárez a Natural Law Ethicist?," 154.
33. Schaffner, 154.
34. Schaffner, 155.
35. Francisco Suárez SJ, *de legibus ac Deo legislatore*, Vol II, ed. Luciano Pereña et al. (Madrid: Consejo Superior de Investigaciones Cientificas, 1975), introduction.
36. Suárez, I.iii.17.
37. Suárez, II, introduction.
38. Suárez, III.xii.5.
39. Suárez, I.iv.5.
40. Suárez, I.iv.14.
41. Suárez, I.iv.5.
42. Suárez, I.iv.5.
43. Suárez, III.xi.4.
44. Suárez, III.xi.4.
45. The emphasis on the awareness of the dissimilarity between God as Lord and humans as lord, articulated in the exercises of the Jesuit charism, was developed in more depth by Eric Pryzwara, who was also influenced by Suárez. This dissimilarity does not lead to a nullification of the individual's service, but rather leads to an understanding of its proper ends and values. "At no point, not even at the eschaton, is the *maior dissimilitudo* of the servant/Lord analogy of proportion overcome. At the same time, Przywara's stipulation that the individual remains one of the Lord's servants entails that service maintains a real integrity. The individual is not ultimately annihilated as he is subsumed into God or into some kind of undifferentiated 'world soul.' Rather, he retains and offers his own unique service." Brian Dunkle, "Service in the *Analogia Entis* and Spiritual Works of Erich Przywara," *Theological Studies* 73 (2012): 348–49.
46. See Suárez, *De Legibus*, III.6.
47. Suárez, *De Legibus*, III.xi.8.
48. Although it is outside the realm of this work, it is worth noting that this equivalency between pagan and Christian rulers provides a key building block for understanding Suárez's concept of religious freedom.
49. Suárez, *De Legibus*, III.xi.11.
50. Suárez, III.xi.3.
51. Suárez, III.xi.6.
52. Jean-Paul Coujou, "Political Thought and Legal Theory in Suárez," in *A Companion to Francisco Suárez*, ed. Robert Fastiggi and Victor Salas (Leiden, The Netherlands: Brill, 2015), 33–34.
53. Antonio Molina Melia, *Iglesia y Estado en el siglo de oro español: el pensamiento de Francisco Suárez* (Valencia: Universidad, Secretariado de Publicaciones, D.L. 1977), 185.
54. Paul Murphy, "God's Porters: The Jesuit Vocation according to Francisco Suárez," *Archivum Historicum Societatis Jesu* 70, no. 139 (2001): 28.
55. István Pieter Bejczy, *The Cardinal Virtues in the Middle Ages: A Study of Moral Thought from the Fourth to the Fourteenth Century* (Leiden: Brill, 2011), 183.
56. Suarez, *De Legibus*, III.xii.8.
57. Suárez, III.xii.11.
58. Suárez, I.xiii.6.
59. Suárez, I.xiii.6.
60. Suárez, I.xiii.7.
61. Suárez, I.xiii.6.

62. Suárez, I.xiii.7.
63. Suárez, I.xiii.7.
64. For further discussion, see Thomas M. Osborne Jr., "Perfect and Imperfect Virtues in Aquinas," *The Thomist* 71, no. 1 (January 2007): 43. For an analysis of the psychological reality of the unity of the virtues, see Jean Porter, "The Unity of the Virtues of the Ambiguity of Goodness," *Journal of Religious Ethics* 21, no. 1 (1993): 137–63.
65. Suárez, *De Legibus*, III.xi.3.
66. Suárez, III.xi.4.
67. Suárez, I.xiii.8.
68. See Tobias Schaffner, "Is Francisco Suárez a Natural Law Ethicist?," 154. See also John Finnis, *Natural Law and Natural Rights* (Oxford: Oxford University Press, 2011) 47; William Daniel, SJ, *The Purely Penal Law Theory in Spanish Theologians from Vitoria to Suárez* (Rome: Gregorian University Press, 1968), 200–208; and Germain Grisez, "The First Principle of Practical Reason," in *Natural Law Forum* 10 (1965): 184n40.
69. Walter Farrell, OP, *The Natural Moral Law According to St Thomas and Suárez* (Ditchling, UK: St. Dominic's Press, 1930), 52.
70. Farrell, 52.
71. Farrell, 50.
72. See, for example, Daniel, *The Purely Penal Law Theory*, 205–6: "Moral obligation and the threat of punishment were parallel forms of authority."
73. Suárez, *De Legibus* I.xii.3, citing Aquinas, *Summa Theologiae*, I–II q. 90, art. 4.
74. Suárez, *De Legibus*, introduction.
75. Suárez, I.xii.3.
76. Suárez, I.i.7.
77. See Schaffner, "Is Francisco Suárez a Natural Law Ethicist?," 153–54, for a critique of the limited engagement with Suárez's corpus, which he believes results in this view.
78. Suárez, *De Legibus*, I.xiv.11.
79. Suárez, I.xiv.11.
80. Suárez, I.xiv.11.
81. Suárez, I.xii.4.
82. Suárez, I.xiv.11.
83. Suárez, I.xii.5.
84. Suárez, I.xiv.1.
85. Suárez, I.vi.1.
86. Suárez, I.xiv.2.
87. Suárez, I.iii.2.
88. Suárez, I.i.5.
89. Suárez, I.i.2.
90. Suárez, introduction. See also I.ii.17 for an acknowledgment that angelic law is not a topic in this work.
91. Suárez, I.iv.5.
92. Suárez, I.iv.5.
93. Suárez, I.i.9.
94. Suárez, I.iv.5.
95. Suárez, I.iv.3.
96. Suárez, I.xv.14–16. The connection between Suárez's understanding of obligation and coercion is another of the allegations against his theory of law. For example, Jerome

Schneewind writes: "Suárez explains the motivational force of obligation in terms of the threat of penalties. I have already noted that he thinks many people are unable to understand the rationale for the laws that govern them. This means that they will not see the good that compliance brings about, and therefore that they cannot be moved by a desire to attain that good. In its place Suárez puts the motive of avoiding threatened punishment." Jerome B. Schneewind, "Modern Moral Philosophy: From Beginning to End?" in *Essays on the History of Moral Philosophy*, ed. Jerome B. Schneewind (Oxford: Oxford University Press, 2009), 89–90. While Schneewind is correct that Suárez does claim that the natural law is "binding under pain of eternal punishment" (II.ix.3), this is not the same thing as implying that it is binding *because of* eternal punishment.

97. Suárez, *De Legibus*, III.xxxiv.21.
98. Suárez, I.xii.4.
99. Suárez, II.iv.2.
100. Suárez, III.i.1.
101. See Terence Irwin, "Obligation, Rightness and Natural Law," in *Interpreting Suárez: Critical Essays*, ed. Daniel Schwartz (Cambridge: Cambridge University Press, 2011), 142–43, citing John Finnis's *Natural Law and Natural Rights*. See also Thomas Pink, "Reason and Obligation in Suárez," in *The Philosophy of Francisco Suárez*, ed. Benjamin Hill and Henrik Lagerlund (Oxford: Oxford University Press, 2012), 175–208.
102. Irwin, "Obligation, Rightness and Natural Law," 158.
103. Irwin, 162.
104. Suárez, *De Legibus*, I.vii.5.
105. Suárez, I.vi.20.
106. Suárez, I.vi.20.
107. See J. P. Sommerville, "From Suárez to Filmer: A Reappraisal," *Historical Journal* 25, no. 3 (September 1982): 537–38. An important point that Suárez makes contra the absolutist is a repeated sundering of the link between family government and civil law. While absolutists such as King James I claimed that their power developed from the patriarchal power but at a higher level, Suárez cuts the connection. Since laws must be generally applied and grounded in an authority derived from the community, family precepts will never possess sufficient authority, since they are not sufficiently communal. Rather, laws by definition are perpetual and apply to the whole community. The faculty of prudence is architectonic for the making of laws, and prudence looks to the community.
108. Suárez, *De Legibus*, III.ii.3.
109. Suárez, I.iv.6.
110. Suárez, I.iv.6.
111. Suárez, I.iv.4.
112. Suárez, I.iv.6. Suárez's use of this verse is important in his rejection of the claims of the absolutists. Often in absolutist literature the verse is used to justify a divinized understanding of human kingship. However, by reminding his readers that it is actually Wisdom who utters these words, Suárez recontextualizes it to place a higher standard and burden on human lawgivers, rather than letting it be used as a justification for stronger legislative authority.
113. Suárez, I.iv.6.
114. Suárez, I.iv.7.
115. Suárez, I.iv.9. The moral obligation comes from God ultimately, not from the will of the legislator. God is the author of the binding obligation that law places on the subject,

although in human law it is mediated (unlike eternal, natural, and divine positive law, whose obligations are directly imposed).
116. See, for example, Thomas E. Davitt, SJ, *The Nature of Law* (St. Louis, MO: B. Herder, 1951): "Suárez, in giving the will the power of regulating, enlightening, and ordering, is making the will independent of the intellect and of any necessity deriving thereof" (39). Similarly, William Daniel writes, "There can be no reasonable doubt that [Suárez's theory of law in general] is purely voluntarist" (Daniel, *Purely Penal Law Theory*, 88).
117. Suárez, *De Legibus*, I.v.23.
118. Suárez, I.v.23.

4

The Work of the People

THE POWER OF CUSTOM
FOR POSITIVE LAWMAKING

In his analysis of the significance of the term "custom" in 42 U.S. Code § 1983 of the Civil Rights Act, George Rutherglen describes custom as if it were a malevolent ghost haunting American jurisprudence. Section 1983 explicitly creates a cause of action for violations of federal rights "under color of any statute, ordinance, regulation, custom, or usage, of any State."[1] However, modern case law relating to section 1983 does not address uses or customs, focusing instead on laws made by legislative officials (i.e., statute, ordinance, and regulation).[2] Why then, Rutherglen asks, does section 1983 expressly refer to "custom" and "usage" as if they had equivalent legal significance to the more commonly recognized legislatively imposed statute or regulation?[3]

The answer, Rutherglen argues, is that when the statute was drafted, an understanding of custom as a freestanding source of law, capable of imposing obligation and even counteracting statutory law, was still present in the American legal system and at certain times played a "pervasive role."[4] In post–Civil War America, where custom was used to justify continued exploitation and domination of former slaves, the pervasive role was pernicious, and section 1983 was intended to combat custom's authority.[5] Faced with this problematic manifestation of customary law to justify oppression, the American legal system turned to an imposition of law from above in order to combat racism, enshrining customary law as a hazard to a morally functioning democracy. Although the influence of racist customs on legal interpretation in the South provided the instance for custom's decline, Rutherglen argues that the erosion of custom's authority of law can be traced back further to mid-nineteenth-century positivist philosophers of law.[6] Most prominent among these early legal positivists was Jeremy Bentham, who argued, contra Blackstone and the legal establishment of the day, that custom could never have law's authority.

However, another story might be told about the power of custom for shaping law to be *more* just, rather than less. Sociologists studying faith-based community organizing within the Latino community in the United States have described the immense political power that those involved in community organizing believe is present if the entire community can be mobilized. Cesar Chavez alludes to this power in the introduction to *Forty Acres*:

> I have always believed that, in order for any movement to be lasting, it must be built on the people. They must be the ones involved in forming it, and they must be the ones that ultimately control it. It is harder that way, but the benefits are more meaningful and lasting when won in this fashion. It is necessary to build a power base. Money by itself does not get the job done.[7]

Chavez claims that this power of the people, which changed and challenged the laws that kept workers in poverty and subjected them to unjust treatment, was only actualized when a group of people came together intentionally and engaged in sustained communal action with a common goal. The problem with poverty programs, he argues, is that their proponents believe money alone can solve poverty disconnected from sustained popular involvement with law directed to the common good as ascertained by each specific community. Although Chavez does not actually mention the word custom, his theory, that popular power achieved through sustained communal action, provides an example of a potential positive retrieval of custom's power for positive lawmaking.

We discover the same claims in a more explicitly theological vein in the liberation theology of Gustavo Gutiérrez. Gutiérrez writes that "the process of liberation requires the *active participation of the oppressed*; this certainly is one of the most important themes running through the writings of the Latin American church."[8] Gutiérrez describes the role of the Church as "addressing the oppressed" to describe for them the agency and power they already possess for standing against the oppressor and addressing the oppressor through "prophetic denunciation of these grave injustices."[9]

Suárez's theory of law as custom runs in the same intellectual and theological stream as these claims. Given the genealogical connection between Suárez and liberation theology, this similarity is not surprising. In this instance, retrieving the thought of Suárez alongside contemporary resources adds two things. First, Suárez's theory of law as custom is a helpful thematization and theological description of popular praxis's power to make law. Suárez, like Chavez, believes custom has the potential to be a powerful communal engagement tool for challenging and even reforming unjust laws instead of being inevitably a tool of oppression in creating unjust laws. Second, as Gutiérrez argues in his retrieval of the thought of Bartolomé de las Casas, engaging with the theology of sixteenth-century Spain in relationship to these questions of injustice and oppression is not an attempt to "reset the watch of history." Rather, in considering how Christians answered the pressing moral questions of earlier epochs, we are better able to understand "the density of our present and the promises of the future."[10]

A retrieval of Suárez's theory of custom must demonstrate how Suárez's theory overcomes the critiques of custom provided by legal philosophers from Jeremy Bentham to the present day and offer a concept of custom worth retrieving for our contemporary context. A brief overview of the historical background that shaped Suárez's understanding of custom is followed by consideration of how Suárez's theory of custom as law satisfies modern appropriations of Bentham's four critiques. We will conclude by considering how Suárez's theory of custom is constructively embodied in two contemporary examples of custom changing law to promote justice and enhance the common good. On a global scale, how has custom contributed to the development of international law regarding questions of environmental justice? Turning to a more particular example, Suárez's theory of custom as law provides an important theological articulation of elements of faith-based community organizing inspired in part by Cesar Chavez. The focus of the analysis is on one of these groups: Communities Organized for Public Service (COPS), based in San Antonio, Texas.

The Decline of Custom

In his article "Custom Redeemed by Statute," Jeremy Waldron identifies Bentham's four primary critiques of custom.[11] First is Bentham's questioning of custom's authority. Can custom, which arises from the actions of the people not from the will of the sovereign, actually be law? Second, how can we distinguish legally authoritative custom from the decisions of judges, who impose their own interpretation? Third, can customs, by definition the actions of the majority, become law without endangering the rights and freedoms of the minority? Fourth, even if custom as law is valid in some societies, can custom function as law in the highly regulated modern world? These challenges, in various forms, have been taken up and adapted by Bentham's positivist successors.

However, despite this rejection among legal positivists, consideration as to whether custom can function as law has recently revived in legal scholarship—most prominently in the context of international law.[12] To provide just a few examples, in his challenge to H. L. A. Hart's legal positivism, Lon Fuller argues for at least some acknowledgment of the force of custom to change and shape civil law.[13] Even Joseph Raz, one of the leading voices of contemporary legal positivism, has presented a brief claim that custom, although it is not issued by a legislative authority, can have legal authority in certain contexts because it provides an exclusionary reason for acting.[14] Gerald Postema has also defended law as custom. Postema's argument is that most traditional concepts of law as custom are deficient because they depend upon the "additive concept"—the belief of the people involved that the customs should be law—in order to discover when custom has evolved into law.[15] In supposed contrast, he argues that customs functioning as laws should be understood as "norms that arise from discursive normative practices embedded in rich contexts of social interaction."[16]

Contemporary Developments of Bentham's Critiques

Hart's revised legal positivism unconditionally rejects the possibility that custom can ever have its own legal authority. Rather, custom must be "recognized by a legal system," or, in other words, by statutory law.[17] Otherwise, it is simply "pre-legal . . . one class of primary rules of obligation, which is sufficient for governing only 'a small community closely knit by ties of kinship, common sentiment, and belief.'"[18] Only the introduction of rules of recognition can create a legal system and make laws valid.[19] Neil MacCormick denies that customs can have the same validity as statutory laws. MacCormick acknowledges that customs and common usage contribute to legal systems, but only because they uphold the tradition that law "ought to be respected in carrying out its functions as these are constitutionally conferred."[20] Custom can provide guidance as to how separation of powers should be respected and interpreted, but cannot establish laws.[21]

Like Bentham, Hart also raises epistemological questions. Custom cannot become law on its own and can be made into statutory law only according to the appropriate rule of recognition, that is, by establishing that the sovereign has granted it legal status.[22] Frederick Schauer, drawing on Norwood Hanson, raises a slightly different objection when considering the role of judges. Is it possible to ever be sure that the customs that judges do recognize as law accurately capture and describe the authentic actions of the people, as opposed to being simply the articulation of the judge's own norms? Schauer argues that judges are inevitably trapped by interpreter's bias of assuming that her own perspective constitutes the most likely, most reasonable, or most widely accepted understanding of a situation.[23]

The question of whether the customary law actually "works itself pure" through repetition remains one of the most important critiques of custom.[24] Clearly, Bentham's concern that the custom of the majority can be used to trample on the rights of the minority is vindicated by the state and local laws of the Jim Crow South. David Bederman traces through other historical contexts this same concern, that custom may be used as simply "a method of social control by elites."[25] He demonstrates that a history of common usage does not necessarily provide any guarantee that the actions of the community will lead to the enactment of laws better than laws instituted by the legislator.

Bentham's final objection is that custom alone is insufficient for meeting the needs for law in our modern, diverse, and complex legal systems.[26] While Hart does grant that custom may fill the gaps of a developing legal system and function as a "pre-legal" source of obligation, it is static, uncertain, and too inefficient to adapt to our current fast-moving, bureaucratic, and highly regulated society.[27] Bederman draws on ethnographic research on customary law practices to elaborate on Hart's concern about custom's static nature. Often by the time the custom has achieved sufficient broad usage to function as law, the cultural tide has moved past the communal justification or need of the custom, leaving behind only a pattern of behavior "hardened into formalism and ritual, empty of meaning and divorced from social context."[28] It is in these situations that customs become oppressive instead of constructive, when the underlying rationale has vanished and only the obligation remains. In the discussion of culture in the medieval context, we can see this shift from constructive to oppressive in the attempt by the new feudal lords to claim the duties owed by the peasant class without acknowledging the reciprocal obligations of care and protection that had originally been the ruler's responsibility. Schauer is also concerned about how custom can function as law in the context of diverse modern societies. While some coherent and connected communities who can establish customs do still exist, it seems likely that any claim that they have established a law according to custom likely directly conflicts with a custom advanced by another group.[29] How, then, can custom ever become sufficiently established as law for a united community?

Custom in Medieval Jurisprudence

These same questions concerning the role of custom as law arose out of the political and theological conflict of the Middle Ages. As political authority declined across much of eleventh-century Europe, existing statutory law was no longer enforced and new statutes were never enacted. Often monarchs lacked not only the ability to enforce laws against local feudal warlords but even the capacity to have laws promulgated in writing.[30] Feudal lords rose to fill the resulting power gaps, making repeated demands for new services and money upon the helpless inhabitants of a region. These tyrannical demands "quickly turned into legal dues based on custom: the hated *consuetudines*— an old word with a new meaning, that is, "of seigniorial rights"—which appear in the texts around AD 1000 and for whose reduction the peasants would fight with a good deal of success in the twelfth century."[31]

Over the course of the eleventh and twelfth centuries the development of centralized sovereign power seemed to offer the only hope for achieving peace and order.[32] Seeking protection against tyranny and protesting the abuses of custom, the people called upon the ruler to promulgate and enforce statutory laws invalidating bad and unjust customs enforced by the feudal aristocracy.[33] This popular impetus to place more authority in the hands of the ruler was also supported by a shift in legal theory. The recovery of Justinian's *Digest* and the subsequent reclaiming of the tradition of Roman law resulted in a shift in emphasis on the legislative authority of the emperor to the power of local custom.[34] In the eyes of many contemporary legal scholars, "customary procedure devoid of intellectual justification yielded to the reasoning that informed the Roman law of sale or the new canon law of marriage."[35]

However, the substitution of legislation for customs was not uncritically accepted. Ordinary citizens were aware that the ruler did not hesitate to use legislative power to his or her own advantage rather than simply to rein in rapacious nobles. In addition, in many places the new *consuetudines* had not fully erased earlier communal practices. At times, ancient custom seemed to be the only power that could oppose the tyrannical demands of the "new" customs. In Anjou, for example, "imperial precepts of redress were long dead in this burgeoning new society, while regional custom, precocious though it was in Anjou, was slow to develop a jurisprudence of security. . . . But by resisting the arbitrary imposition of new customs and by holding to comital authority in defense of old immunities, monks and canons (and surely also lay people of whom we have no record) preserved a façade of public order."[36] The people were therefore not always willing to permit rulers to erase all governing customs. In this skepticism and concern regarding expanding royal power, they were often supported by Church officials, who had their own reasons for skepticism about rulers appropriating too much power.

These same tensions between local custom and legislative authority were also arising within the Church, as local customs came into conflict with attempts to universally systematize canon law.[37] In his *Decretum*, or *Concord of Discordant Canons*, Gratian (ca.1100–1155) argued for upholding as law the good parts of custom, while jettisoning the bad. Gratian begins by defining two sources of human law: natural right and practices.[38] Natural right, defined as "that which is contained in the Law and the Gospel," clearly judges human practice.[39] However, natural right as it exists alone "has no such direct juridical force. The basic principles of reason, truth and justice must be formulated—and therefore restricted in scope, made determinate—in order to serve as a base for adjudication."[40] This means that natural rights can only be applied through the human practices of promulgating written law and of establishing customs. As Jean Porter writes, "the subordination of practices to natural right is thus qualified and balanced by the indeterminacy of natural right apart from the specifics of human practices, and custom and written law can be considered together as two alternative and (ideally) complementary ways of giving expression and force to natural right."[41]

On one hand Gratian believes that the existence of one central authority, within both the Church and the civil government, is necessary to promote unity, stability, and justice.[42] On the other hand he has both pragmatic and theological justifications for upholding the continuing importance of custom.[43] Custom is important because it enables local communities to be governed in a way that acknowledges their particular contexts and practices, such as local Church customs of piety and worship.[44] When the law is deficient or fails in justice, custom may be written down and become civil law.[45] However, where the law is not deficient, custom must yield to the written law.

The end result of this harmonization is that priority is eventually granted to the written law. Porter argues that this prioritization is not meant to diminish the fact that custom can be an authoritative expression of natural rights. Rather, it is simply the recognition that "written law will normally represent a more perspicuous and clearly authoritative expression of natural right than does custom."[46] Still, the statute does not always offer the final word. Rather, "when an ordinance is irrational or unjust, or in some other way at odds with natural right, the non-reception by the people offers one way of rejecting and correcting the putative ordinance in question."[47]

Gratian's paradigm, in which both statutory law and custom exist in harmony and are not in competition, defined the broad outlines under which custom was considered by his successors. Both custom and statutory law were acknowledged to be important, but the exact terms of the harmonization were subject to debate. The development of this debate is captured in Aquinas's treatment of custom. Aquinas argues that custom can establish law, but only in proportion to the power maintained by the community. If the community retains its full sovereignty it can establish law through custom without permission. If the community does not retain full lawmaking power but rather delegates some of it, the ruler must tolerate the custom in order for it to become law.[48] The type of repeated actions that become custom are restricted to those that "proceed from the inner judgment of reason."[49] If it is a valid custom, custom is sufficient to establish law, interpret law, and even abolish law by indicating through popular rejection that the statutory law has lost its reasonableness.[50]

Suárez's Theory of Law as Custom

In developing his theory of custom as law, Suárez clearly sees himself as the bearer and articulator of this long tradition that provides rich resources to answer the questions and challenges raised in his own time.[51] However, unlike his medieval predecessors, Suárez's early modern context meant that he had to engage with different challenges related to custom's authority as law: both the increased statutory regimes of the nation-state as well as the theological challenges to fundamental understandings of custom as law posed by the Protestant Reformers.[52] By drawing upon these traditional resources and reflecting upon the challenges posed to custom as law, Suárez ends up responding to challenges that are very similar to those posed by contemporary philosophers of law.

Suárez's Definition of Custom

Suárez distinguishes two types of custom: customs of fact and customs of law. Any repeated moral action (with "moral" implying "free") performed frequently in the same way by the majority of the community creates a custom of fact—that is, custom understood formally.[53] This repetition of actions inevitably has an "aftereffect [*relinquitur*]."[54] In the individual, the aftereffect is physical: the development of a "personal habit [*habitus*]."[55] Under certain conditions, "customs of fact [*consuedutine*]" can also produce an aftereffect relating to the communal moral order.[56] These repeated actions by a community can generate what Suárez refers to as a moral "power"(*facultatem*) or a moral "obligation, which we call law" (*vinculum, quod jus appellamus*).[57] But only the "common and public" actions of the entire community can give custom the force needed to become law.[58] Therefore, according to Suárez, custom has the potential to be not simply a pre-legal popular reflection nor an indicator of what the law may be. Rather, under the right conditions, custom *is* law: "custom is not settled law, but rather it settles law."[59]

Although Suárez claims that popular custom developed by the people can become law, he is also well aware of the danger that unchecked development of custom can pose to the stability of the community. Not every custom is capable of generating a law, just as not every declaration of a lawmaker can create a law. Just as there are pronouncements of a lawmaker that might appear to be law but are actually only counsel, there are some types of communal actions that might appear to be customs of law but in reality are simply customs of fact. These are customary actions that are not capable of producing the moral effect that creates law.[60] This includes customs developed out of existing laws.[61] In such cases, while the repeated actions of obedience strengthen the force of the law, the actions do not create the law, but rather the law mandates the actions.[62] Furthermore, laws creating customs must be distinguished from private rights or privileges created by custom. While rights or privileges might be binding on individuals in specific situations, they cannot be considered law because they do not govern the whole community.[63]

In addition, just as the commands of the lawmaker must contain specific elements in order to become law, so too must the custom. The elements that must be present in both instances are fitness of subject matter, appropriate power of lawgiver, and the will that the practice be law "sufficiently manifested externally."[64] These three elements correspond to three of the key objections raised to custom. Appropriate power responds to the question of authority. Fitness of subject matter addresses to questions of custom's moral goodness. Human will "sufficiently manifested externally" is related to the question of how we know that a custom is no longer a custom of fact but has become a custom of law. Suárez considers each of these elements, plus the question of the relevance of custom in the modern world, in a way that addresses the critiques raised by legal positivists.

The Authority of Custom

Suárez addresses the question of the authority of custom in civil society by recognizing both the importance of the lawgiver and the role of the people in establishing any form of law, including custom.[65] Suárez claims that God has given each perfect community the power to create law—either through statutes or custom. Almost every community, for its own more efficient government, delegates to a legislative authority various degrees of power to make statutory law. However, no matter how total the authority of the ruler may be, the "legal right" to establish law through custom can never be fully transferred away.[66] Any community that possesses the capacity to receive law also always possesses the capacity to establish law through custom.[67] Therefore, each community can introduce a legal custom exactly in relationship to its capacity to receive law—as long as the custom receives the tacit consent of the lawgiver.

In his emphasis on the importance of the lawmaker's tacit consent, Suárez shows that, like Gratian, he does not seek to eradicate the legislative authority's role.[68] The chaos of the eleventh century had demonstrated that some form of central authority was needed to avoid chaos and corruption. However, where Gratian believes that legislative authority can eventually overrule custom, Suárez affirms the equally important roles of the lawmaker and the people. The proximate cause of custom's establishment as law is the people who create the custom through their acts. The primary cause is the sovereign power, exercised through tacit consent.[69] Both powers are necessary for the custom to become law, and accepting one does not require denying the other. Suárez draws on Aquinas for support for this position. Aquinas writes that custom can be established either by a commonwealth, in which the people have retained sovereign power, or through the ruler's tacit consent to the custom.[70] Suárez interprets this to mean that upholding the people's authority to establish custom does not mean a rejection of legislative authority.

Suárez explains how these two powers are complementary when he considers how custom can abrogate law. Does saying that custom can abrogate law really mean that laws are not enacted unconditionally, and only with the proviso that the people have to accept them for them to possess any force?[71] Suárez rejects this claim: law cannot depend for its authority upon the acceptance of the people, since this would mean that law had no intrinsic power and maintaining its authority is subject to the people's whim.[72] Rather, the power to enact a custom that can abrogate an existing law results from the union of power between the lawgiver and the subjects. The people have the power to factually establish a custom, and custom is completely formed into law when the ruler has decided to "tolerate and give consent to the popular will."[73] Thus, rather than choosing one party or the other, Suárez claims that the power to abrogate law through custom results from a union between the people's factual power to advance a different law and the ruler's legal power to confer implicit consent through toleration, with both leading to annulment.[74] The people's power does not depend on how much legislative power the people retain for themselves, since "this act of repudiating law by custom is not one of jurisdiction, or of public authority, but it is rather one that proceeds from those under a duty of obedience to the law."[75]

Suárez supports the claim that the people have an intrinsic power to make law through custom by considering two factual examples. Within the Church, lay people, who lack any legislative power, are still able to establish customs of worship that bind with moral authority and even abrogate ecclesiastical ordinances.[76] This is exactly what has happened, Suárez argues, in the acceptance of infant baptism and lay communion under one kind as a rule in many churches.[77] Within a civil community, merchants functioning as a perfect community with respect to commerce may, with the ruler's consent, establish a custom that stands in as "statutes of a quasi-municipal character."[78] This example is one that most modern theorists skeptical of custom as law would find hard to deny, considering that the United Commercial Code itself developed out of customary mercantile law, and custom continues to inform much of international law related to trade.

In a certain sense Suárez seems to be making a similar argument to Hart. It would be possible to read Suárez's argument as claiming that the people's authority is sufficient to establish a primary rule, but the legislative consent, given through a secondary rule, is actually necessary to make the rule into law. This reading would miss the full force and significance of Suárez's view of custom. It is the practices of the people that provides the initial power to make law. The consent of the ruler is also necessary, but only when the two powers are combined can custom become law. Thus, custom serves as a constant reminder of where true power lies, and it can function as a check on the power of the executive, rather than the other way around. Suárez offers a more thoroughly grounded and developed version of Postema's view of law as created by interaction, without sacrificing the insights from his own cultural context, that legislative authority is important for maintaining a functioning and efficient legal system. It is the people and the ruler, interacting together, who are able to give custom the proper moral force to become law.[79]

Suárez is anxious to establish custom as a source of law whose authority is equal to statutory law, in the same way he seeks to make the people and the ruler mutually complementary sources of authority. Where Gratian ultimately subordinates custom to written law, Suárez makes them equal and capable of coexistence.[80] Suárez emphasizes this point in responding to the claim of jurists who argue that customs that have been encoded in statutes by one in authority to make laws cease to count as a custom (since they are no longer authorized by the tacit consent of the people, but rather by the express command of the lawgiver).[81] It is true that custom is usually unwritten and typically introduced "by usage."[82] However, while custom is normally unwritten, this is not always the case. Customs that are sufficiently established in action and then later written down as laws may still retain their separate authority as customs.[83] In these situations, the law's authority stems from "two obligations [*vincula*] simultaneously—that is, of custom and of written law," in the same way that the same action might be mandated by two different statutes.[84] The two sources of authority do not fuse, but operate together, alongside and strengthening each other. Thus, custom "retains its own force and the essential character of custom, unless it is abolished by a special written statute."[85]

Suárez draws this argument from both jurists and canon lawyers. A number of jurists make the claim that custom retains its own force and essential character unless it is abolished by a special written statute."[86] In canon law, this claim is demonstrated by the fact that customs established by the apostles have been written down in canon law. These customs do not lose their apostolic authority simply because they have been recorded and promulgated in the laws of the Church. Rather, the recording in canon law "adds new force to it; and, as the Gloss on that law observes, from being a particular custom it thus becomes a common law."[87]

In making this argument, Suárez presents a more authoritative view of custom than even a modern advocate of viewing law as custom, such as Fuller, might make. Fuller, like Gratian, believes that custom can become law only where a lacuna exists. However, Suárez's claim that custom continues to maintain its obliging power, even with the existence of a subsequent written law, actually prioritizes custom even over legislative enactments.

The Knowledge of Custom

Suárez considers the question of how we can know that a custom has become law through the requirement of promulgation. Like any other "juridical entity," custom requires public promulgation.[88] However, unlike many other theories of custom, this promulgation never depends upon the actions of the judge. Suárez is clear that while a judge's ruling to ratify a custom may "declare" the custom, it is never required for "completing" it.[89] If a judge's decision were required for a custom to become established law, it would create a contradiction. If the judge's imprimatur were necessary, this would indicate that custom is not sufficient to establish law on its own. By removing the necessary involvement of the judge, Suárez removes multiple complications, such as how the judge's judgments can be trusted and the question of who actually establishes law, both of which are raised by Bentham, Hart, and Schauer.

In contrast, the standard of promulgation for custom requires the actions of two wills: the ruler's and the people's. The people demonstrate their will by their repeated enactment of the custom, thus satisfying the public requirement for promulgation.[90] In the same way that the publication of written words is necessary for a statute's promulgation, the repetition of the customary acts, "may be called the unwritten words by which this kind of law is engraved upon the memory of men."[91] The challenge for determining the will of the people is how to differentiate between the desire to promulgate a custom of law and a repeated action that is simply a custom of fact.

The "base form" is the same for both types of custom: the repetition of acts of "moral goodness and usefulness ... uninterrupted for a sufficient time."[92] The difference lies in the "intrinsic form": the will of the people that the custom should become law, "which under another aspect is the efficient cause of the obligation created by the custom."[93] This intrinsic form is determined by considering whether or not the people externally manifest the belief that the custom is legally obligating.[94]

One example of this internal form is the differentiation between many of the ritual customs of the worship of the Church. Practices such as receiving ashes on Ash Wednesday or a palm on Palm Sunday are customs of fact, since it is obvious that there is no intention to make them a law for all the faithful.[95] In contrast, the practice of infant baptism is understood not just as an important ritual practice but as morally obligating to the faithful. The custom of infant baptism departs from earlier practices but does not contradict positive commands found in scripture and instead supplements it. At some point this customary practice began to oblige as a law. For Suárez, only external actions can indicate that a custom has become a law, not the investigation of internal attitudes alone.

The detection of the will to establish a custom of law is not exact, but should be left to the standard of the "judgment of a prudent man," with the default assumption being in favor of a custom of fact rather than a custom of law.[96] However, as James B. Murphy points out, this standard actually provides its own objective criteria. Thus, to use Murphy's terminology, determining the will of the people does not depend on subjective guesswork, but rather on the deployment of different types of filters which limit that customs are intended to become law.[97] To further paraphrase Murphy, in considering the people's action, the first filter is that of the reactions and judgment of the people concerning the practice. The second filter is that of natural and divine law. The third is the judgment of the prudent man as to the common good.

Determining the will of the ruler is in a certain sense simpler. First, it can be assumed that the ruler agrees that a custom has become law if he actively passes a law approving the custom. Second, he is assumed to have given tacit consent simply by letting the custom continue, once he has knowledge of its existence.[98] When the custom is sufficiently general and public, the assumption is made that the ruler must know of it and has therefore given his tacit consent by allowing the custom to continue.[99] This does not mean that the ruler necessarily agrees with or supports the law, but simply that he acknowledges that the costs of trying to outlaw the custom are too great.

In many ways Suárez's understanding of how culture becomes law is close to Postema's description of the role of discursive normative practices.[100] For the people to will that a custom become law is as simple as their deciding that the custom should be law. The process develops slowly and gradually out of a common consciousness, which, over time, begins to determine that a series of acts are for the common good and, because of their goodness, are binding. The slow, gradual, and, in Postema's words, "discursive" development of a custom into law is illustrated by Suárez's explanation as to how one custom as law can give birth to another custom as law.[101] Often over time a new custom develops that departs from the original form of the law, not simply as an auxiliary custom serving the primary custom. This custom is eventually "superadded" to the existing custom and then becomes contrary to the existing law, since it introduces changes. For example, when the custom establishes that the jurisdiction of secular law is extended to clerics, it may do so in imitation of existing law but does not do so out of observance of that law. Rather, it is motivated by the realization that it advances the common good for certain laws to be applied to all citizens. Eventually this new custom becomes its own customary law.[102]

The Morality of Custom

The question of whether a custom can be morally evil is as crucial for Suárez and his contemporaries as it is in our own day. Suárez distinguishes two questions related to this category: Is the custom good or bad?; and Is the custom reasonable or unreasonable?[103]

The first question is one of morality. Customs that are simply repetitions of the natural or divine law are always customs of fact. Of course, these customs are morally beneficial, since they are useful for "adding strength (so to speak) as far as we are concerned, to the natural law, by keeping fresh its memory and by facilitating its observance on the part of the whole community."[104] But they do not establish new law. Customs that contradict the natural or divine law are by definition evil, so therefore they cannot generate the moral force to become customs of laws.

However, the natural law, according to Suárez, does not regulate every category of moral action. While there are some acts that are strictly prohibited by natural law and some that are rigorously enjoined, many other acts are unregulated. These other acts might have natural law requirements as to "mode or precise character" if and when they do occur but they are by no means mandated by the natural law as to absolute performance.[105] This leaves a large swath of human life that is underdetermined by natural law. If some customs developed for one particular context constitute "some usefulness essentially good, some law might be introduced through them as custom, or at least human law abrogated."[106] For example, the price of any specific good, unless it is exorbitant, is not intrinsically moral in its nature. However, in order to ensure something useful in the community—perhaps that a staple is within the financial reach of all purchasers—custom might set the price at a certain level.[107]

The same requirements for goodness that apply to statutory law are applied to determine whether a custom promotes "a usefulness essentially good." These requirements are that the subject matter of the established law is "useful for the common welfare, not excessively onerous, or a deviation from the general mode of upright living."[108] The requirement of usefulness to the common welfare sets a limit: that customs that can establish law are only those whose subject matter relates to the common good.[109] So, for example, customs relating to aesthetics cannot become law because they do not relate to the common good and are not moral. They produce "facility or skillful usage in actions of that kind, but impose no obligation of exercise as custom."[110]

However, this does not mean that a custom needs to be absolutely good to establish law (i.e., good in object, intention of the agent, and circumstances)—an almost impossible standard to meet for communal action. Rather, "it is sufficient that it be concerned with an object good by its nature, that is, either with acts which are in their object good or with those which could be performed with moral rectitude or done from a just motive."[111] Even if a custom is not introduced in a good way, but arises from evil actions, if its object has turned out to be good, then in this sense it still has the nature of a good custom and may establish law.[112] The only thing that can constitute an absolutely evil custom is a custom that is comprised of acts so intrinsically evil by reason of their object "that they cannot be made good actions by any human power."[113]

Suárez considers some important circumstantial limits on the people's ability to give consent. He rejects the claims of several jurists who uphold the authority of a custom that has been introduced through error regarding subject matter. In response, he argues that error precludes the introduction of custom into law because error makes it impossible for the people to consent to a custom becoming law and, for this reason, the law is not based on right reason.[114] This holds whether the error pertains to a falsely presumed legal obligation or erroneous consent as to facts of action. So, for example, if people limit their own rights because they misunderstand their rights under the law, their actions cannot mean that they establish a law to their own detriment, since they were only consenting through error.[115] In the same way, custom cannot be established by acts performed through compulsion or out of fear, which remove the element of intention necessary for establishing custom.[116] As Murphy points out, this exclusion of customs enforced by fear or coercion removes all possibilities that customs of exploitation and domination can become law—the very types of pernicious customs that section 1983 intended to exclude from possessing legal authority.[117]

Suárez considers reasonableness as one requirement that is supplemental to the requirement of goodness. In this he takes account of the cultural contingency and specificity that particularly distinguishes custom as law. A custom may be good but also unreasonable for a certain culture at a certain time. The question in determining this is one of "fittingness." An unfitting custom, while not evil, might create negative "moral effect" or an "element of danger, or possibilities for harm if it should be introduced into common public observance; and this, despite the fact that it is neither evil in itself, nor forbidden by any positive law." For example, although a custom of daily mass attendance is unquestionably good, to perceive such attendance as a law-creating custom would be clearly unreasonable because it would create an obligation that would be imprudently burdensome if it were established by a positive law.[118]

However, there are two objections to this understanding of custom as capable of abrogating law that Suárez must address. First, any valid law by definition is not unjust. Therefore, could a custom that opposes a just law be capable of having a good subject matter? After all, "in general, the revocation of a just law without cause is unreasonable."[119] Suárez answers this question by stating that simply because a law is just does not mean it cannot be abrogated. Rather, the question becomes, which law is better? In order to abrogate an existing law, a custom can be justified by showing that some reasonable cause exists explaining why it would be better than the existing law. As long as the custom, if it were law, meets the conditions of subject matter necessary for justice, then it has passed the subject matter requirement, even if the law it opposes is also just.[120]

Contrary to our intuition perhaps, Suárez sees far less conflict around the requirements of the subject matter for custom abolishing a law than the requirements for the subject matter establishing a law. The standards for the subject matter establishing law are much stricter as far as utility and rectitude are concerned. As far as abrogation, however, "it is enough that the annulment of the obligation in question be not contrary to the public advantage, since, although some advantage is taken away, there is a corresponding compensation, either in the removal of an occasion of a greater evil, or in conciliating the minds of subjects to a milder government."[121] Although the standard is lower, there must be some reason to justify the repeal of a just law. It is not enough that the custom is not opposed to divine law or natural reason; there must also be a good reason to remove the law.[122]

Suárez also considers whether human law's prohibition of the actions constituting a custom make the subject matter of the custom intrinsically evil. He does agree that the initial action establishing the custom is evil in that it goes against the law. However, it is not essentially evil, since "human power and will" can remedy the situation, either through making the custom into law or withdrawing the prohibition against the action.[123] Under this logic custom can only be intrinsically evil if it is contrary to natural or divine law. A second question regarding subject matter is whether a custom can be reasonable if it abrogates a law that is itself reasonable. Suárez's solution is that the abrogated law should be understood to be replaced by a custom "that may be reasonable under other aspects, which are also good and fitting."[124] Even the good and reasonable may be improved upon and adapted to better serve in a changing circumstance.

In considering this requirement, Suárez is obviously drawing upon the rich heritage of reflection from the scholastic approach to custom. He addresses concerns regarding the introduction of bad customs by definitively stating that a custom cannot contradict the commands of the divine law or the natural law. However, beyond this definite limit, he presents a view of the good and reasonable custom that makes it an appropriate and powerful tool to preserve and advance the common good of each specific and particular community. Because customs develop in the space between the natural law and the already existing civil law, they are uniquely able to address the needs expressed by a particular community. Rather than being tools of the elites, customs offer the potential to give the people a voice against the power of elites, who are often the ones imposing legislation from above. Customs, the products of the acts of the people and the interpretation of wise and prudent communities, provide a countersource of communal knowledge and understanding of the common good, which does not necessarily overrule the wisdom of the ruler but always checks, balances, and corrects the ruler's will in achieving and promoting the common good.

The Appropriateness of Custom for the Modern World

Unlike many of his scholastic predecessors, Suárez's exposure to the complexity of the early modern nation-state gives him the context to begin to consider questions regarding custom in contemporary discourse. A first contemporary claim regarding the practicability of custom in modernity is that the complexity of the nation-state makes it unlikely that the ruler will be aware of all customs and thus cannot grant direct consent. Suárez considers this same question when considering how to approach a conflict between laws issued by the pope and local customs serving as laws for religious observance. If the law is general in nature, then it is assumed that it is not intended to abrogate a local custom, of which it is assumed the pope had no knowledge, unless the revocation of local customs is specifically noted.[125] In fact, unless there is strong evidence to the contrary, the assumption is that the pope would not want to overrule a custom, since forcing people to change one "is contrary to a general law ... [and] is attended by difficulties beyond the ordinary."[126] Suárez believes that the default presumption is always in favor of custom. The burden falls upon the ruler to both know the custom and specifically overrule it, even if that ruler has divinely granted universal jurisdiction.

Another argument is that rule by custom forecloses the diversity within human community and inadequately addresses the plurality of modern liberal democracy. While Suárez does not explicitly address this idea, his insistence on law's dual sources of authority—the ruler and the ruled—creates a strong system of checks and balances that also serves to protect minority interests. Suárez has not forgotten the lessons of earlier exploitation of local custom by local warlords, and he is well aware that making the consent of the ruler necessary provides a strong legislative check upon either the tyranny of the majority or the exploitation of popular practice for corrupt ends. It also provides protection against attempts by other sources of authority to exploit claims of custom for private ends.

On the other hand, the requirement that a community can establish and authorize a custom protects the rights of particular communities against the more universal power of the ruler or against the tyranny of the majority, at least in a legislative democracy. The ability of each discrete group to create customary law is always a check on the power of the ruler, while at the same time preserving room for change and development at the communal level. It enables each community, even those within a larger nation, to develop forms to pursue the common good unique to each specific community, without retreating into sectarianism.

By community, Suárez does not mean only the type of perfect community necessary for forming a state. Rather, communities can be imperfect and only bound by some common interests or concerns, yet still have the power to establish custom in relationship to those identities or concerns that bind the community together. Thus custom in the community of merchants enables them to do their job better and be more productive, but they do not have the ability to create customs that will govern other groups not engaged in commerce within their own civil community. However, even the ruler must respect the customs of commerce that relate to the communal bond.

The critique of custom's unsuitability for the modern world is often phrased as a fear that customs are incapable of adjusting to changing times and can end up being formulistic and controlling. Suárez addresses this charge directly in his work and rejects it. Rather than necessarily being oppressive and controlling, custom can itself place a limit upon the overweening power and reach of statutory law. Custom's inherent openness to change and flexibility is a key component of law's ability to promote the common good. If a custom is no longer suited to the times or begins to introduce harm, "then there may be a positive duty not to observe the custom."[127] This change can often more easily be effected by smaller communities modifying their own customs to fit the time than revisions made by the apparatus of a large and bureaucratic state. We can demonstrate custom's continuing relevance to the modern world and the accuracy of Suárez's description in two very different contemporary examples.

Custom in International Environmental Law

Customary law plays a significant, although contested, role in international law. However, most often, the customs considered are the customs that govern the relationships between nation-states, not customs concerning the internal interactions within a community between the ruler and the subjects.[128] Suárez addresses this type of custom primarily in his analysis of the *ius gentium* rather than the civil law. In some areas of international law, the actions of nonstate actors in developing the customs that shape international law are beginning to gain greater significance. Communities have come to impact international environmental law by developing customs in a way like that identified by Suárez.

Environmental legal scholar Nancy Kubasek has identified four different customs or principles that shape international environmental law. The first principle is "good neighborliness": each state has an obligation to use its land and resources in ways that do not negatively impact other nations.[129] This custom is the most relevant to air and water pollution.[130] The second is an obligation not only to not infringe on the environmental rights of other states but also to exercise due diligence to proactively protect those rights.[131] This can include a duty to regulate a state's output of pollutants so as to avoid impacting the air quality of others. The third custom is a fair and equitable use of shared resources. The fourth is a duty of fair notice and full disclosure of important environmental information to other nations.[132]

While most nations share in articulating a commitment to these customs, the reality is that each nation-state has a different understanding of the actual content of the operating custom and a different level of commitment to putting customs into practice. For example, it was only in the 1980s that the United States began to consider that it had an obligation to regulate factory disposal of hazardous waste, a practice that was clearly in violation of the first three types of custom Kubasek identified.[133] While this failure to properly dispose of waste was censured by international courts as early as 1941, it took fifty years for US federal legislation to be enacted to bring practices into a more full compliance with this international environmental custom.[134] In another example, "sustainable development" is a commitment often considered a normative custom of international environmental law, perhaps under the custom of protecting the rights of others. However, the exact description of what "sustainable development" constitutes in legal terms is still unclear, despite its appearance in treaties and "soft law" declarations such as the 1992 Rio Declaration and the 2002 final Johannesburg Declaration on Sustainable Development."[135] To simply say that a custom exists in international environmental law does not mean that the custom actually has any type of significant environmental impact. Rather, the international legal custom's content and effectiveness varies depending upon the understanding of the custom within each nation-state.

Kubasek argues that environmentalists in the United States have attempted to overcome this difficulty by focusing primarily upon convincing lawmakers to adopt more environmentally friendly regulations. Some environmentalists have argued for change on the grounds that market pressures support changes to environmental policy. Others have turned to activism, attempting to appeal to concerns grounded in long-term claims concerning the common good. Both approaches have often ended in failure and legislative gridlock.[136] Daniel Bodansky makes a similar argument. Based on treaties and public statements, there is wide international recognition of accepted customs of international environmental law. However, when analyzing how much these customs are actually reflective of practices of nation-states, he finds the actual praxis falls far short of the descriptions of customs that appear in treaties and international codes.[137]

Both Kubasek and Bodansky claim that part of the solution to this gap between "customs" of international law and actual customary practice depends on the actions of the communities, not on the decisions of lawmakers or officers of the nation-state. Kubasek calls for greater communal involvement through a promotion of communitarian discourse among environmentalists. She argues that developing a practice of communitarian discourse instead of antagonistic rhetoric will contribute to an empowerment of the various stakeholders who are affected by environmental preservation processes and provide a more powerful, unified approach to political advocacy for legislation that mandates more environmentally friendly practices.[138] Bodansky, likewise, describes part of the failure of international "custom" to function normatively as a result of an exclusive emphasis among state actors and legal scholars on the role of third-party controls, such as courts and arbitration tribunals. Currently, these judicial bodies have very little authority to compel environmentally friendly actions that are in line with customary environmental law or to enforce punishments on state actors in violation. One potential solution he recommends is a change in focus, to the role that "interactions among the subjects of the legal system (second-party control)" can play in making custom normative.[139]

These calls for communal engagement create a situation where an understanding of Suárez's theory of morally binding custom developed by the people is useful and impactful. Suárez's emphasis on the people's role in forming custom captures the core of both Kubasek's and Bodansky's claims that communal practices are crucial for making nation-states take the customs of international environmental law seriously and act in compliance with them. Three of the four customs identified by Kubasek apply equally to the practices of businesses and government entities. If businesses formed a custom of acting to minimize their release of pollutants in both air and water and made equity and reasonableness key criteria in their use of resources, the legislature could more easily establish a regulatory framework of abiding by these customs of international law. Doing so would contribute dramatically to minimizing the release of pollutants and maximizing the appropriate use of natural resources. In addition, if these practices were adopted by a significant majority of the business community, corporations would expect these practices to be considered normative for government and business competitors' actions as well, in line with Suárez's observation that the community of merchants is more than capable of enacting customs that are as morally binding as laws.

The Paris Climate Accord of 2015 provides the most recent and most forceful affirmation that the development of customs within business communities may be effective at reducing environmental pollution. Unlike other previous accords such as Kyoto, the Paris Accord acknowledged the substantial role played by nonstate actors, including business communities. "The shift to a more systematic inclusion of non-state actors reflects growing recognition that nation states are no longer the only actors tackling global warming and that subnational governments, cities, and private capital will have an important role to play in mobilising, funding, and implementing global decarbonization."[140] Although limits on the international shipping industry were not explicitly mentioned in the Paris Accords, the imposition of private standards within the shipping industry provide an example of the success of this approach. Several studies demonstrate that private industry standards have resulted in demonstrable reductions in emissions within that industry while at the same time resulting in improved efficiencies and even increased profit margins.[141] A report on these standards by the Clean Cargo working group in 2015 "indicates that average CO2 emissions per container per kilometer for global ocean-based transport routes have declined by 8.4 percent from 2013 to 2014 and by more than 29 percent since 2009."[142]

The pressure that customs developed by communities outside the business world exert adds incentive and moral persuasion to push the business community into the development of customs. For example, the recent trend among institutional investors, under pressure from their own constituents, to divest or severely limit investments in fossil fuel companies is currently having an unprecedented ripple effect upon even corporate behemoths like Exxon Mobil.[143] Another example on a more populist level is the repurposing of the Roman Catholic custom of abstaining from meat on Fridays to the contemporary environmental movement's call for "meatless Mondays." This practice is driven by the conviction that reducing meat consumption will reduce the amount of methane produced by animals contributing to global pollution.[144] Another example of a custom beginning to transition into a law: in spring 2019 the mayor of New York announced that all New York City public schools would serve only plant-based foods on Mondays to institutionalize this practice.[145]

Community Organizing and Customs of Law

While environmental issues show how change may be effected on a global scale, the effectiveness of community organizing shows the power of customary change on the local level. In *Blessed Are the Organized,* Jeffrey Stout explains the common consensus regarding the lawmaking practices of community organizing:

> What kind of practice is it, then, to cultivate one's power as a democratic citizen and use it well? It is a *political* practice because it attends to shared human arrangements in light of concerns and judgments that are not always in harmony. It is a *social* practice because the ends it pursues and the means it employs involve building up human relationships of certain kinds. It is an *egalitarian* practice in the sense that it is open to anybody who wishes to master it and in the sense that it aspires to create a society in which no one is in a position to dominate others.[146]

This threefold definition of the practices by which citizens can actualize their power—political, social, and egalitarian—shares the same qualities that distinguish Suárez's theory of custom. For a custom to become law it must express the political wisdom of the community and attempt to balance the needs of a specific community, taking into account different societal challenges and requirements. The development of custom is inherently social, because legal custom always advances the common good. It is inherently egalitarian because it depends upon the actions of the whole community, not just the ruler, for a custom to be developed from the start.

Stout identifies the power and importance of custom in considering how leaders can be raised up within communities to challenge the power and dominion of elites. The true leader, he writes, is one who is grounded in the power of the community for whom he or she speaks. Such a leader realizes that the community does not need to assume a "posture of submission" toward politicians and lawmakers but understands that the community possesses its own authority and its own power.[147] Such leaders may be gifted and talented, but their strength comes from the authority of the community and their connection and ability to give voice to the practices that challenge the dominant forces. Quoting Saul Alinsky, he writes: "All communities are shaped by traditions of some sort, which Alinsky defined as the 'collective habits, experiences, customs, controls, and values of the whole group.' In democratic politics, Alinsky wrote, '*the tradition is the terrain*.'"[148] Only by accepting this power of custom are leaders and community organizers empowered to speak for the group and understand that the group "has the capacity to achieve significant change and the moral capacity to demand a hearing."[149] These grounding principles of community organizing express exactly the same conviction as Suárez does when he argues that some lawmaking power given by God always remains with the people and can never be fully surrendered to the legislature.

COPS and the Authority of the Community

The similarity between the details of Suárez's theory of custom as law and community organizing practices become more obvious when considered in the specific case of the growth and development of the San Antonio group Communities Organized for Public Service (COPS). Founded in 1973 by Alinsky-trained organizer Ernesto Cortés, COPS grew out of a tradition of neighborhood organizing, where most early focus and training is centered on techniques of action and confrontation—confrontation with the target or the meetings within the community necessary to build the communication and network that Alinsky viewed as crucial to developing mass power.[150] Some activists involved in the movement argue that the more militant aspects of community organizing are crucial as key tools to solidify neighborhood organizations and hold community leaders to account.[151] However, in the transition between the 1960s and the 1970s, many of the more militant and issue-focused organizations in the Alinsky tradition ceased to exist, either dissolving when funds or leadership energy ran out or gradually winding down because their goal was accomplished.[152] The most successful organizations of the 1970s were defined less by militant tactics and more by the depth of their connection to specific communities. By analyzing COPS as one of the most successful examples of this new model, we will see that successful community organizing depends not only on tactics but more fundamentally on the exercise of the political authority inherent in a community's intentional repeated acts oriented to the common good: in short, the development of customs of political action leading to legal change.

The story of the early days of COPS shows this transition away from an exclusive emphasis on confrontational tactics to an understanding that the ability to change laws depends most on communal power, communal action, and communal goals. This development incorporated key elements of Alinsky's original vision: specifically the importance of the "process of organization . . . not [as] a top-down exercise imposing an alien structure . . . but enlisting and collaborating with the existing institutions and traditions already present."[153] In addition, it maintained Alinsky's focus on community organization as a "form of political *ascesis* or disciplined formation: it educates and apprentices people into the practices necessary for sustaining public or civic friendships."[154] These two elements of Alinsky's theory as instantiated in COPS overlap perfectly with Suárez's theory of the development of law from below through the development of communal custom.

COPS was organized intentionally to combat the unjust processes and practices instituted by Anglo politicians and real estate investors from the north side of the city, who had formed a civic organization intended to maintain control of the city: the Good Government League.[155] Early research by COPS leaders found that city laws and regulations were permitting the reallocation of community resources away from the most needy Mexican American communities to the more affluent new developments. Money allocated to improve roads on the poorer south side often ended up being redeployed to the north side.[156] COPS intentionally began its first successful advocacy project by demanding the reallocation of funds to cover the repair and improvement of the storm drainage system in southwest San Antonio. When COPS advocates confronted city leaders with the city's repeated failure to use funds allocated to remedy this life-threatening situation, the city manager could only respond at first with a feeble "we dropped the ball." However, under repeated pressure from COPS, within a week the mayor and council agreed to reallocate money to fund crucial repairs.[157]

Unlike the militant organization of the 1960s, COPS leaders viewed this early success as opening the door for later successes, but not necessarily defining their group or limiting the way successes could be achieved. Although the tactics remained important, members came to perceive that COPS's power arose not from the successful deployment of organizing tactics alone; rather, it was grounded in its ability to develop and train members of the community to sustain community customs that challenged unjust laws. At the first COPS convention in 1974, Bishop Patrick Flores, the auxiliary bishop of San Antonio, described the power and authority inherent to the community: "You are here today not as supplicants with downcast eyes, not as welfare recipients, not as beggars; you are here as equals, as responsible, law-abiding, tax-paying people. You are a people that, with your sweat, have helped shape this country, this state, and this particular city. You seek no special favor. You seek a just share of your tax monies to have a decent community."[158] In a report on neighborhood organizing presented to Congress in 1979, COPS leaders identified two unique features, both grounded in the power of specific communities, that they believed were key to their success. First, the organization drew specifically from the Mexican-American communities in San Antonio. "The common culture, heritage, color of skin, experience, values, and church that they share has enabled COPS to develop as an extended family. For example, when leaders were asked if they printed a newsletter, they said it wasn't needed—they already have their communication networks. COPS is a reflection of the Mexican-American culture, values, and church."[159] Second, they noted that the organizational structure was inextricably bound to the specific communities, since it was developed to only function in coordination with the Roman Catholic Church in San Antonio, with membership open to entire parishes only, not to individuals.[160] This emphasis on the power of community rather than simply one-size-fits-all tactics resulted in COPS becoming "less one-dimensionally conflictive in its relations with political officials. The organization developed a sophisticated political capacity for contestation and compromise."[161] Even the architecture of San Antonio's city hall was changed to reflect the custom of citizen engagement, including an expansion of the city council room to accommodate crowds that attended hearings of community significance.[162]

The continued success of this approach can be found looking forward across the decades. In 1979 the COPS leaders could write to Congress that "COPS' list of revitalization accomplishments is extremely impressive. Leaders indicate that the importance of these achievements is that they are symptomatic of a major power shift which was taking place. The power of developers to utilize the people's tax money for their own gain has been broken."[163] In 1992 Virginia Ramirez, co-chair of COPS, described in a statement to Congress the success of COPS in reorganizing job placement training in San Antonio. She claimed that this success was primarily due to intensive focus on communal needs being achieved through communal practices.[164] In a 2002 case challenging planned development along the Edwards Aquifer in which COPS was one of the plaintiffs, the court noted COPS's continuing importance in the community, describing it as a "long-established public watch-dog."[165]

Intentionality of Establishing Customs of Law

The leaders of COPS realized that only communal customs that are intentionally developed to effect legal change are effective—the same element of intention that Suárez identifies as key for distinguishing between a custom of law and a custom of fact. COPS succeeded because its members understood that they possessed power as a community and they intended to use that power to change the law, not simply to change community patterns or to build an esprit de corps. Their emphasis on training that established a law-defining custom is clear in leaders' descriptions of the COPS leadership training process. One leader "spoke of the training session held in her parish church before major meetings with city officials where the residents were taught all about city budgets, or water mains, or CDBG monies. When they went to the meetings they knew why they were there and what they were fighting for."[166] Describing her introduction to COPS, Beatrice Cortez describes how attending her parents' meetings at her local parish to train COPS organizers taught her that the exercise of communal power could also teach her how "to stop being a victim" and act with authority to change laws and processes. This conviction, that successful legal change can arise from intentional communal action, motivated her service as the fourth president of COPS.[167]

COPS and the City Council

The COPS model also operates based on an understanding of the relationship between communal action and legislative leadership, similar to that expressed by Suárez when describing the dual roles of the ruler and the people in making law. From its initiation, COPS intentionally removed itself and its leaders from campaigning in elections or running its own candidates. "It was not going to be the launching pad to send heroes to city hall to fight for the people."[168]

Rather, its exclusive focus has been on developing the custom that citizens work alongside elected officials to change unjust laws and policy applications, especially as related to the provision of basic city services and the organization of the city government itself.[169] COPS does not make the laws, but it uses popular pressure to motivate elected officials to ratify the community's actions already in progress, correcting legal inequities or passing new and equitable laws. For example, in part because of the pressure exerted by COPS to provide more space for the voice of underrepresented minorities, the San Antonio city council was forced to hold a referendum to amend the city charter to change the council membership from being comprised only of members elected at large to a district-based system, where each member is elected from an individual district.[170] This change broke the control of the Anglo majority and began to provide a voice for African Americans and Mexican Americans in the city. Importantly, COPS did not choose or endorse the new candidates, but rather set the process in motion to change the system.

COPS and the Common Good

Despite the remarkable long-term success of COPS, it should only be considered a successful example of Suárez's theory of customary lawmaking because the customs it establishes actually advance the common good. Therefore, it is important to note that reasonable questions about COPS's ability to advance the common good, understood broadly as the common good of the city, have been raised by those involved in studying the movement. The success of COPS resulted in a dominance on the political scene, meaning that citizens in other areas of the city often had no idea as to how to make their voices heard in order to resolve their own neighborhood issues.[171] COPS itself identified these issues in the report to Congress: "Because COPS is placing such a demand on resources to revitalize and rebuild their communities, the other neighborhoods are pretty much being neglected."[172] In an article on community organizations, Georgette Poindexter poses a similar question relating to COPS and the common good, in this instance related to COPS's advocacy for a living wage. She traces the argument of the economic development agencies in the city, which claimed that the requirements of a living wage would stifle the city's ability to attract and retain the businesses crucial for economic development and the flourishing of the city's economy as a whole.[173]

Both of these scenarios raise the question as to what standard of the common good is necessary for custom to become law. Here especially Suárez's pragmatic analysis of the relationship between custom and the common good is important for explaining and justifying COPS. In both scenarios, Suárez likely would argue that for a custom to become law it does not need to embrace the perfect fullness of the common good. Rather, it must simply be both good in its object and more just and more reasonable than the law it replaces. Under this logic, while the dominance of customs developed by COPS in San Antonio is not the perfection of the common good because some voices were lost, COPS did improve the former laws, which until then had limited political engagement to an even smaller and more exclusive group. Because the interaction between customs and laws never ceases, COPS's customs should not be understood as foreclosing the engagement of other neighborhood groups, but simply one step forward in developing and improving the existing legal structure of the city. Imposing a minimum legal wage also should not be understood as the end of economic advancement, but simply the setting of a new minimum standard for just laws of economic development and leaving room for further customs of economic advancement to be developed by all participants in the economic system.

Conclusion

While four hundred years separate Francisco Suárez from the community organizers in Texas and environmental activists around the world, Suárez's theory of custom provides the theoretical descriptions for exactly their development of customs advancing the common good into law. Unlike the pernicious customs that Rutherglen describes, understanding custom as Suárez articulates it—as a tool of communal empowerment and resistance—provides a way to advance the common good, not to limit it. Suárez's view of custom is not the overweening force of oppression and control by the minority. Rather, it provides a way to create space for gradual and positive change in response to new challenges, such as the environmental movement, or old oppressions, such as systemic limitations being placed on one economic group. While Suárez's ideas complement theologies of liberation and social organizing, they also expand the idea of what different groups can achieve to promote the common good for societal change. Rather than shutting others out, Suárez's notions expand the options open to communities engaged in the active formation of law for the common good.

Notes

1. 42 USC § 1983 (2000). A portion of this chapter originally appeared in "Settling Law: Suárez's Theory of Custom for Contemporary Contexts," in *Francisco Suárez (1548–1617): Jesuits and the Complexities of Modernity*, ed. Robert Aleksander Maryks and Juan Antonio Senent de Frutos (Leiden, The Netherlands: Brill, 2019), 178–201.
2. George Rutherglen, "Custom and Usage as Action Under Color of State Law: An Essay on the Forgotten Terms of Section 1983," *University of Virginia Law Review* 89 (2003): 926.
3. Rutherglen, 929.
4. Rutherglen, 929.
5. Rutherglen, 928.
6. Rutherglen, 929–30.
7. Cesar Chavez, introduction to *Forty Acres: Cesar Chavez and the Farm Workers*, ed. Mark Day (New York: Praeger, 1971), 9.
8. Gustavo Gutiérrez, *A Theology of Liberation: History, Politics, and Salvation*, rev. ed., trans. Caridad Inda and John Eagleson (Maryknoll, NY: Orbis, 1988), 67. Italics in the original.
9. Gutiérrez, *A Theology of Liberation*, 68.
10. Gustavo Gutiérrez, *En busca de los pobres de Jesucristo: El pensamiento de Bartolomé de las Casas* (Lima, Peru: Instituto Bartolomé de las Casas, 1992), 14. Translations are my own.
11. Jeremy Waldron, "Custom Redeemed by Statute," *Current Legal Problems* 51 (1998): 102–13.
12. See, for example, David V. Snyder, "Language and Formalities in Commercial Contracts: A Defense of Custom and Conduct," *SMU Law Review* 54 (2001): 617–54; Michael Byers, *Custom, Power and the Power of Rules* (Cambridge: Cambridge University Press, 1999); and David Bederman, *Custom as a Source of Law* (Cambridge: Cambridge University Press, 2010).
13. Lon Fuller, *The Morality of Law*, rev. ed. (New Haven, CT: Yale University Press, 1969), 234.

14. Joseph Raz, *The Authority of Law: Essays on Law and Morality*, 2nd ed. (Oxford: Oxford University Press, 2009), 29.
15. Gerald Postema, "Custom, Normative Practice, and the Law," *Duke Law Journal* 62 (2012): 714–15. Postema identifies Suárez's theory of custom as a paradigmatic example of this allegedly problematic view.
16. Postema, 707.
17. H. L. A. Hart, *The Concept of Law*, 3rd ed. (Oxford: Oxford University Press, 2012), 45.
18. Hart, 92.
19. Hart, 94.
20. Neil MacCormick, *Institutions of Law: An Essay in Legal Theory* (Oxford: Oxford University Press, 2008), 42.
21. MacCormick, 45. MacCormick does note that at least one culture (on the Micronesian island of Yap) has been documented to show custom that seems to provide an equally morally obliging legal force as the laws of the state. However, he acknowledges this could be an accurate description of the state of jurisprudence in other cultures as well, although the question could be open to study (60–70).
22. Hart, *The Concept of Law*, 44–45.
23. Frederick Schauer, "Pitfalls in the Interpretation of Customary Law," in *The Nature of Customary Law*, ed. Amanda Perreau-Saussine and James B. Murphy (Cambridge: Cambridge University Press, 2007), 22.
24. Schauer, 31.
25. Bederman, *Custom as a Source of Law*, 4.
26. David Bederman astutely points out how easy it is for value judgments and moral freighting to inevitably creep in, by asking these questions and attempting to distinguish between societies that are "primitive" and "modern"—let alone, he points out, the problematic practice of referring to customary law in earlier treatises as the "law of savages" (3).
27. Hart, *The Concept of Law*, 93.
28. Bederman, *Custom as a Source of Law*, 5.
29. Schauer, "Pitfalls," 30–31.
30. R. van Caenegem, "Government, Law and Society," in *The Cambridge History of Medieval Political Thought c. 350–c. 1450*, ed. James H. Burns (Cambridge: Cambridge University Press, 1988), 183.
31. Caenegem, 182–83.
32. Caenegem, 187–88.
33. Caenegem, 187–88.
34. Kenneth Pennington, "Law, Legislative Authority, and Theories of Government, 1150–1300," in *The Cambridge History of Medieval Political Thought, c. 350–c. 1450*, ed. James H. Burns (Cambridge: Cambridge University Press, 1988), 425.
35. Thomas Bisson, *The Crisis of the Twelfth Century: Power, Lordship, and the Origins of European Government* (Princeton, NJ: Princeton University Press, 2015), 459.
36. Bisson, 136–37.
37. Bederman, *Custom as a Source of Law*, 23.
38. Jean Porter, "Custom, Ordinance, and Natural Right in Gratian's Decretum," in *The Nature of Customary Law*, ed. Amanda Perreau-Saussine and James B. Murphy (Cambridge: Cambridge University Press, 2007), 84.
39. Porter, 80.
40. Porter, 91.

41. Porter, 91.
42. Porter, 94.
43. See, for example, D12, in which Gratian defends a variety of local customs under the heading of promoting and upholding justice. Gratian, *The Treatise on Laws* (*Decretum DD 1–20*), trans. Augustine Thompson, OP (Washington, DC: Catholic University of America Press, 1993), 42.
44. Porter, "Custom, Ordinance and Natural Right," 95.
45. Gratian, *Decretum*, 5–6.
46. Porter, "Custom, Ordinance and Natural Right," 96.
47. Porter, 97.
48. Thomas Aquinas, *Summa Theologicae*, trans. by Fathers of the English Dominican Province (New York: Benziger Bros. edition, 1947), I–II q. 97, art. 3, ad. 3.
49. Aquinas, I–II q. 97, art. 3.
50. Aquinas, I–II q. 97, art. 3.
51. See, e.g., Dominique Bauer, "Custom in Francisco Suárez' *de Lege non Scripta*: Between Factuality and the Legal Realm," *Anuario de Derecho Canonico* 4 (April 2015): "Suárez's approach to the subject, the originality of which cannot be denied, in many respects also takes further aspects of legal doctrine and theory that appear with his predecessors and that underline the longevity and continuity of the tradition that led up to *De legibus*" (35). See also Brian Tierney, "Vitoria and Suárez on *Ius Gentium*, Natural Law, and Custom," in *The Nature of Customary Law*, ed. Amanda Perreau-Saussine and James B. Murphy (Cambridge: Cambridge University Press, 2007), 115–17.
52. See for example, David Steinmetz, "Luther and Calvin on Church and Tradition," *Michigan Germanic Studies* 10, no. 1 (April 1984): 108.
53. This type of repeated action may be designated by *consuedutine*, *mos*, or *usus*. See Francisco Suárez, *De Legibus*, in *Opera Omnia* (Paris: Apud Ludovicum Vives, 1856–78), 6:VII.1.4. Translations come from *Selections from Three Works of Francisco Suárez, S.J.*, trans. Gwladys L. Williams, Ammi Brown, and John Waldron (Oxford: Clarendon, 1944; rprt: Indianapolis, IN: Liberty Fund, 2013). I have also consulted the *Vives* edition; when a Latin term is of significance for the argument it is inserted in the text or note.
54. Suárez, *De Legibus*, VII.i.4.
55. Suárez, VII.i.4.
56. Suárez, VII.i.4.
57. Here, Suárez distinguishes between *mos* and *consuetudo*, with *mos* referring to the after-effect of habit and *consuetudo* referring to the effect that creates a law.
58. Suárez, VII.i.2.
59. Suárez, VII.viii.1.
60. Suárez shares Hart's insight that some communal activities do not carry the normative force of law but are still significant to the community's functioning. See Hart, *The Concept of Law*, 91–93.
61. For example, although Luke refers to the "custom of the law" regarding the circumcision of Christ, it should not be understood as a custom that produces a law, but rather a custom that grows out of the original law God gave to Moses. Suárez, *De Legibus*, VII.i.5.
62. Suárez, VII.i.9.
63. Suárez, VII.i.8.
64. Suárez, VII.xiv.3.
65. For further discussion of scriptural authority for the binding nature of custom within the Church, see Suárez, VII.iv.10.

66. Suárez, VII.iii.10, VII.i.9.
67. Suárez, VII.ix.10.
68. Richard Ross and Philip Stern present a similar description of Suárez's emphasis on both the importance of the consent of the ruler and the development of custom by the people to provide a significant account of early modern legal pluralism. They argue against the voluntarist genealogy that traces Suárez's view of custom as simply absolutist and describe how much he leaves up to the people in "the wide dark shadow of tacit consent." Richard Ross and Philip Stern, "Reconstructing Early Modern Notions of Legal Pluralism," *Legal Pluralism and Empires: 1500–1850,* ed. Lauren Benton and Richard Ross (New York: New York University Press, 2013), 80–81.
69. Suárez, *De Legibus,* VII.ix.2. To define tacit consent Suárez again draws on Aquinas (I–II q. 97, art. 3), defining it as the sovereign permitting a custom to continue if it "be morally evident that the toleration is not merely permissive, but an active or approving one; whether it is such will be easily seen from the circumstances and from usage, especially either when the approval is reasonable, or when, by a permission alone, the safety and well-being of the subjects is inadequately provided for" (VII.xiii.12).
70. Suárez, VII.ix.7. See Aquinas, *Summa,* I–II q. 97, art. 2, ad 2.
71. Suárez, *De Legibus,* VII.ix.7.
72. Suárez, VII.xviii.3.
73. Suárez, VII.xviii.3.
74. Suárez, VII.xviii.3.
75. Suárez, VII.xviii.4.
76. Suárez, VII.xviii.4: "*Abrogantem legem ecclesiasticem.*"
77. Suárez, VII.iv.12.
78. Suárez, VII.ix.11, VII.ix.8. Suárez also considers the objection to the claim that a community of women can make laws for their community because, according to some, women lack lawmaking authority. Suárez quickly dismisses this objection on the grounds that it is based on an erroneous assumption that women's nature is such that lawmaking authority does not inhere within them as a community.
79. Suárez, VII.xviii.3.
80. James Bernard Murphy, in *The Philosophy of Customary Law* (Oxford: Oxford University Press, 2014), discusses this claim further: "Suárez sometimes emphasizes the priority of the consent of the people and sometimes the priority of the consent of the prince. Sometimes he defines the essence of custom in terms of the consent of the people. . . . But at a deeper level, in every regime the consent of the people seems to be logically prior, in the sense that unless the people first practice a custom, thereby signaling their consent, there is nothing for the prince to consent to. The consent of the people sets the stage for the toleration or suppression of a custom by the prince. The consent of the prince has no bearing unless and until the consent of the people is manifest. The logical priority of the consent of the people makes customary law seem uniquely democratic: even in a polity in which the people have irrevocably alienated their law-making powers to a prince, customary law must still originate among the people" (48).
81. Suárez, *De Legibus,* VII.ii.4. One modern-day example of this is the English constitution. Although much of the constitution has been codified into statutes by Parliament, there is a strong sense within English jurisprudence that the constitution's authority still rests on its customary status.
82. Suárez, VII.ii.2.

83. Suárez, VII.ii.4.
84. Suárez, VII.ii.4.
85. Suárez, VII.ii.4.
86. Suárez, VII.ii.4.
87. Suárez, VII.ii.4.
88. Suárez, VII.ix.1.
89. Suárez, VII.xi.4.
90. Suárez, VII.xvi.1.
91. Suárez, VII.ix.1.
92. Suárez, VII.ix.1.
93. Suárez, VII.ix.1.
94. Postema, "Custom, Normative Practice, and the Law," 714.
95. Suárez, *De Legibus*, VII.xiv.6.
96. Suárez, VII.xv.13. Obviously, using the standard of a prudent person's judgment is somewhat contextually specific, but Suárez does provide several common-sense guidelines, including a sense of scandal if the custom is not followed, a sense of obligation to abide by the custom even at great personal cost or inconvenience, or a clear sign that the custom contributes greatly to the general welfare. See Suárez, VII.xvi.4.
97. Murphy, *The Philosophy of Customary Law*, 57.
98. Suárez, *De Legibus*, VII.xviii.15.
99. Suárez, VII.ix.12, 13. Suárez includes within this majority all people except infants and those lacking mental capacity. He includes women and those under twenty-five years. See Suárez VII.ix.14.
100. Postema, "Custom, Normative Practice, and the Law," 707.
101. Postema, 720.
102. Suárez, *De Legibus*, VII.iv.17.
103. Suárez, VII.vi.1.
104. Suárez, VII.iv.4. Suárez also notes that custom may be useful for interpretation even of divine and natural law.
105. Suárez, VII.iv.3.
106. Suárez, VII.iv.4.
107. See Suárez VI.ix.9. for a discussion of the role of custom in setting a price. While it is beyond the scope of this book, the difference between Suárez's view of the role of custom in setting a price in a way that advances the common good versus the free market capitalist approach, wherein prices should be set as high as the market will bear, would be worth a more in-depth comparison.
108. Suárez, VII.xiv.3.
109. Suárez, VII.ii.5.
110. Suárez, VII.iii.6.
111. Suárez, VII.vi.3.
112. Suárez, VII.vi.3.
113. Suárez, VII.vi.4.
114. Suárez, VII.xii.2.
115. Suárez, VII.xii.5.
116. Suárez, VII.xii.11.
117. Murphy, *The Philosophy of Customary Law*, 53. "When those customs are ruthlessly enforced by violence (say, by the KKK), Suárez would deny that conformity to such

custom is a sign of any kind of consent. But most customs of social subordination are enforced by much subtler threats and incentives: if we 'know what is good for us' we will show proper deference. In these more common cases in which customs may well be practiced with resentment, Suárez seems to say that we should not interpret conformity to these customs as evidence of consent to binding customary law. So the customary deference of black to white Americans in the South should not be interpreted as consent to the legal enforcement of racial customs."

118. Suárez, *De Legibus,* VII.vi.13, VII.vi.11, VII.vi.7.
119. Suárez, VII.vi.16.
120. Suárez, VII.vi.17.
121. Suárez, VII.xviii.9.
122. Suárez, VII.xviii.10.
123. Suárez, VII.vi.4.
124. Suárez, VII.xviii.25.
125. Suárez, VII.xx.9.
126. Suárez, VII.xx.11.
127. Suárez, VII.xx.1.
128. Mark S. Blodgett, Richard J. Hunter Jr., and Hector R. Lozada, "A Primer on International Environmental Law: Sustainability as a Principle of International Law and Custom," *ILSA Journal of International and Comparative Law* 15 (2008): 16.
129. Nancy K. Kubasek and Gary Silverman, *Environmental Law,* 2nd ed. (Upper Saddle River, NJ: Prentice Hall, 1996): 432–34.
130. Blodgett, Hunter, and Lozada, "Primer," 21.
131. Kubasek and Silverman, *Environmental Law,* 432–34.
132. Kubasek and Silverman, 432–34.
133. Nancy K. Kubasek, M. Neil Browne, and Michael D. Meuti, "Communitarian Discourse as a Catalyst for Emergent Environmental Law," *Environmental Law Reporter News and Analysis* 32 (2002): 1.
134. See *Trail Smelter Case* (U.S. vs. Canada), 3 United Nations Reports of International Arbitration Awards 1905 (1941).
135. Pierre-Marie Dupuy, "Formation of Customary International Law and General Principles," in *The Oxford Handbook of International Environmental Law,* ed. Daniel Bodansky, Jutta Brunnée, and Ellen Hey (Oxford: Oxford University Press, 2008), 462.
136. Kubasek, Browne, and Meuti, "Communitarian Discourse," 2–3.
137. Daniel Bodansky, "Customary (and Not So Customary) International Environmental Law," *Independent Journal of Global Legal Studies* 3 (1995): 111–12.
138. Kubasek, Browne, and Meuti, "Communitarian Discourse," 6.
139. Bodansky, "Customary (and Not So Customary)," 117.
140. Peter Christoff, "The Promissory Note: COP 21 and the Paris Climate Agreement," *Environmental Politics* 25, no. 5 (2016): 780.
141. *See* Joanne Scott et al., "The Promise and Limits of Private Standards in Reducing Greenhouse Gas Emissions from Shipping," *Journal of Environmental Law* 29, no. 2 (2017): 231–62.
142. Clean Cargo Working Group (CCWG), *Collaborative Progress:* 2015 Progress Report (BSR August 2015), as cited in Scott et al., "The Promise and Limits," 244.
143. See, for example, William Neuman, "To Fight Climate Change, New York City Takes On Oil Companies," *New York Times,* January 10, 2018, https://www.nytimes.com/2018/01/10/nyregion/new-york-city-fossil-fuel-divestment.html.

144. See, for example, the website of the organization Meatless Monday, a part of the "Monday Campaigns" started by Johns Hopkins University promoting Monday as a day to achieve health goals, https://www.mondaycampaigns.org/meatless-monday.
145. See the press release issued by the mayor's office at https://www1.nyc.gov/office-of-the-mayor/news/135-19/mayor-de-blasio-chancellor-carranza-brooklyn-borough-president-adams-citywide#/0.
146. Jeffrey Stout, *Blessed Are the Organized* (Princeton, NJ: Princeton University Press, 2010), 93.
147. Stout, 96.
145. Stout, 101–2. Italics in the original. Citing Saul Alinsky, *Reveille for Radicals* (New York: Vintage Books, 1989; originally published 1946), 72–73.
149. Stout, 99–100.
150. Helena Lynch, "Industrial Areas Foundation," *New York Law School Law Review* 50 (2005–6): 572.
151. Robert A. Rosenbloom, "The Neighborhood Movement: Where Has It Come From: Where Is It Going?," *Nonprofit and Voluntary Sector Quarterly* 10, no. 2 (April 1981): 6.
152. Rosenbloom, 7.
153. Luke Bretherton, *Christianity and Contemporary Politics: The Conditions and Possibilities of Faithful Witness* (Malden, MA: Wiley-Blackwell, 2010), 74.
154. Bretherton, 77.
155. Jeffrey Berry, Kent Portney, and Ken Thomson, *The Rebirth of Urban Democracy* (Washington, DC: Brookings Institution Press, 1993), 52.
156. People Building Neighborhoods, *Final Report to the President and the Congress of the United States* (Washington, DC: National Commission on Neighborhoods, 1979), 466.
157. People Building Neighborhoods, 464.
158. People Building Neighborhoods, 465.
159. People Building Neighborhoods, 459.
160. People Building Neighborhoods, 459.
161. Richard L. Wood, "Fe Y Acción Social: Hispanic Churches in Faith-Based Community Organizing," in *Latino Religions and Civic Activism in the United States*, ed. by Gastón Espinosa et al. (Oxford: Oxford University Press, 2005), 146.
162. People Building Neighborhoods, *Final Report*, 474.
163. People Building Neighborhoods, 469.
164. US House of Representatives, "New Alternatives to Community Distress," Hearing before the Joint Economic Committee, 102nd Congress, 2nd session, April 30, 1992, 2–3.
165. *Save Our Aquifer v. City of San Antonio*, U.S. District Court, W. D. of Texas, 2002, 237 F.Supp. 2d 721, 723.
166. People Building Neighborhoods, 476.
167. Mark R. Warren, *Dry Bones Rattling: Community Building to Revitalize American Democracy* (Princeton, NJ: Princeton University Press, 2001), 51.
168. People Building Neighborhoods, *Final Report*, 465.
169. Berry, Portney, and Thomson, *Rebirth*, 52.
170. Warren, *Dry Bones Rattling*, 5.
171. Berry, Portney, and Thomson, *Rebirth* 59.
172. People Building Neighborhoods, *Final Report*, 474.
173. Georgette C. Poindexter, "Economic Development and Community Activism," *Urban Lawyer* 32, no. 3 (Summer 2000): 402.

5

Doubts and Deliberation

COMMUNAL ENGAGEMENT IN LEGAL INTERPRETATION

In a world filled with ever-proliferating statutes, regulations, and court cases, the claim that legal interpretation is a challenging task is hardly a controversial statement. Francisco Suárez recognizes this same challenge in Book I of *De Legibus*, where he writes, "There is hardly any human diligence that can be used by which doubts that arise about the understanding of laws will be avoided."[1] This difficulty arises because human laws are given in human language, a system of signs produced and interpreted by fallible and finite humans, and they are, therefore, always susceptible to vagueness or ambiguity. There is always a danger that laws, given generally, may in a specific context appear too narrow or overly broad for the challenge at hand, may imply claims that go beyond the law's intended scope, may breach procedural rules, or may simply appear to be an example of a lawmaker's mistake.[2] For all of these reasons, laws always require interpretation.

For Suárez, interpretive engagement with law is not an optional or part-time activity only carried out from the judge's bench or solely dependent upon a lawmaker's intent. Rather, interpretation is an intrinsic element of lawmaking and of law's reception in which all citizens, not just judges and lawmakers, are actively engaged. Engagement in law's interpretation is one of the essential components of the development of law through the dialectical engagement of the lawmaker and the subjects. Interpretation, therefore, provides another mechanism by which citizens can engage with law from below to work to effect change.

Suárez develops his understanding of legal interpretation as a tool for engagement and improvement of law through a focus on the people's role in legal interpretation. Suárez's theory of law as an interpretive act can be differentiated from several contemporary approaches to legal interpretation, all of which emphasize the role of the judge or the lawmaker's intent. His broad framework, developed out of both theological and legal sources, provides an important resource for Christian engagement with law. Suárez applied this theory of interpretation in his own context. When placed in dialogue with these contemporary theories, his work is also adaptable to explain contemporary legal interpretation by the people such as the development of environmental regulations and the actions of churches offering refuge to political asylees as part of the sanctuary movement.

What Is Interpretation?

Suárez provides two definitions of interpretation. The most rigorous sense of the word means only "the clarification and comprehension of the true sense, and, so to speak, the immediate sense of that law, considering only the usual and proper sense of the words and the meaning of the law which results from them so understood."[3] The other sense is broader and encompasses many meanings; it defines the law and "acts in some manner around the law."[4] This second creative mode of more expansive interpretation can include the correction as well as the abrogation of law: the amplification, the restriction, the exception, the excuse, or the cessation of the obligation of the law. However, while Suárez adopts this broader definition, he does so only in part. When speaking strictly of the interpretation of human laws that continue to oblige, he claims that this includes the changing of laws only by amplification or restriction.[5] The other modes of changing laws, at least for individuals, only occur with the exercise of the virtue of equity. Thus, determining the correct meaning of the words can function to either expand or retract the scope of the law but neither completely abolishes or creates it.[6] The goal of all of this amplification or restriction is to bring laws into greater accordance with their proper end: the promotion of justice and the common good. Judicious interpretative engagement can result in the improvement of a whole system of laws when human efforts have introduced prior errors contrary to justice and the common good.[7]

Suárez's theory of interpretation as amplifying or restricting law has some fundamental similarities with legal philosopher Ronald Dworkin's understanding of legal interpretation as inherently "creative."[8] For Dworkin, interpretation *is* law. By making this association, Dworkin attempts to escape what he describes as "the flat distinction between description and evaluation that has enfeebled legal theory."[9] Dworkin claims that practices, including legal theory, develop through interpretation and therefore claims that interpretation comes to constitute the practice. "Interpretation folds back into the practice, altering its shape, and the new shape encourages further reinterpretation, so the practice changes dramatically, though each step in the process is interpretive of what the last achieved."[10]

Both Dworkin and Suárez assert that the interpreter should not just report back on what the law is, but should engage with it and, through this engagement, perhaps change it. As Dworkin writes, when considering the metaphor of a social scientist engaged in studying the tradition of courtesy within a culture,

> he can, if he wishes, undertake only to report the various opinions different individuals in the community have about what the practice demands. But that would not constitute an interpretation of the practice itself; if he undertakes that different project he must give up methodological individualism and use the methods his subjects use in forming their own opinions about what courtesy requires. He must, that is, *join* the practice he proposes to understand; his conclusions then are not neutral reports about what the citizens of courtesy think, but claims about courtesy *competitive* with theirs.[11]

Suárez considers this type of engagement by the interpreter located within the community necessary. Given his understanding of the lawgiving and law-modifying community as comprising one *corpus mysticum*, there is no neutral space apart from within the community where the interpreter can either stand or act.

The Theological Grounding of Interpretation

Suárez's theory of legal interpretation is developed from his theory of scriptural interpretation as a practice of both the people and the ruler. The importance of interpretation depends on the identification of three forms of law: as it exists in the intention of lawgiver, as an external sign, and as it exists in the understanding of the subject.[12] Moving from the lawmaker's intention to the external sign requires an interpretive act when the law is written down, just as it does when moving from the sign to the reception of the law. How much interpretation is needed in each phase varies depending on the nature of the law: divine, natural, or civil.

For Suárez, the practice of legal interpretation is as crucial for natural and divine positive law as it is for civil law. Even the divine positive law given in scripture always requires interpretation. The divine Lawgiver has the perfect intention and aim, ensuring that these both are perfectly translated into the sign of the law. In contrast, the recipient of the sign still has to engage in interpretation. The recipient's interpretation is, in certain contexts, made with the perfect lawgiver's perfect assistance, specifically the Holy Spirit, who provides "special direction and illumination." Interpretation of scripture, carried out without the Holy Spirit, is accomplished only by "a purely human spirit which is frequently mistaken, and therefore it cannot be the foundation of a certain faith."[13] Suárez claims that one of the key differences between Protestants and Catholics is the answer to the question of whom the Holy Spirit guides in interpretation. For Protestants, the Holy Spirit gives the gift of authentic interpretation to the "individual faithful."[14] Catholics do believe that the Holy Spirit does at times teach "some privately about the mystery of faith, or about the sense of Scripture, in such a way as to render them certain about the truth of the doctrine or about the revealed sense." However, authentic interpretation occurs when the Holy Spirit assists the Church corporately in the act of interpretation, with different individuals playing different roles. For all the baptized, the Holy Spirit "illuminates them inwardly for believing what he teaches through his preachers." The Holy Spirit also provides a special grace of interpretation for pastors and doctors of the Church, "as far as it is expedient for the common good of the Church; and so, for the most part, this is not done through express revelations nor through infallible judgments but to the extent necessary and as much as the status and duties of each require." Finally, at the highest level of interpretive security, "the Great Pontiff and legitimate counsels, when they define something, teach it through a singular assistance such that they cannot err"

Suárez explicitly connects scriptural interpretation and legal interpretation by using legal terms to distinguish between private and personal interpretation in the Church. It goes without saying that God's interpretation of His own laws is, of course, perfect and fully binding. However, the ecclesial community, when guided by the Holy Spirit, can also provide a binding interpretation on certain limited topics. The authoritative interpretation "pertains to the foundation of faith, and therefore only by him can it be done to whom Christ specifically promised the keys of knowledge." Suárez uses the legal term "authentic" to define this interpretation, since it has the full force of law. The second category of interpretation, carried out by the doctors of the Church, is termed doctrinal. It lacks infallible authority and can be carried out "by private authority, provided it not be done rashly and at will."[15] John Doyle points out that the distinction between authoritative and doctrinal interpretation is not necessarily a difference between qualities of interpretation, but rather between different weights of authority. A saint may provide a better "doctrinal" interpretation, but until that interpretation is legitimized by the pope or ecclesial counsels, even if that interpretation is less clear, elegant, or complete, it will never carry the same interpretive weight.[16] Finally, individuals who are not pastors and doctors of the Church may engage in private readings of scripture. This private reading does not carry any type of interpretative weight, yet is important for personal understanding and everyday preaching.[17]

In interpretation of scripture, then, there are three different options for interpretive weight:

> the authentic interpretation: either God's interpretation of His own law or ecclesial interpretation when guided by the Holy Spirit;
> the persuasive doctrinal interpretation of the doctors and pastors; and
> the nonbinding private reading of the individual.

In contrast, the various forms of interpretation of natural law are not guided by the Holy Spirit in the same way. True, some of natural law is perfectly presented in scripture in the Decalogue.[18] However, people must engage in interpretation of natural law even without revelation in order to live fruitfully in domestic life and in community. Suárez describes the interpretation of natural law as something that not only God but also men can and should engage in: "For it is man himself who ought to inquire into and understand the true sense of the natural law; and if he is unable to grasp this sense by himself, he ought to learn from others."[19] This interpretative action constitutes the substance of most human engagement with the natural law. The ability to interpret correctly, by applying the general precepts of the natural law to specific circumstances, depends on culture, education, training, and development of virtue. The precepts of the natural law do not vary, but each person is always involved in actively determining how they should be interpreted for each context. As discussed earlier, law is developed through a dialectical process, crucial for ensuring that it is suitable for each context and each development or change in a culture. As Suárez points out, "not all natural precepts are equally known or equally easy to understand. They require interpretation in order that their true sense may be understood without taking away or adding anything . . . the good or bad of human actions depends to a great extent upon the circumstances and opportunities for their execution."[20]

Determining how best to incorporate natural law into civil law is a crucial step for the development of civil law. There is always an interpretive act occurring, which results in the determination of exactly how natural law should inform civil law to keep it appropriate for that time and context. However, despite the fact that the civil law should not contradict but should incorporate some of the natural law, they are not identical. Rather, civil law, understood in its proper sense, "is strictly defined as creating a new obligation which would not exist simply under the natural law.... In effect, if the human law is only declarative of natural reason, there is not a doubt that it would have the same force as reason [*ratio*] itself."[21] Civil law requires its own interpretive engagement and cannot simply be understood through interpretation of natural law alone.

Suárez's approach to civil law's interpretation incorporates aspects of the interpretation of both natural laws and divine laws, including the categories of authoritative and doctrinal. In considering natural and divine law, he reserves authoritative interpretation to the Church and doctrinal interpretation to the doctors of the Church and the ecclesial counsels. Both of these are empowered by the Holy Spirit to interpret: the Church, infallibly, with the whole authority of the Holy Spirit, and the doctors and pastors doctrinally, according to special charisms and gifts of the Spirit.

When discussing the analogy between civil law and divine law, Suárez uses the same categories to assess scriptural interpretation, but with different distribution of authority, due to the differences in the parties involved.[22] Suárez's distinctions between the two categories of interpretation require an awareness of the human lawgiver's limitations. Because the ruler acts with God's authority, the ruler still has some authority to interpret authentically, since the authority that the lawmaker possesses to make law also extends to the ability to interpret law. The same power to interpret law resides in the successor who is equal in power. The successor has the power to interpret regardless of whether or not the intention of the original authority who made the law is accessible.[23] This form of interpretation can be more than a clarification; it can be a direct change, whether adding or taking away from the application of the law. Even if the interpretation does not seem adequate to the significance of the words of the original law, it is still authoritative.[24] However, although the ruler and her successor's interpretation may be authentic, it is not final in the way in which God's interpretation of His own laws is authentic and is therefore open to revisions and questions from other sources.

First, since the human ruler is fallible, she might fail in perfectly communicating her intention in making a law. The words of the law might be too vague or ambiguous, or too broad or too narrow, to actually promote the common good in a particular situation. Second, the ruler's aim or intention might be unjust or inappropriate for a specific context. Finally, the ruler might not incorporate the natural law component into the civil law in the most appropriate way. All of these potential failures change who has the ability to interpret.

The second source of interpretation—doctrinal—involves primarily judges and legal scholars. Suárez's discussion of this category has obvious connections to the proportionalist debate in contemporary moral theology.[25] This type of doctrinal obligation is important because "in effect, the human condition is such that the man can scarcely explain his own opinion with clear enough words that ambiguities and doubts do not arise, over all because the human law speaks narrowly and generally; and in its application to diverse cases in particular arises with frequent doubts. This is why we require the judgement of experts."[26] Proportionalist experts often engage in interpretation by comparing one law to another within the same body of law.[27] Although this form of interpretation does not carry the same authority as authentic interpretation, "at times it can be so certain that it can induce obligation."[28] This creation of obligation stems from probability and accumulation of authority: the longer experts agree on an interpretation, the more certain that interpretation is. "When the interpretations of the experts are diverse, one has to form the judgement according to the weight of the reasons and authority of the experts."[29] Wide agreement of experts indicates general acceptance and observation of the interpretation and wide concurrence of experts makes it difficult to give a reason strong enough to convert securely in conscience to the contrary interpretation. However, because this mode of interpretation depends on the judgments of a variety of interpreters in various contexts, this form of interpretation always has some degree of contingency.

The people can also issue authentic interpretations. In the Church, the people can issue authentic interpretations under the guidance of the Holy Spirit and when assembled in ecclesial counsels. In an analogical way in the civil sphere, the community can, through its practices, engage in interpretation of law and legal terms. This interpretation in practice (*ex usu*) has significant force, and can, at times, even be authentic—at the same level of authority as that of the lawgiver.[30] The justification of this claim depends on Suárez's theory of reception: subjects can refuse to receive the law but they can also selectively receive it through interpretation, refining or extending the law rather than completely rejecting it. "Just as we have said in an earlier passage that an interpretation made by law is an authentic one, by reason of the efficacy of such law in establishing that interpretation, so the same [in like circumstances] is to be said of custom which has developed to the point at which it obtains the force of law ... since a custom is effective in securing the establishment of law, it can also, for that reason, interpret a law efficaciously, and can do so in the way which other laws do."[31]

The people's interpretation includes not only an interpretation of the words of the law but also an evaluation of the appropriateness of the lawmaker's aim and the lawmaker's success in applying the natural law through the civil law. This attempt to refine civil law to better accord with natural law, through interpretation, creates a continuous dialogue between a ruler and the people, since "many natural precepts require much declaration and interpretation in order that their true sense may be established. This assertion may be understood to refer both to the natural law as it is in itself and as it is written in positive law [*lege*]."[32] In civil law, therefore, as with natural law, interpretation is always an ongoing activity imposed on an open-textured body of law, not a one-time effort on a closed text. Rather than seeing law as a closed system, Suárez considers law to be consistently open to input from various sources. Engagement between the people, the lawmaker, judges, and legal scholars in interpretation makes interpretation both important for upholding the rule of law but also an important tool for making laws more just.

When considering Suárez's theory of who can interpret, the importance of Suárez's theological convictions shaping his theory of law are very clear. The foundational figure of God the Lawgiver as the ultimate source of all ethical reflection necessarily centers his theory of interpretation first upon the role of the lawmaker making the law. This authority is shared to a degree by the pope, who has the power to make authoritative decrees governing the Church, and to a lesser degree by the human lawmaker. It is this authority that gives law its morally obliging character. Even though the human lawgiver is inherently flawed and limited, the respect due to her office and the fact that she is made in the image of God requires not only respect for her clear and explicitly stated intentions but also a charitable determination of how to read her will as expressed in the law.

However, the importance placed on the role of the lawmaker is balanced out by the role of the people. Because the people are entrusted with God's power to make law, and because the law is originally given for their own good, which they are, to a certain extent, best able to interpret, the lawmaker's will alone (or that of the experts alone) is never sufficient for interpretation. Rather, the interpretive power of the people is also always in play. It is the people who oftentimes can discern how to apply the precepts of the natural law best in their own lives, and this always acts as a check against the lawmaker's power and will.

What Does Interpretation Do?

Suárez identifies four potential ways in which interpretive acts, carried out by any of these actors, can amplify or restrict law. The first, and most obvious, is to read the law and put it into action "according to the natural sense of the words." The second is to interpret according to the civil or legal sense of the words, which can include a reference to "the practice of common right or by some legal fiction."[33] Third is to restrict or amplify the meaning of the words in a way that is not natural, perhaps to the point of impropriety (taken in the strict sense) but still within what H. L. A. Hart would call the "penumbra" of meaning.[34] Fourth is a move beyond the significance of the words to focus only on "the similarity of the things or cases or formal identity in the reasons itself, to the law."[35] In each of these modes of interpretation, Suárez considers how the act of interpretation, whether carried out by the community or by experts, preserves the authority of the rule of law and leaves room for engagement to make the law more just.

Since reading a statute using words in their natural meanings is the most obvious understanding of interpretation, Suárez does not spend much time considering its techniques. He does however consider the reasons that might motivate one to choose to apply a different type of definition over the definition closest to natural language. Such a choice could be motivated first by a systematic concern to maintain the integrity and consistency of a body of law by using terms of art in the same way when they appear in different sections of the same statute or different statutes of the same code. Or it could be motivated by teleological/deontological concerns: an effort to advance the common good and to promote justice by turning to the most favorable interpretation, such as loosely interpreting a sentencing law in order to improve justice, not simply to increase punishment.

This approach may result in the expansion or restriction of a word's meaning beyond its most natural meaning. This does not require the use of an explicitly legal definition, but rather the expansion or restriction within the penumbra of meaning and beyond what would generally be considered "the proper sense of the word." The goal of this restriction or amplification is also motivated by respect both for the intentions of the lawmakers and interpretation's goal in promoting the common good. Suárez writes that in carrying out this interpretive act, "we do not separate ourselves from the mind of the legislator, because then the words really do not show the will of the legislator in their proper sense, but a little modified [*translationem*]. Whence comes text of the Saint Gregory 'Frequently, while attending to the proper sense of the words, the true sense is lost.'"[36] Suárez provides a commonly considered illustration: a summons to appear in court. A summons does not require only that a person literally appear in court and then walk back out the door, but actually to be present for the legal proceedings. "For, one who says that he goes to a place for business, is saying virtually that he is going to stay there all the time that the business requires. And that is what is understood, according to custom of him, who comes by a summons [*praecepto*], that he will wait upon the will of the one who commands."[37] Thus, provisions within statutes should be interpreted in such a way that they have some actual significance and do not contradict other provisions. This mode of interpretation should also be deployed when the plain sense of the law is unjust, absurd, or useless. Since the lawmaker must have desired to make a valid law, an interpretation that saves a law from injustice or impracticability is understood to be in accord with what can be most plainly discerned of the mind of the lawmaker.[38]

Suárez also considers the fourth and most difficult act: the question of whether or not the valid interpretation of a law can completely depart from its text. In other words, can the interpreter use interpretation to make new law? Or should the interpreter always be working within some meaning of the language of the text to use interpretation to refine and define the already existing body of law? It is important to note that Suárez sees the departure from the text as something that should take place in exceptional circumstances only, out of respect for the priority of law's written nature.[39] Suárez is also very clear that obligation and liability under the law ends after the third category. People who are obeying the law are not morally obliged to obey interpretations of the law that depart from the verbal sense of the law's words.

The resources that are already available within the legal tradition must guide any total departure from the statutory language. Carrying out the evaluative judgment of whether a law should be interpreted according to similarity of reason with other laws is the exclusive work of judges or others trained to engage in legal interpretation.[40] Suárez considers whether a departure from the text is permissible because the law has either an identical or a similar reason for existence as another law. Could the interpretation of the law with the similar reason be applied to fill an interpretive gap in the law at issue? For example, many towns have posted requirements in school zones that drivers not only must lower their speed but also are not allowed to use their cell phones, except in hand's-free mode, when children are present. A judge could reasonably assume that older regulations regarding distracted driving in commercial vehicles should be read to include a limitation on the use of mobile devices. In both cases the reasons are similar: protection of pedestrians. Reading a more contemporary interpretation of distracted driving into an older statute would be relatively uncontroversial.

Suárez claims that this idea, that a law may be read according to other similar statutes even when it allows a departure from the text, is supported by the interpretive value of tradition: "Nothing conforms better to reason and prudence than to follow the footprints of those that proceed us, especially if it is approved by the law of the superior." In addition, a study of statutes indicates that often a similarity of reason motivates the lawmaker in issuing a series of laws. Drawing on Aquinas, Suárez claims that considering the similarity of reason between separate laws can also ensure that the judge is able to "judge according to the law," rather than making law.[41] If the statute at hand does not expressly govern the case at issue, considering another statute that was passed for a similar reason will appropriately shield the judge from lawmaking but confine her interpretation to the existing legal patterns. "When the presumption [as to a law's meaning]—although it is not expressly written in the law—has a great affinity or similarity with the written law (and this happens generally when there is given an equal or better reason [in the written law]), it is to be judged by the written law. And therefore it is said 'since the law will not be able to cover all the cases, we proceed from similar to similar.'"[42]

This use of similar reason to fill a lacuna of the law is, according to Suárez, uncontroversial. Where the controversy arises is whether identity or similarity of reason in one law obliges a judge to extend or restrict the scope of the law at issue, even contrary to the words of the law. This form of interpretation is much more limited. There are two strict requirements for carrying this out and for ensuring that "the reason be adequate to the law": "That the reason, alone and by itself, acts in a sufficient and effective mode to constitute the law, [and] that it is the only end plainly intended by the law."[43] It is not enough that the reasons behind the law be similar; they must be identical.

To return to the cell phone use analogy, imagine if the judge was considering an older statute regarding distracted driving that explicitly exempted a mobile device from being considered a cause of distracted driving. The judge could most compellingly read a ban on mobile devices (drawn from the school zone law) into the distracted driving law, contrary to the very words of the statute, only if the reasons for the two statutes were identical and clearly the cause of the law. For example, it would be much more convincing if the statute at issue regulated school bus drivers in town rather than long haul truckers driving on a bypass around the town. It is obvious that the reason for the limitations on using mobile devices in cars driving through school zones when children are present is that children crossing streets and getting in and out of cars require special protection, care, and concern, which might not be considered necessary for adult pedestrians. Extending the limitations on cell phone use to other situations where children are getting in and out of vehicles and potentially crossing streets, such as boarding school buses, provides an equality of reason that would justify imposing a reading on the law contrary to the statute's wording.

This fourth act of interpretation leaves room for interpretation to expand or restrict the law based on the interpreter's understanding of the law's reason in a way that promotes justice and the common good. However, it must be narrowly construed and requires a high degree of certainty. In establishing this strict standard, Suárez is protecting the freedom of the lawmaker's will. There might be many reasons in favor of a law. The lawmaker, in her freedom, does not have to agree with all of those reasons in making a law. Also, for a judge to attempt to interpret a law against its explicit words, based on one reason selected out of a multitude, would risk ignoring the lawmaker's actual reason for making the law.[44] Therefore the judge can only substitute an interpretation from one law against the words of another law when the reasons for making the law are identical. In this way the judge seeks to uphold the lawmaker's will by ensuring that the law reflects the lawmaker's presumed desire to act "with prudence and in the proper mode ... [and] in order to avoid some absurdity or injustice of the law."[45]

Suárez's limitation on interpretation against the words of a law shows his continued commitment to carving out a large area of morally neutral space within the law to preserve the freedom of the lawmaker's will. The interpreter does not apply the reason gleaned from another law simply because the law does not sufficiently act to promote justice and the common good. Rather, it is applied only if the law contradicts justice and the common good.

Thus Suarez argues that the judge does not make law, but rather develops it through creative interpretation. Suárez believes that the law is generally capacious enough to provide the answers and sources for interpretations, rather than full of gaps for the judge alone to fill. The influence of two different legislative forces, the lawmaker and the people, expands the resources available for filling interpretative gaps, beyond what any legal positivist, who only envisions a top-down theory of law, might imagine conceivable.

Components of Interpretation

Along with describing what interpretation does, Suárez names three components of law that must be understood in order to interpret a law. They are, in this order, "the words of the law ... the mind of the legislator in making the law, and the reason [ratio]."[46] Understanding that each of these components has its own type of epistemological uncertainty requires interpretative engagement with each component: "In all of these depends the true interpretation of the law."[47] In other words, the interpreter must simultaneously understand the law's words, the law's purpose, and the legislator's intent.

Legal Language

In his discussion of the need for interpretation, legal philosopher Joseph Raz notes that words carry the meaning that convention has assigned to them. He also comments that some philosophers of law assume that this realization is a modern innovation: "The triumphalism which often accompanies this suggestion, and the implication that conventions were overlooked in pre-post-modern analysis is somewhat surprising. Since the decline of magic no one has ever doubted the dependence of language and other carriers of meaning on conventions."[48] Suárez proves Raz's point: he has no doubt that words are conventional signifiers, since he believes that all law functions as a sign, usually a sign of the will of the lawmaker.[49] Thus, words are the primary signifier of this will. However, the sheer existence of the will alone is not enough to provide a force of obligation. Rather, the will must be expressed in words that indicate obligation. If the will is unclear as it is conveyed in words, it lacks binding authority. This is true even if the will to oblige can be established through other means.[50] Thus, a law's words have no authority unless they derive from the lawmaker's will to establish law. And the lawmaker's will has no authority unless it is clearly expressed in law through words.

In order to resolve this apparent contradiction, Suárez draws upon Saint Hilary to describe interpretation as a dynamic act of relating words to will, which involves its own type of creativity: "This is what the opinion of St. Hilary has in mind, which says 'the sense of the words has to be found out by the motives that there were to say it; because it is not the thing which is submitted to the language but the language which is submitted to the thing.'"[51] Therefore, the act of interpretation involves a dynamic engagement between discerning the will of the lawmaker and the generally accepted meaning of the words. While the words are more certain, the will is the principle of the law, although it can only be discerned through conjecture.[52] Whatever sense of the words comprising the law was intended by the will of the lawmaker can often be conjectured by considering the lawmaker's reason for making the law.[53]

The first and clearest way to determine purpose is to consider the words of the statutory text at hand, from the words "the true interpretation of the law must be deduced, and always preferred, *if there is nothing opposed to it.*"[54] After all, when the law is written, it is given in words that are recorded and not subject to easy change. "If the words were not so, there would be nothing certain in the laws, nor would it be possible to regulate by them the actions of people, since the will of each one would derive improper senses."[55] Words, however, are signs that change and evolve over time. John Doyle lists up to eight different ways in which Suárez indicates how the meanings of words related to sacraments have changed and which must be taken account of in sacramental theology.[56] Because words are signs, not the inward reality themselves, they can change over time in their usefulness as signposts. Words are necessarily ambiguous because they cannot fully convey deeper realities. Add to this the complication that words have an entire range of meaning, with constantly added and discarded different significances over time and through various contexts. Though words are essential, the use of words always necessarily contributes to ambiguity. Suárez grounds this understanding primarily in a theological sense. According to Doyle, Suárez first develops his ideas relating to the indeterminate meaning of words within his sacramental theology, where he considers the importance of words and materials in the celebration of the Eucharist. In the celebration of the Eucharist, the priest's words are necessary to accomplish the Eucharistic transformation but are also signs pointing to an inward reality.[57] The sense of the word must remain the same even if the form of the word changes for the Eucharist to be effective.[58]

Given this instability in language, Suárez identifies two types of meaning that must be considered in interpretation: the ordinary meaning and the juridical meaning. Suárez possesses an undoubted preference for interpretation according to the clear sense of the words understood in their most common usage, that is, as they are actually used in ordinary conversation.[59] Just as with custom, Suárez gives the first priority to the understanding and interpretation *of the people*. He claims support both from jurists and from the patristic fathers, both of whom used the ordinary meaning as the prima facie, but not exclusive, tool for interpreting law.

This understanding he describes as the "natural one," not in the sense of being *essentially* imposed by nature, since "all words of the human laws receive their significance according to convention and by imposition," but rather because it belongs to the "simple and primordial" understanding of the words in each particular context.[60] The natural meaning should not be understood to refer to historical roots and derivation, but rather the most common use by the common people.[61] Because of the importance of the natural meaning of words, the people are the primary source for developing this understanding. So, we see that before they even actively engage in interpretation themselves, the people's knowledge and practices shape the law.

However, the people alone do not determine the meaning of a law's language. In Suárez's theory of the development of law as a dialectical process, there is another sense that must also be considered in a legal context: the word's juridical significance. For example, although the same word is used, describing a natural death and a death in the eyes of the law (such as by those making a religious profession) are very different things. The first act of interpretation, therefore, is to determine whether the natural sense or the juridical sense is being referenced.[62] Following this determination, the act of interpretation instantly gets more difficult. The reality, of course, is that words rarely have one clear and indisputable natural significance. Rather, they often have several different significances, or at least different valences and implications that significantly alter the perception. Thus, interpretation of law develops out of a consideration of the language of the people and the language of the courts, read together.

Consideration of the Legal System

Suárez considers the analysis of the actual words of the law as the first step to determining the intention of the lawmaker. However, the law must not only be interpreted according to its own language; it must also be interpreted within the broader corpus of laws. This systematic approach helps mediate between the multiple possible meanings words may accrue over time. In this approach, the interpreter might consider the various valences that a word has acquired across a series of legal texts to indicate which meaning of the word the lawmaker intended in a particular statute, with greater weight always given to the meaning that is, given equality of circumstances, the most benign and least rigorous.[63]

Suárez is not unique in this approach. In their analyses of legal interpretation, both Ronald Dworkin and Joseph Raz emphasize the importance of coherence within a body of law. Raz calls it "continuity/tradition" and Dworkin calls it "fit."[64] Given his cultural context, it is not surprising that Suárez shares this same commitment. The political instability that preceded the development of medieval jurisprudence meant that the internal coherence across time of the written law was of prime importance for the maintenance of social stability.

Suárez then develops a theory of systemic engagement to expand our understanding of the lawmaker's intent. This systemic engagement is based on the presumption that the lawmaker, unless she specifies otherwise, seeks to preserve laws. Therefore, the default presumption is that the lawmaker willed that the words would be understood in a way that does not contradict or oppose other texts.[65] Although this interpretation may result in what might appear to be an improper or unnatural reading of the text of the later edict, it should be considered as a definition that has developed out of juridical custom or understanding of right.[66] At times the use of the word in the rest of the body of law may provide a clue as to which significance is to be preferred. Suárez emphasizes the crucial cultural point that no lawmaker exists in a vacuum and all are limited by the constraints of the end of the law: to promote the common good.

Suárez is not naïve in arguing that the tradition is static or comprised of only one source. Like other scholastics, he is working from a body of established texts within a tradition, including scripture and writings by theologians, jurists, and canonists, as well as the actual civil laws of various countries. Although he does not hesitate to disagree with at least some of the established authorities at various points, up to and including Thomas Aquinas (although never Church teaching itself, nor scripture), much of his work is an attempt to discern a middle ground between sources that at first appear to be opposed in order to continue to develop a theory of law within the established tradition. In using this strategy he is following in the footsteps of Gratian and the Decretalists. This commitment to a synthesis of a wide variety of texts shows that drawing upon more than one source for interpretation does not necessarily result in rampant subjectivity. Indeed, it privileges the introduction of more than one voice and leaves room for further contributions both from below and from outside the communal tradition of interpretation.

Purpose of the Law

Suárez at first appears to argue that the purpose of the law is the same as the reason or intention the lawmaker had for making that law. If one can be certain of the law's purpose, one can also have a good indicator of the mind of the lawmaker, and thus the meaning of the words.[67] However, he then nuances this approach by dividing the process of determining the lawmaker's reason for the law into two categories: reasons that are included in the text of the law and reasons that are deduced by those interpreting the law regarding the lawgiver's actual internal intention.[68] Failing to distinguish between these two types of reasons for the law has contributed to much of the confusion surrounding the discussion of reason in law. In one sense reason is always indicated only remotely, since it is impossible to discern exactly what intentions motivated the lawmaker.[69] However, the reason or purpose included in the text of the law can be determined with somewhat greater certainty than reasons for the law that were in the lawmaker's mind.

It is important to note that although they are related, the reason for the law and the lawmaker's intent are not the same thing. The lawmaker may make a law according to a private intention, but not necessarily promulgate a law that requires everything included in his intention. The lawmaker's intention is, therefore, often more expansive than the purpose of the specific law developed from it. Additionally, the purpose expressed in law can capture what the lawmaker's intention was at one point in time, but cannot capture all of it. "It can occur that starting from one reason the will may be moved by diverse means and to diverse reasons. Therefore, in order to know thoroughly the will of the legislator, which is his own mind, the reason expressed in the law is not enough, but all reasons must be weighted and examined attentively."[70]

Because this gap between purpose and intention exists, relying on the purpose expressed in the law is not an infallible tool of interpretation. Even if one purpose is stated, the reality is that human laws are not always created for one purpose alone, or even for several purposes. In fact, sometimes there may be so many purposes for creating a law, and these purposes may be so vaguely defined or inchoately sensed even by the lawmaker, that it is difficult to give a precise reason for everything required by the law. "In effect, even though the law will always be in conformity with reason, nevertheless the choice between the things which are reasonable will not always have one reason and therefore the [specific] reason is not always there to investigate, as it says in the Digest."[71] Discerning the lawmaker's purpose for the law is therefore an inherently uncertain undertaking, since the reasons for the law's existence may be much greater, and less clear, than what the lawmaker is able to name, even to herself.[72]

This skepticism about the possibility of grasping the purpose for a law might seem to indicate that Suárez is taking a purely voluntarist and positivistic approach to legal interpretation, defining it simply as interpreting the lawmaker's will. It is authority that matters, with other components of interpretation coming in a distant second. However, we will see that Suárez's theory is significantly more complex.

Intention

For Suárez, the core task of true interpretation is determining the lawmaker's intent in making the law, which may go beyond the words or the stated purpose of the law's text. Suárez's terminology in referring to intent varies somewhat. He generally refers either to the will or the mind of the lawmaker (or sometimes both, together) in order to indicate intent.[73] He claims that it is this act of the lawmaker's willing a law into existence that makes laws obligatory and therefore binding. This is why he describes will as constituting the "soul of the law."[74] Establishing intent as the "norm of interpretation" also creates a standard of objectivity in interpretation, since the key to understanding any law is determining the lawmaker's will.

However, determining the lawmaker's private and personal intent is not the primary source for interpretation for Suárez. Rather, for Suárez, the lawmaker's intent is always interpreted through a lens of the good, the just, and the useful. Suárez is able to seamlessly combine these two apparently contradictory sources for interpretation because the primary presumption in determining intent is always the assumption that the lawmaker, in fact, intends to issue a valid law. Since an unjust law is no law, the presumption is also always that the lawmaker willed the law to be just. Therefore, the words are always given the reading that would promote the most justice, within the range of possible meanings, since the assumption is that the lawmaker willed to act justly. The same hermeneutic is applied if the natural sense of the words would indicate that the lawmaker had willed something against the common good or some form of impossibility or absurdity that made the law impossible to perform, making it invalid.[75] This type of interpretive analysis does not just come into play when the words cannot be determined or the systemic direction of the law is vague. Rather, it is a background question being raised during all interpretive activity and thoroughly pervades Suárez's theory of legal engagement.[76]

Furthermore, if the injustice of the law is unclear, then the presumption is that the people should give prima facie deference to the judgment of the lawgiver. This second tenet of engagement with the question of intention is what Ernesto Garzón Valdés refers to as the assumption of the "just and rational legislator."[77] Under this rule, the person receiving the law should assume that the lawmaker intended to produce a law that was just, promoted the common good, and did not fall into absurdity and impossibility. This assumption will radically shape any interpretive activity.

There are several reasons for this charitable response in civic interpretation. First, by the nature of the divine grant of lawmaking authority, the lawmaker "is in permanent possession of a superior right."[78] Second, the lawmaker's responsibilities to promote the common good, along with having access to the resources that accompany her office, often mean that the lawmaker "is directed by superior counsel and may be moved by general reasons hidden from [her] subjects."[79] Finally, the people should be motivated by a general concern for the common good and should seek to uphold the general authority of the rule of law wherever possible. If the presumption in favor of the lawgiver is widely disregarded, the people "would assume an excessive license to disregard the laws, since the latter can hardly be so just that it is impossible for them to be treated as doubtful."[80]

But this requirement is only a presumption. Suárez recognizes that the human lawmaker may not always desire the common good or that her will may also result in a failure to enact a just law.[81] Nevertheless, the law may actually achieve good, contrary to the lawmaker's flawed intent. Thus, the common good can be achieved whether or not the intention of the lawgiver is actually to promote it. The question to be asked in this situation is not what the lawgiver intended to have happen, but rather what the law is actually accomplishing. Thus "if the legislator makes a law from hatred, for example, or from some other perverse motive, if, in spite of this, the law itself yields the common good, that is enough for its validity."[82] Therefore, the lawmaker's intent, in some form or another, is still prioritized, even as interpretation becomes a tool to advance legal justice and the common good.

For Suárez this nuanced engagement with intent is also grounded in theological suppositions. A consideration of actual results rather than of sinful motivations is analogous, he claims, to the understanding that the sacraments do not depend on the goodwill of the person administering the sacrament to actually be effective. "The perverse intention of the sacred minister who administers [a sacrament] does nothing to hinder the sacrament, if [the intention] is not opposed to its substance [*substantiam*]."[83]

This inclusion of a moral component as a standard of interpretation, along with intent, inevitably raises questions of objectivity. Who can determine what and whose good is being advanced by a particular law? The legal positivists' concern, that the introduction of moral elements into interpretation opens the door to subjective judicial interpretation based upon personal preference and belief, remains a challenge. The key element in Suárez's theory, which safeguards against this subjective failure, is the fact that the interpretation is not simply carried out by judges alone but is also authoritatively decided by the people and the lawmaker, aided by the interpretive ability of experts. Although this combined effort toward interpretation does not guarantee that the good will be perfectly realized, it acknowledges the discernment of the common good as a communal enterprise, carried out from four important and overlapping but still separate perspectives. The task of interpretation is not set up as a competition, with judges opposed to the lawmaker opposed to the people. Rather, the engagement in interpretation of all three additional groups is essential. The doctrinal expert provides the wisdom gained from study and knowledge of tradition; the lawmaker provides the broad perspective from the top down; and the people provide the more narrow and focused understanding of what advances the common good, from the ground up.

While this explanation does not perfectly resolve the question of objectivity, it provides some important limits against any one group's limited perspective. For example, the application of natural law by the people is developed out of natural reason and is grounded in the exigencies of created human nature, which provides one element of objectivity. As Suárez says, "All that is deduced from a necessary dictate of natural reason has, necessarily, its roots in nature, and is derived from a natural inclination, whether the dictate is formed either directly or mediated through argumentation [*discursum*]."[84]

This is apparent in how Suárez combines both elements when turning to what Paul Pace identifies as Suárez's "three-tiered description" of the purpose of civil laws.[85] Civil laws are not intended to promote either the happiness of the future life or the happiness of the individual alone in the present life. Rather, their end is the natural happiness of the perfect community. As Suárez says, this happiness depends upon "living in peace and justice"; "possessing sufficient goods that are necessary to maintain and make life comfortable"; and having "the normal rectitude of customs that are necessary for the social peace, the prosperity of the public, and the adequate conservation of human nature."[86]

In this schema, the emphasis includes both peace and justice (rights-oriented goods) and the physical well-being of prosperity and comfort of the whole. There is also an emphasis on the good of the individual and of the community, as both are natural ends of the law. This understanding is a continuation of Suárez's emphasis on law's role in promoting the good of the individual as well as the good of community.[87] Suárez then subdivides the common good into two categories: one that directly relates to the needs of the community and one that promotes individual good in a way that is to the advantage of the whole community.[88] Contra Hart's description of natural lawyers, Suárez does not depend on an understanding of natural law only as "a universal natural law discoverable by human reason and applicable to all men at all times and places."[89] Rather, the common good must be understood with a high degree of particularity for both individuals and community as well. As Suárez says, "There exists an authentic law, and it may be truly valid only so far as the material of which it treats is useful and suitable [*util et conveniens*] to the common good of that time, that place and for that people and community."[90]

Interpreting laws to achieve these goals requires the engagement of the lawmaker, the people, and the experts. The people have the best discernment into the needs of their own community, both for material goods, for peace, and for justice. The lawmaker and the experts have the broad perspective and personal distance to protect justice for individuals and minorities, as well as the capacity to think strategically about how laws can be developed to promote the common good.

The third goal is that laws should promote the customs necessary to achieve these other goals. This goal, which depends on a broad view and understanding of each context, demonstrates the importance of all three groups engaging together in creation and interpretation of law. As the people and the rulers become more virtuous, both the laws made and the ways in which they are interpreted will be even more likely to promote the common good, peace, justice, and prosperity of all.

Interpretation in Action

Let us consider two different instances of an application of Suárez's theory of interpretation. The first, where Suárez engages in the type of interpretive action described earlier, ends with the conclusion that there is no possibility that the law at issue could be justly interpreted, even though it provides a useful demonstration of how Suárez applies his own theory. The second example, more contemporary to our times, demonstrates how Christians today can engage in this type of interpretive engagement and actually change the laws.

King James and the Oath of Allegiance Controversy

In his polemical work *Against the Anglican Heresy*, Suárez carries out a clause-by-clause interpretation of the oath of supremacy that James I demanded from every English subject, following the failed attempt of the Gunpowder Controversy to destroy the Houses of Parliament. This oath had become an item of significant controversy across Europe and resulted in a battle of pamphlets and papal bulls involving the pope, the king, Cardinal Bellarmine, and eventually Suárez himself.

Suárez joined the controversy at the request of Pope Paul V in order to defend Bellarmine.[91] While the controversy had personal significance to him—one of the Catholics executed by James I for alleged treasonous involvement in the Gunpowder Controversy, Henry Garnett, was a fellow Jesuit whom Suárez had known during his time at the Roman College—it also enabled him to put into application many of the ideas developed in *De Legibus*. In the last section of the two-volume treatise, Suárez engages in a rigorous interpretation of the text of the oath of allegiance demanded by the king. Several key points he makes there demonstrate his theory of interpretation.

Suárez begins by noting that the first part of the oath contains a profession of obedience to "our Supreme Lord, King James."[92] In order to interpret what "our Supreme Lord" means, Suárez, finding the natural definition of the word unclear, turns to other sources within the body of law, namely, oaths and formulas that James has previously published and never retracted, as well as James's theological writings. Together these indicate that the phrase is intended to "signify that he is supreme simply, as well in spiritual things as in temporal."[93] These other legal sources indicate that the meaning goes beyond that expressed in the natural language of the oath and should be understood as a vow of allegiance without limits. "The following denial, that the 'Pope ... does not have any power or authority to depose the king,' points to the reason the king has for requiring the oath: to establish his own claims to the throne free of outside interference which might occasion resistance by the citizens whom he governs."[94]

Suárez carries out a similar analysis upon the second part of the oath, which requires that each citizen make "a special promise to reveal all treacheries in these words, 'and I will expend all my effort to reveal and make manifest to both His Majesty and to his heirs and successors all treasons and treacherous plots that against him or any of them may come to his notice or hearing.'"[95] According to the natural sense of the words, revealing treachery would be a reasonable expectation (outside the seal of the confessional) for any ruler to have for his subjects.[96] However, understanding the king's reasons for the oath, as demonstrated by the earlier sections of the oath—namely, rejection of papal authority—it becomes clear that by treachery the king means "everything that is *in his own judgment* and according to the errors of the preceding sections reckoned to be treachery."[97] Because of this wording and similar language, Suárez argues that the law that forces Catholics to swear this oath is contrary to justice, since it demands that Catholic citizens of the realm either place a temporal authority (the king) over a spiritual authority (the pope) or else perjure themselves. The king's judgment and intention in making a law, his own interpretation of what constitutes treason, is not enough to overrule either the natural good—that citizens cannot be forced to perjure themselves—or the supernatural good—that the authority of the pope is superior in spiritual matters to that of any earthly king.

Suárez does consider whether or not it is possible to interpret the oath in such a way that it could be understood as just, even if that was not the king's original intention. It is possible that "the words of this oath are not so clear that they cannot be taken and sworn in some other sense ... although the one proposing the oath is demanding it in a corrupt sense and with a bad intention, the one swearing it is not bound to conform with the former's intention, but can use the amphiboly that the words allow."[98] In this instance Suárez considers explicitly whether or not creative interpretation of the law by the people in service of the common good, contrary to the ruler's intention, is permissible. Sadly, for James I (and even more for English Catholics, who were in danger of losing property and even their lives for refusing to take the oath), Suárez finds that the claims of the oath are in fact so clear (and so repetitive) that to place any meaning on the words of the oath other than a blanket acknowledgment of the king's spiritual superiority, would be impossible and would result in perjury on the part of any Catholic who took the oath.

Interpretation within the Sanctuary Movement

In the late 1970s and early 1980s, a network of churches and synagogues, based primarily in Arizona and California, organized into a loose network to provide "sanctuary" to Guatemalan and El Salvadoran refugees who were attempting to claim asylum in the United States in order to escape violence and persecution stemming from civil war at home. Christians and Jews involved in this movement were spurred to action when they realized that the Immigration and Naturalization Service (INS) was systematically refusing to grant any of the asylum claims of refugees from these countries. Rather, the INS was deporting all asylum seekers back to their home countries, heedless of the danger and threat of imminent death they would face upon their return.

As these congregations became aware of the danger that these refugees faced, they felt compelled by their beliefs or their consciences to do what they could to protect these people from deportation and ensure that they were granted the immigration status of extended voluntary departure. To achieve this goal, churches invoked the medieval practice of sanctuary, a practice with deep roots in scripture and the earlier Christian tradition, and offered immigrants safe spaces to live within their church buildings. Documents from many meetings at the churches that decided to become sanctuary churches, as well as eyewitness testimonies, make it clear that one of the key questions among the churches was not whether the refugees needed help or whether the Christian faith called upon these churches to provide it, but whether as Christians and as citizens they were called to place obedience to the civil law over righting the wrongs of injustice. A number of those involved drew upon the civil rights movement and Vietnam War protests to claim that morality trumped legality. They were saving lives, which they considered more important than obeying the law, and considered the entire sanctuary movement as an act of civil disobedience.

However, others involved in the movement offered another theological understanding. Rather than seeing what they were doing as civil disobedience, they claimed that they were actually following the law. In fact, they were following it in a more correct and accurate way than the governmental agency they opposed.[99] The key for them in making these interpretive claims was the use of the term "refugee" in the statute at issue in this case: the 1980 Refugee Act, passed by Congress just two years before the sanctuary movement came into existence.

This act had been passed out of a concern that previous laws governing refugees created a situation where a person fleeing a country whose government was friendly to the United States would have a harder time gaining refugee status than a person whose government was unfriendly.[100] The new refugee act adopted the same general language as the wording used by the United Nations (UN) in 1951: that asylum should be granted based upon "a well-founded fear of persecution on account of race, religion, nationality, membership in a particular social group, or political opinion."[101] The adoption of this new language was intended to ensure that the US political involvement in international politics did not influence asylum standards. Those involved in the sanctuary movement found that the law's application seemed to be different from the law's language. In reality, the INS generally applied one standard of proof for people fleeing countries at odds with the United States, such as communist nations, and another standard of proof for people whose government was either an ally of the United States or aligned with US interests. According to a study carried out by the UN High Commissioner for Refugees in 1981, after the passage of this allegedly neutral law, only one El Salvadoran had been granted refugee status in the United States in fiscal year 1981, and none had been granted temporary asylum, leading to a conclusion that there was potentially systematic discrimination against El Salvadorans.[102] A later study (in 1987) by the General Accounting Office, confirmed this finding of systemic discrimination.[103]

These moves to organize to protect people seeking asylum did not go unnoticed. Although the government at first did not prosecute people involved in the sanctuary movement, eventually a number were brought to trial on different charges. At the largest trial, in 1985, a group of eleven defendants were brought to trial on charges of alien smuggling. In pretrial motions the defendants argued that what they were doing was legal, both because it was moral and because their interpretation of the relevant statutory language was correct (i.e., that the refugees qualified because they were in fear for their lives given the political situation in their home countries, and therefore qualified for refugee status).[104] The presiding judge refused to allow this argument to be admitted in their defense on the grounds that he did not want to be forced into ruling on the executive branch's conduct.[105]

Despite this judicial restriction on producing evidence, the publicity surrounding the trial and the limited testimony presented in court still told a compelling story. People across the country began to learn about the plight of people seeking asylum, about the sanctuary movement, and about the legal specifics of the activists' claims regarding the interpretation of "refugee status."[106] Eight of the defendants were eventually convicted (although none served jail time), but a broader awareness of the problematic limitations on refugee status drew many more churches, lawyers, and politicians into sympathy with the movement. In the end it was the advocates' interpretation of the statute that eventually prevailed. Through a number of legislative enactments, many of the Guatemalan and El Salvadoran refugees were eventually granted asylum and allowed to stay.[107]

Conclusion

In *The Concept of Law*, H. L. A. Hart describes his account of law as "descriptive in that it is morally neutral and has no justificatory aims."[108] Suárez's theologically grounded theory of interpretation is never intended to be "morally neutral." On the other hand, his inclusion of aspects of his theory in *Against Heresies* is clear proof that it is intended to be descriptive. As a teacher and participant in Reformation-era controversies, he proposed his theory because he believed that it actually describes how interpretation, carried out by the people, the lawmaker, and the experts, can change the substance of law without abandoning law's authority. In the sanctuary cases, the defendants were not hiding refugees and parsing statutory language because they necessarily had considered whether or not they could change the law. Rather, they saw people in need of help and felt that, as Christians, they were called to care for them. Eventually their challenges to existing law were based along the lines of interpretive activity that Suárez developed: rather than completely rejecting the law, they offered a different description and drew upon a meaning of "refugee" that made more sense in common usage, even if not in politics. Using this interpretation did not require the sanctuary advocates to completely deny law's authority, including the government's ability to make prudential decisions about granting asylum status. Rather, they interpreted the legislature's reason for the law in the way that most promoted the common good: that the lawmakers intended asylum as a humanitarian service for all in danger, rather than as a political tool. They then acted upon that belief. Over time their lived interpretation of the law convinced more people, more so than the INS's actions or the judge's interpretation at trial, bringing the law more into line with an interpretation that promoted justice and the common good.

Notes

1. Francisco Suárez, *Tractatus de legibus ac Deo legislatore*, ed. Luciano Pereña VicenteI (Madrid : Consejo Superior de Investigaciones Científicas, 1972), VI.i.5.
2. For a more extensive analysis of each of these issues, see Jim Evans, *Statutory Interpretation: Problems of Communication* (Oxford: Oxford University Press, 1998).

3. Francisco Suarez, *Tractatus de legibus ac Deo legislatore,* ed. Carlos Baciero (Madrid: Consejo Superior de Investigaciones Científicas, 2010), VI.ii.1.
4. Suárez, VI.ii.1.
5. Suárez, VI.ii.1.
6. Suárez, VI.ii.1.
7. Suárez, VI.ii.6.
8. See Ronald Dworkin, *Law's Empire* (Cambridge, MA: Belknap, 1986), 62–64.
9. Ronald Dworkin, "How Law Is Like Literature," in *A Matter of Principle,* ed. Ronald Dworkin (Cambridge, MA: Harvard University Press, 1985), 148.
10. Dworkin, *Law's Empire,* 48.
11. Dworkin, 64.
12. Suárez, *De Legibus,* I.iv.5.
13. Francisco Suárez, *Defense of the Catholic Faith Against the Errors of Anglicanism,* trans. Peter L. P. Simpson (Createspace, 2012), I.xi.4. I also consulted the Latin edition in the *Vives Opera Omnia* to ensure correct translations. See Francisco Suárez, *Defensio Fidei Catholicae et Apostolicae contra Errores Anglicanae Secta,* in *Opera Omnia,* vol. 24 (Paris: Apud Ludovicum Vives, 1856–78).
14. All remaining quotes in this paragraph are from Suárez, I.xi.7.
15. Suárez, I.xi.15.
16. John P. Doyle, "Francisco Suárez on the Interpretation of Laws," in *Collected Studies on Francisco Suárez, SJ,* ed. Victor M. Salas (Ithaca, NY: Cornell University Press, 2010), 371.
17. Suárez, *Defensio,* I.xi.15.
18. Suárez, *De Legibus,* II.xv.2.
19. Suárez, II.xvi.6.
20. Suárez, II.xvi.6.
21. Suárez, VI.iii.3.
22. Suárez, VI.i.1.
23. Suárez, VI.i.2.
24. Suárez, VI.i.3.
25. While I was not able to determine whether Suárez had been exposed to Islamic legal theory, it is worth noting that this emphasis on the role of outside jurists has much in common with Islamic law's emphasis on the role of the *mufti* in providing legal interpretations outside the courtroom setting, which carries substantive, but not binding, authority. See Muhammad Khalid Masud, Brinkley Messick, and David Powers, "Muftis, Fatwas, and Islamic Legal Interpretation," in *Islamic Legal Interpretation: Muftis and Their Fatwas,* ed. Muhammad Khalid Masud, Brinkley Messick, and David Powers (Cambridge, MA: Harvard University Press, 1996), 3–4.
26. Suárez, *De Legibus,* VI.i.5.
27. Suárez, VI.i.3.
28. Suárez, VI.i.5.
29. Suárez, VI.i.6.
30. Suárez, VI.i.4.
31. Suárez, VII.xv.11. The practices of the people can also serve to interpret divine law, but only when interpreting the intention of the lawgiver. The standard for certainty here is either that the interpretation is observed "by the tradition of the Universal Church or one that has had the approval of the Pope" (VII.xvii.6).
32. Suárez, II.xvi.6.

33. Suárez, VI.ii.2.
34. Suárez, VI.ii.2; VI.i.16. See also H. L. A. Hart, *The Concept of Law*, 3rd ed. (Oxford: Oxford University Press, 2012), chap. 1.
35. Suárez, *De Legibus*, VI.ii.2.
36. Suárez, VI.i.16.
37. Suárez, VI.iii.17.
38. Suárez, VI.ii.7.
39. Suárez, VI.ii.5.
40. Suárez, VI.iii.14.
41. Suárez, VI.iii.14 (referencing Aquinas, *Summa*, II–II q. 60, ad 5).
42. Suárez, VI.iii.14. In seeking to avoid judicial legislation Suárez is much more similar to Dworkin than Hart. The judge is not using interpretation to make new law but rather is extending his interpretation along an already existing web of laws.
43. Suárez, VI.iii.19.
44. Suárez, VI.iii.20.
45. Suárez, VI.iii.22.
46. Suárez, VI.i.7.
47. Suárez, VI.i.7.
48. Joseph Raz, *Between Authority and Interpretation: On the Theory of Law and Practical Reason* (Oxford: Oxford University Press, 2009), 229.
49. Doyle, "Francisco Suárez on the Interpretation of Laws," 369.
50. Suárez, *De Legibus*, VI.i.13.
51. Suárez, VI.i.14.
52. Suárez, VI.i.15–16.
53. Suárez, VI.i.19.
54. Suárez, VI.i.7 (emphasis added).
55. Suárez, VI.i.8.
56. Doyle, "Francisco Suárez on the Interpretation of Laws," 370.
57. Doyle, 370.
58. Suárez, *De Sacramentis* in *Opera Omnia* (Paris: Apud Ludovicum Vives, 1856–78), q. LX, art. 8, p. 42: "Ratio vero est, quia sensus est veluti anima verbi, quia verbum no profertur propter sonum, sed propter sensum, et ideo, si idem sensus maneat, idem verbum, atque adeo eadem forma manere censetur: si autem mutetur sensus, et verbum et forman substantialiter mutari necesse est."
59. Suárez, *De Legibus*, VI.i.8.
60. Suárez, VI.i.9.
61. Suárez, VI.i.10.
62. Suárez, VI.i.9.
63. Suárez, VI.i.18.
64. Ronald Dworkin, *A Matter of Principle* (Cambridge, MA: Harvard University Press, 1985), 143.
65. Suárez, VI.i.17.
66. Suárez, VI.i.16.
67. Suárez, VI.i.19.
68. Suárez, VI.i.20.
69. Suárez, VI.i.19.
70. Suárez, VI.i.20.
71. Suárez, VI.i.19.

72. Suárez, VI.i.19.
73. Suárez, VI.i.12.
74. Suárez, VI.i.12.
75. Suárez, VI.i.17.
76. Interestingly, MacCormick discusses how the requirement of mutual interplay between the three strategies of interpretation, informed by avoidance of injustice and uncertainty, has altered his own theory of interpretation. All absurdity "for the purpose of the Golden Rule includes conflict either with justice or with other aspects of what is deemed the public good. . . . It is in the relevant sense 'absurd' to read a statute either in such a way as to generate injustice by reference to some legally recognized principle of justice, or in such a way as to be self-defeating in terms of presumed objectives of public policy pursued through legislation. So it would not be correct to say that the category of teleological/deontological arguments comes into play only if the other two categories fail to yield an unequivocal result. Consideration of arguments in that category may show such an absurdity as will displace a prima facie binding conclusion about the meaning of the legislative words in their (fully contextualised) 'ordinary signification.'" Neil MacCormick, "Argumentation and Interpretation," *Ratio Juris* 6, no. 1 (March 1993): 27.
77. Ernesto Garzón Valdés, *Derecho, Ética y Política* (Madrid: Centro de Estudios Constitucionales, 1993), 123.
78. Suárez, *De Legibus*, I.ix.11. In this analysis he draws on Aquinas, who also provides the standard for certainty in I–II q. 96, art. 4.
79. Suárez, *De Legibus*, I.ix.11.
80. Suárez, I.ix.11.
81. Suárez, I.vii.4.
82. Suárez, I.vii.9.
83. Suárez, I.vii.9.
84. Suárez, II.vii.10.
85. Paul Pace, SJ, "Francisco Suárez and Justice: A Common Good Perspective," *Gregorium* 93, no. 3 (2012): 503.
86. Suárez, *De Legibus*, III.xi.7.
87. Suárez, I.vii.4.
88. Suárez, III.xi.7, I.vii.8.
89. H. L. A. Hart, "American Jurisprudence through English Eyes: The Nightmare and the Noble Dream," *Georgia Law Review* 11, no. 5 (1977): 978.
90. Suárez, *De Legibus*, I.vii.9.
91. Suárez, *Defensio*, preface.
92. Suárez, VI.ii.1.
93. Suárez, VI.ii.1. In light of current controversies concerning what statements by a lawmaker are admissible and required to establish intent, including those made on social media, it is interesting that Suárez claims that the published materials containing statements made by a ruler, including nonlegal sources, may serve to indicate intent.
94. Suárez, VI.ii.3.
95. Suárez, VI.iii.7.
96. Whether a priest can be forced to break the seal of the confessional in the interest of national security was another controversial issue circulating in England at this time. This question likewise has present-day moral implications. For example, the Royal Commission into Institutional Responses to Child Sexual Abuse in Australia recommended in 2017 that priests should be required to break the seal of the confessional to report child

abuse. See "Australia Abuse: Archbishop Rejects Call to Report Confessions," *BBC News*, December 15, 2017, http://www.bbc.com/news/world-australia-42370543.
97. Suárez, *Defensio*, VI.iii.8 (emphasis added).
98. Suárez, VI.viii.5.
99. Miriam Davidson, *Convictions of the Heart: Jim Corbett and the Sanctuary Movement* (Tucson: University of Arizona Press, 1988), 32.
100. David Michels and David Blaikie, "'I Took Up the Case of the Stranger': Arguments from Faith, History, and Law," in *Sanctuary Practices in International Perspective: Migration, Citizenship and Social Movements*, ed. Randy K. Lippert and Sean Rehaag (New York: Routledge, 2013), 32.
101. Davidson, *Convictions of the Heart*, 44.
102. Davidson, 44.
103. See Gil Loescher, *Beyond Charity* (Oxford: Oxford University Press, 1993): "A 1987 U.S. General Accounting Office study of asylum compared the treatment of four nationalities—Salvadorans, Nicaraguans, Poles, and Iranians. The study found that 'aliens who stated on their application forms that they were arrested, imprisoned, had their life threatened, or were tortured had much lower approval rates if they were from El Salvador and Nicaragua than if they were from Poland and Iran.' . . . Moreover, of the four groups examined in the GAO study, only Salvadorans were deported to their home country after having been denied asylum (at the rate of 300 per month)" (104).
104. Davidson, *Convictions of the Heart*, 100; Michele Altemus, "The Sanctuary Movement," *Whittier Law Review* 9 (1987–88): 707–9.
105. See Davidson, *Convictions of the Heart*, 109. See also Altemus, "The Sanctuary Movement," 709.
106. Jay Matthews, "Sanctuary's Point Being Made: Movement that Aids Illegal Aliens Is on Trial in Arizona," *Washington Post*, January 30, 1986: "[Judge] Carroll has insisted that only the defendants' deeds, not their motives, are relevant. But through adept cross-examination or the judge's inattention, the Sanctuary Movement's argument is coming through, raising defendants' hopes that the jury will sympathize with their actions. They have been unable, however, to present their more sophisticated legal argument, that they behaved in accordance with the 1980 Refugee Act providing U.S. asylum to anyone with a 'well-founded fear of persecution on account of race, religion, nationality, membership in a particular social group or political opinion.'"
107. Susan Gzesh, "Central Americans and Asylum Policy in the Reagan Era," Migration Policy Institute, April 1, 2006, https://www.migrationpolicy.org/article/central-americans-and-asylum-policy-reagan-era/. See also, for example, Peter Applebome, "In Sanctuary Movement, Unabated Strength but Shifting Aims," *New York Times*, October 27, 1987: "Others point to what they say is the profound effect the movement has had in increasing attention given by churches to Central American issues. 'In terms of influence, it is perhaps the single most successful effort to help people become aware of our policies in foreign countries,' said William R. Farmer, a professor of the New Testament at the Perkins School of Theology at Southern Methodist University. 'It's a powerful movement. When people see and listen to the refugees, they are transformed. It's not mainstream, but it's having an effect on the mainstream.'"
108. Hart, *The Concept of Law*, 240.

6

Falling between the Legal Cracks

PRACTICES OF EQUITY
IN THE FACE OF INJUSTICE

In 2015, Joan Cheevers, a chef and an attorney, was issued a citation and a cease and desist order by the police of the city of San Antonio for offering a meal to an unhoused person from out of her personal vehicle. The citation could carry a fine of up to $2,000. Rather than accepting a plea bargain, she chose to challenge the citation and requested a trial by jury.[1] The year before, Arnold Abbott, a ninety-year-old World War II veteran was cited for feeding four homeless people in a park in Fort Lauderdale, Florida. Along with two local pastors, he faced up to a $500 fine and potential jail time.[2] Both Abbott and Cheevers claimed, in subsequent interviews, that their actions were motivated by a belief that the city ordinances against public food service were unjust in their application to people and organizations involved in feeding the homeless.

When working within the paradigm of using the law to change the law, the instinct that many Americans might feel when confronted with these scenarios is to argue that the justice of these citations should be considered through the lens of established legal rights.[3] Are these actions protected by a right to free expression or right to freedom of religious exercise? Does the city possess a superior right to determine how best to care for the homeless and to regulate the use of public spaces such as parks?

Along with recourse to the juridical approach of rights language, American citizens often turn to nonviolent protest to work to change unjust laws. The civil rights movement, most iconically under the leadership of Martin Luther King, demonstrated the effectiveness of this practice to change hearts and minds and to reclaim rights that have been disregarded by the legal system. However, while important, each of these approaches have their own limitations.

Using Suárez's doctrine of equity, the actions of individuals such as Cheevers and Abbot can expand our process of moral reasoning and decision-making beyond the simple application of competing rights as criteria. Suárez's theory of equity presents an alternative to rights-based reasoning alone. Rather than seeing equity as simply a general theory of justice, he describes it as a specific external principle of legal action through which individuals may licitly respond to laws that are not generally unjust but are unjust or burdensome to a specific individual or in a specific situation. In such situations, individual subjects can determine the extent of a law's authority over themselves by invoking the doctrine of equity, and they can even act against the letter of the law without needing to engage in any type of rights-based reasoning. In addition, equity, a moral virtue, can guide citizens in determining when a law does not oblige in a specific situation. Equity, for Suárez, is not equivalent to civil disobedience, but it does create room for personal exemptions from law's authority in order to make law globally more just and complement practices of nonviolent protest.

Placing Suárez's concept of equity in the context of contemporary legal discourse can illuminate contemporary understandings of equity. Suárez's analysis of equity highlights three key components of his theological jurisprudence, which are essential to his view of lawmaking from below. His analysis demonstrates his conviction that resistance to unjust laws does not require a rejection of the rule of law but does show how promoting the individual good and the common good are intrinsically connected rather than competitive ends. He emphasizes how at times an individual's freedom of determination according to conscience should not be understood as in competition with the good of the community, but rather as a component of that same good. Two contemporary situations of legal controversy—feeding the homeless as lawbreaking and breaking the seal of the confessional—provide a good platform for discussing this determination. Suárez's concept of equity can provide helpful guidance and the possibility for creative moral discourse with law that transcends rights discourse. Although his concept develops out of a critique of law's application, it is always constructive when oriented to a more expansive conception of the common good through modification of an excessively rigorous law. A creative and constructive approach to law can both transform a particular law and transform an entire conception of law, from simply an arbitrator judging between opposing claims of rights to an ever-developing instrument of human flourishing.

Nonviolent Protest: Benefits and Limits

Almost all contemporary Christians agree that nonviolent protest against unjust laws is at times justified and an important act of public witness. Many times such protest is oriented to changing laws through outside pressure rather than changing law from within. However, at least for MLK, there is an assumption that nonviolent protest simultaneously affirms the value of law even while challenging it. He was well aware of the danger of losing the importance of the rule of law. As he stated in *Letter from Birmingham City Jail*:

> In no sense do I advocate evading or defying the law, as would the rabid segregationist. That would lead to anarchy. One who breaks an unjust law must do so openly, lovingly, and with a willingness to accept the penalty. I submit that an individual who breaks a law that conscience tells him is unjust, and who willingly accepts the penalty of imprisonment in order to arouse the conscience of the community over its injustice, is in reality expressing the highest respect for law.[4]

However, for King, respect for the law never means blind obedience. Nor does it mean that the only possible way to change the law is by influencing politicians or through the political process. Rather, in his last book, *Where Do We Go from Here: Chaos or Community?*, King provides a compelling vision of the potential development of "new methods of participation in decision-making," which will enable the poor to work for justice in their own communities and to advance the common good while seeking out new and more comprehensive solutions to correct systems that sustain poverty.[5] In many ways, King's call contains echoes of Suárez's theory of equitable engagement.

Turning to a contemporary of King also committed to nonviolence, American theologian Dorothy Day, we find a similar complementary between her writings and Suárez's theory of law's change through equitable engagement with law. Day is explicit that the Catholic Workers should rely on nonviolent action, such as organizing strikes of oppressed workers; this principle is driven by a commitment to the teachings of Jesus Christ since nonviolent resistance to injustice is the true form of "conform[ing] our lives to the folly of the Cross."[6] Day's imagination for the proper response to injustice goes far beyond protest. When Catholic Worker members reject anarchism and nihilism in favor of nonviolence, they also reject the vision of those who seek to destroy what exists instead of "building a new society in the shell of the old."[7] In one sense they are set free not to live under the law of violence in the world and instead in the freedom in Christ. However, as Day explores in another letter, one way this important freedom is demonstrated is through actions of individual responsibility to promote the common good. These actions do not depend on or wait for individual structures to naturally improve, but rather seek to transform them, through such actions as feeding the homeless.[8] In many ways Suárez's theory of equitable revision of law exactly parallels Day's call to nonviolent action.

Theories of Equity

When contemporary English and American lawyers and judges discuss the concept of equity they are typically referring to a judicial action in common law, not to the response of an individual citizen. For example, in one textbook on modern equity and trusts, the author defines three different perspectives of equity in a legal system: equity as a form of "natural justice" that guides a court to correct the strict application of a common law or statutory rule; equity "as constituting the collection of *substantive* principles developed over the centuries by the Courts of Equity, principally the Court of Chancery, to judge people's consciences"; and equity as the "*procedural* rules and forms of action developed by the Courts of Chancery over the centuries."[9] Each of these forms of equity arose out of a desire to ensure that the potential harshness of the common law and statutes were limited. The role of the chancellor is to exercise "the residual discretionary power of the King to do justice among his subjects in circumstances in which, for one reason or another, justice could not be obtained in a common-law court."[10] Catholic canon law has developed a similar understanding of equity, drawing a direct parallel between practices of equity and the Christian understanding of the grace-filled message of the gospels. Even in a very early articulation, the *Decretum's* theological justification of canonical equity, the focus is on equity as a reprieve from the law's severity, out of love and mercy: "We are not to be severe toward penitents, but we have been advised to be merciful.... Man as man is to be shown mercy ... the Bishop ruling his flock ... the judge ruling his province, the king ruling his people ... are to show human consideration to them because they are human."[11]

These three understandings of equity contain several key distinctions from Suárez's understanding of equity. First, they limit the application of equity to the judiciary alone. Second, because it is exercised by a judge, equity can be only compensatory and reparative. Because prevailing theories of equity developed historically through the actions of the courts of the chancellery (as opposed to rulings by common-law judges), this reparative function in modern law is often conceived as an "escape valve" to compensate for the complexity of developing legal systems and to fill in "gaps" in the law.[12] The progressive historicist nature of this description means that "in a fully developed modern legal system, there will be very little room for equity in the original sense at all.

The law of equity is now constituted by legal rules of an orthodox kind; and is one specific branch of the law among others."[13] Also, the difficulty of obtaining some sort of normative standard for "natural justice" has ensured that equity understood according to the first definition is most often considered the domain of philosophers rather than lawyers and judges.[14] Finally, the view of equity as an act of love and mercy does not consider the chance that the law may have been unjust in an individual instance, meaning that the person who broke it did not require forgiveness but an equitable exception.

Suárez's theory of equity does not develop out of this common-law approach, but rather is directly within the tradition of Aquinas's and Aristotle's understanding of the concept of *epikeia*. This tradition, as interpreted by Suárez, differs from the common-law approach primarily in that it describes the application of equity as the responsibility of all citizens, not simply judges. It also does not view equity as a "gap filler" in a developing legal system or as opposition to or modification of the justice of law. Rather, it emphasizes a connection between the application of equity and a commitment to advancing the justice of law and the common good.

In this sense the doctrine of equity fits neatly into Aquinas's understanding of the cardinal virtue of justice. As Jean Porter convincingly argues, Aquinas's account of justice encompasses both the significance of natural justice— "preconventional standards for fairness and equity"—and the importance of "norms and structural forms of fairness and equality."[15] Porter argues that Aquinas and his interlocutors understand that the conventional forms that instantiate justice are "expressions, perhaps distortions, of a kind of natural justice that is grounded in the values intrinsic to our way of life."[16] When describing the virtue of equity, Aquinas identifies one way by which the mediation between natural and institutional justice occurs: through the actions of virtuous individuals.

The relationship of equity to civil law in Aquinas has not been widely explored in contemporary scholarship. In fact, the standard work on equity in relationship to civil law in the Thomistic tradition is a doctoral thesis written by Lawrence Riley at the Catholic University of America and published in 1948.[17] This lacuna may be due to the fact that most contemporary theological engagement with Aquinas's theory of equity is focused on whether or not equity can be applied to modify natural law or canon law, not on the application of equity to civil law.[18]

Rather than providing a comprehensive overview of Aquinas's theory of equity, we turn to a brief consideration of the key points that form the scaffolding upon which Suárez builds his theory, focusing on the two questions from the *Summa* that Suárez himself seems to consider the most important:

I–II q. 96, art. 6 and II–II q. 120. In I–II q. 96, art. 6, Aquinas does not mention the word equity but does discuss when it is possible to act against the letter of human law. In II–II q.120, Aquinas explicitly discusses the virtue of equity and refers back to I–II q. 96 art. 6, thereby explicitly tying his comments to a discussion of equity.

Aquinas refers to the standard example of a person who refuses to return the deposit of a sword to a madman or one who seeks to fight against his country. In normal situations, civil laws, and even the natural law, would require that deposits be returned. However, in following the letter of the law, the person holding the deposit would clearly be acting against the common good by letting loose on the community an insane or dangerous person armed with a deadly weapon. Discerning how to respond in the morally correct way to this situation requires the virtue of "*epikeia*, which we call *equitas*."[19]

How does this example of equity provide an instance of justice and, if it does, how can equity be related to legal justice?[20] For Aquinas, legal justice is understood in two ways. First, it can be understood as justice that complies with the law, "either the letter or the intention of the lawgiver, which is of more account."[21] In this understanding equity is a part of legal justice because it is the discernment of the intention of the lawgiver—to promote the common good—even when it may contradict the letter of the law.[22] For example,

> suppose that in a besieged city, it be an established law that the gates of the city are kept closed, this is good for public welfare as a general rule: but, were it to happen that the enemy are in pursuit of the certain citizens who are defenders of the city, it would be a great loss to the city if the gates were not opened to them: and so in that case the gates ought to be opened, contrary to the letter of the law, in order to maintain the common weal, which the lawgiver had in view.[23]

Obeying the law in this one specific instance would surely violate its end of promoting the common good and run contrary to the lawmaker's intent to preserve the safety of the city. Therefore, preserving law's ultimate end of advancing the common good may, in times of great urgency and civil danger, permit citizens to act against the letter of the law. However, if legal justice is understood narrowly as complying *only* in strict accordance with the letter of the law, then equity should be understood as a part of a more general form of justice that "exceeds" this spirit of strict compliance.[24] Equity is, therefore, a subjective part of legal justice, and in fact directs it, functioning as "a higher rule of human actions."[25]

Aquinas's example indicates that equity should be understood as distinct individual actions, not the transformation of normative standards of interpretation. Equity is a practice only for the singular and extraordinary situation. Therefore, the application of equity in a specific situation should not be understood as setting a precedent for changing the normal interpretation of the law. The citizens' decision to let the riders into the city gates does not mean that the law should be interpreted at all times as permitting the city gates to be opened. The application of equity is valid only in this specific situation to protect the entire city.

Aquinas is concerned that this description of interpretation outside the letter of the law should not be viewed as an opportunity for license, or as negating the authority of the law. Normally, dispensations from the letter of the law are provided only to those in authority, to avoid the situation in which each person judges on his or her own what is "useful and not useful to the state."[26] This type of interpretation by the citizen should occur only in the case of "sudden risk needing instant remedy," when the suddenness of the danger would make it impossible to contact the authorities. In this case alone "the mere necessity brings with it a dispensation, since necessity knows no law."[27] However, this dispensation is limited to situations when the necessity is clear beyond a doubt. In cases of doubt, preference should be given to consultation with the lawgiver or following the letter of the law, rather than citizens acting in equity upon their own initiative.[28]

In the objections, Aquinas considers several more questions related to the practice of equity. First, does the belief that one should consider the intention of the lawmaker—to advance the common good—over the letter of the law constitute imposing a judgment on the lawgiver? Since the practice of equity is confined to specific cases that the lawmaker does not envision, the people are not seeking to evaluate the lawmaker's specific intention for the law.[29] In addition, the practice of equity should not be understood as a failure on the part of the lawmaker or the law, considered generally. The human lawmaker, unlike the divine lawgiver, is simply not capable of envisioning every single case that might arise under a particular law and therefore cannot be responsible for knowing when a just law might fail. In fact, were the lawmaker to attempt to list every possible case in which the law might not apply, the lawmaker would fail in her duty. This expansive approach to lawmaking would not generally advance the common good, since delving into so many specifics would create confusion and loss of the clarity necessary for the law's general just application.[30]

As well as considering equitable actions, Aquinas considers equity as a virtue. As in all exercises of the virtues connected to justice, the act of judgment in the will must be guided by the proper functioning of prudence in the intellect. In the virtue of equity, the judgment of the will is moved by a special type of prudence: called *gnome*.[31] Just as prudence perfects the practical intellect, gnome enables the citizen to determine the perfection of the law and grasp its true goals, rather than perceiving only the letter of the law. Thomas Bushlack describes both gnome and epikeia as functioning similarly in relation to different cardinal virtues: "*gnome* and *epikeia* serve as corrective parts of prudence and justice, respectively, that maintain the balance of fairness and equality that is an essential component of the common good, and that law is intended to serve."[32] Therefore, the proper functioning of the virtue of equity requires the proper discernment of prudence—that the law is not just in a specific situation—and of course the just act of the will.

Suárez's Theory of Equity

These texts from Aquinas provide the foundation for Suárez's development of his own theory of equity. Rather than contradicting Aquinas, Suárez seeks to resolve ambiguities and develop his theories with more specificity and precision in order to address questions that have developed out of Aquinas's theory and to explain how equity can be used to protect individual citizens in a way that does not limit the common good. Suárez's theory of equity indicates both his indebtedness to and his development of Aquinas's theory, specifically two key developments that Suárez makes. First, he is even more explicit than Aquinas that equity is a virtue practiced by the people, not by the lawmaker. Second, equity is understood to apply to laws that are unduly burdensome to an individual, not simply laws that are unjust.

Definitions

In order to adequately explain his theory of equity, Suárez, in his customary style, carefully defines his terms. Throughout *De Legibus* he distinguishes four ways by which the law may be changed. First, any law may be changed due to some intrinsic cause: by change in person, motive, time, or circumstances related to the law. Second, any law may be changed due to some extrinsic cause: by change enacted by the lawmaker. Both of these types of changes may be partial or total: an exception for a single case or a suppression of the entire law.[33] Crucially, Suárez argues that the application of equity to the law can make only an intrinsic change to the law. This distinction means that equity can be enacted only by the people, not the rulers. Equity can also be only a partial change, because it is applied only in situations in which the general law cannot, for considerations of justice, be applied to a specific case.[34] Thus, like Aquinas he understands equity as an intrinsic practice of the individual citizen and as applied only in specific cases where the generally applicable law should not apply.

It is important to note that Suárez does not engage with the description of equity as being concerned with mercy or remission of the law out of grace or kindness. Suárez acknowledges the role of mercy in relationship to law, but mercy is something given out of kindness by the ruler or the lawmaker. His version of equity is not the gift of the ruler nor is it dependent on the lawmaker's will; it is a God-given capacity of the people, which they can and should exercise as they pursue justice in law. In this approach to equity, as opposed to equating it with mercy, Suárez's legal theory remains grounded in the doctrines of creation and human agency. This core *loci* for his legal theory contributes to his expansion of the doctrine of law from below and the empowerment of the common people.

Suárez also distinguishes between the just (*iustum*) and the equitable (*aequum*), and justice (*iusticia*) and equity (*aequitas*). The definition of what is just (*iustum*) has two meanings: natural ("what is right (*rectum*) according to natural reason and which never fails if reason does not err"), and legal ("which is constituted by human law, which is often defective in particular cases, though just in a general sense."[35] This same division can be applied when talking of justice and equity. Equity can be identified as "natural equity, which is the same as natural justice" and can occur in statutory language as a substitute for a claim that a legislation is naturally just.[36] This form of equity is not "an emendation of [legal] justice but rather its rule or origin as the *Digest* (L.xvii.91) indicates in the statement: 'in all matters, but especially in law (*ius*) equity must be considered.'"[37]

Equity can also be considered as the "prudent moderation of the written law (*lex scripta*), beyond the rigor of its words and, in this sense, it is said to be opposed to strict law (*stricto iuri*)." Using these definitions, "the terms 'equitable' (*aequum*) and 'good' (*bonum*) are applied... to that which is indeed thus, even though it may appear to be in discord with the letter of the law (*lex*)."[38] Suárez claims that this second use of equity is the sense in which Aristotle understands equity "when he spoke of it as the amendment of that which is just, that is to say, legal, and he called *epiikiam* the virtue which proceeds from that act."[39] By expanding upon this double definition of equity Suárez answers one question that had been posed to Aristotle and Aquinas in saying that yes, equity can both be above legal justice (in its natural definition) and opposed to it (in its moderating sense). These two definitions are related to each other, since the moderation of the civil law can be appropriate only when it is aligned with natural justice. But the distinction is a helpful clarification of the relationship.

According to these definitions, equitable interpretation can be applied only to laws that are generally just and advance the common good. Equity is never a rejection of the rule of law. Rather, Suárez argues, equity furthers the rule of law because it is an acknowledgment that all good laws contain an intrinsic understanding on the part of the lawmaker: that there may be specific cases in which the law ceases to apply, due to the limitations of the human lawmaker and the contingency and sinfulness that characterize human existence.[40] The lawmaker is both incapable of anticipating all of these contingencies and is incapable of drafting a law that is sufficiently broad to encompass them all while also sufficiently simple and direct to the extent that it is useful and accessible. Leaving room for the application of equity in a law that is generally just "requires greater prudence and a more universal justice" than simple lawmaking.[41] In prioritizing the justice of equity, instead of the strict justice of the letter of the law, the true end of the law is in fact achieved.[42] Suárez emphasizes here the importance of the distinction of the different types of equity and justice: natural equity is intrinsic to the justice that informs the law at its very foundation. Legal equity is simply the practice and application of that natural equity to critique and improve legal justice. Like Aquinas, Suárez identifies this second type of equity as a virtue.

The practice of equity, although in one sense an interpretive action, should therefore be distinguished from legal interpretation, strictly conceived. As discussed previously, general interpretation can be exercised authoritatively by two parties acting together: the lawmaker and the people. However, general interpretation addresses only questions regarding the potential meaning of the statutory language.[43] When defining equity, on the other hand, Suárez considers a practice of interpretation that goes beyond discerning the meaning of the words of the law and, potentially, beyond discerning the intention of the lawmaker as well. Interpretation proper to equity is an interpretation not of what the law means generally but rather as to whether or not the law would justly apply in a specific circumstance. As Suárez writes, equity "is the reform of the law in regards to its universality."[44] Thus the concern is not what the specific will of the lawmaker was behind the specific words, but whether there should be an exception from the law completely, according to the general will of the lawmaker to promote the common good. Equitable interpretation relates only to the "rectification of legal justice, since it interprets law as not to be observed in cases in which it would be an error in practice against natural justice or equity."[45] The other key distinction is that equity is defined as a virtue, whereas it seems as if the broader type of interpretation should be understood as an art or skill (hence the importance of the opinion of outside learned experts, something that is not as important in a discussion of *equity*).

Equity and the Natural Law

A consideration of how Suárez analyzes the question as to whether equity can be applied to the natural law leads to the theological grounding of his theory of equity. Natural law exists for Suárez in two modes: as it exists in itself and as it is expressed in positive law. The types of natural law expressed in the civil law "are merely declarative or (so to speak) a recollection of the natural law, as were the moral precepts of the Decalogue in the Old Law, and as those human laws which contain formulas of natural justice—that a deposit must be returned, that a promise must be fulfilled."[46] Even the civil law, which expresses some natural law, can never incorporate the entirety of the natural law. Yet the civil law must include more than the natural law to ensure that it is sufficiently particular to be appropriate for each community and context.

Unlike interpretation, it is not possible to carry out epikeia, understood as judgment, on the natural law per se, whether by God, angels, or humans.[47] The argument against this claim is articulated most clearly by Cajetan, who argues that epikeia is being applied to the precept of the natural law—that deposits must be returned—when the responsible person does not return a sword to a madman.[48] Suárez rebuts this claim by pointing out that Cajetan is working under a fundamental misunderstanding of the nature of natural law. Epikeia in this case is not being applied to the actual precept of the natural law itself. This would be impossible, since the precept itself is right reason (or natural epikeia). Epikeia cannot correct or contradict right reason: "The precept in question, as such, resides in right reason, and right reason does not dictate that deposits must absolutely be returned, but under the conditions which justice and charity demand."[49] The wise person interprets the precept with greater nuance and depth in this situation, taking into account and weighing all the claims of justice and charity that might apply in each situation. This evaluation, while it draws upon the virtues of justice and charity, is not the same as the act of applying equity. The wise neighbor is not claiming that she should not return the sword because she is excused from the obligation of obeying the general precept of the natural law in this specific situation. Rather, she is attempting to discern what the precept of the natural law demands. The natural law in itself "is not able to amend, since it is placed in right reason, which is not able to be amended, inasmuch as it is founded upon right reason, which is not able to fall short of the truth. For if it fell short, it would no longer be right reason."[50]

However, when the natural law is considered as it is revealed through human civil law, the question is different. This form of the natural law does leave room for "exception by *epikeia,* over all in order to determine the intention of the human legislator." In this case the exception by epikeia is in relation to the will of the lawmaker and her intention in giving the law, not to the natural law itself. Rather, "it is merely an explanation of the change which has occurred in the subject matter, the reason of which the act in such circumstances does not *per se* involve any evil, nor does it fall under the natural law."[51] Thus, the natural law, given by God, can stand as the rule by which human law is measured, but natural law itself is not subject to human judgment. Suárez's development of the connection between natural justice and the enactment of equity leaves room for a civil law that is morally informed but not simply a translation of the natural law into morality. For example, the wise neighbor who refuses to return the sword to a madman is not acting with epikeia toward the natural law. However, if a civil law had incorporated this precept of the law—that deposits should always be returned—then for a wise person to refuse to restore a sword to a madman would be an act of epikeia.

Equity as a Virtue

Having considered natural equity and the natural law, the standard of goodness and justice to which the law must adhere, consideration must also be given to equity as a virtue. Possessing the virtue of equity prepares citizens to engage in the equitable interpretation of the law in a specific case so as to bring it into accord with the objective standards of natural equity. Although this broad outline of how equity functions as a virtue does not differ from Aquinas's understanding, there is one crucial difference: Suárez delimits equity explicitly as solely a virtue in the people, not the ruler, by dividing up the acts of the will that are proper to the virtue of justice in the lawmaker (legal and commutative) from those that are proper to the people (equity).

Like justice, equity first requires an exercise of prudence in judging that the law does not apply in the particular instance at hand. In the ruler this type of interpretation, that the law does not apply, would be an act of political prudence. However, when it occurs in the people, it is a judgment of general prudence similar to what guides the other practices of individual virtues. Suárez connects this specific type of prudential judgment with Aristotle's *sententiam* or gnome.[52] The virtuous subject may discern through gnome that her unique circumstances make it "excessively rigorous or unjust" for the obligation of the law to be imposed.[53]

Second, all practices of justice require the act of the will, which in equity "obeys this judgment [of the intellect] and works against the words of the law."[54] The will to do justice has a different object on the part of the lawmaker than on the part of the people. The exercise of the will on the part of the ruler is not an exercise of equitable justice, but of general legal justice. Because the lawmaker sets the terms for legal justice, she should will that the law is interpreted in the most just way in order to advance the common good and according to commutative justice, in order to not overburden the people.[55] In contrast, the equitable person wills to set the judgment of gnome into effect and therefore may be led to act contrary to the claims and obligations of legal justice, because she has discerned that her unique circumstances make it "excessively rigorous or unjust" for the obligation of the law to be imposed.[56]

Equity's Engagement with the Law

When are these equitable actions needed? The common belief—held not only by Aquinas, as developed from Aristotle, but also by Duns Scotus, by the modern theologians and commentators such as Cajetan and de Soto, and by numerous modern jurists—is that "it is a certain thing that at times the obligation of the law in a particular case, ceases, even though the words of the law appear to include this case and in no other law is it excepted nor is it dispensed from the law by the sovereign."[57] The question to be asked, therefore, is Does the law ever cease to oblige in a specific case? Or, as Suárez puts it, quoting Aquinas, "if the subject is able at times to work against the words of the law?" This is the question he believes Aquinas is asking, when determining whether the "hand of equity may be laid on the practice and execution of the law."[58] For it to be morally acceptable for a subject to disobey a law issued by a proper authority there must be some other reason why the law does not oblige, as discerned by the exercise of prudence on the part of the people.

Here we see Suárez's elaboration upon the theory established by Aquinas and Aristotle and its practical application. First, Suárez considers the types of precepts to which equity can apply. It can apply to negative precepts, positive precepts, or can even extend to damages as well, since equity may also govern demands for restitution.[59] Suárez identifies theorists who claim that equity applies when the reason of the law ceases negatively, that is, when there is no longer a positive reason for the law to be obeyed. This theory is based on the belief that law is only authoritative because it is based on reason. Under this view, if the reason of the law ceases then it is as if the soul ceases to inhabit the body. Just as the body can no longer live or move, the law can no longer oblige.[60] The same argument is given with concepts of the common good and justice standing in the place of reason. If the law does not advance the common good, then it loses the force by which it obliges.

Suárez returns again to the importance of the lawmaker's will in establishing legal obligation to rebut this claim. He argues that it is not enough for the reason of the law to cease negatively for equity to be applied. Rather, it must also cease "contrarily": when to obey the law would no longer be morally neutral, but might require acting against justice, reason, or the common good. Thus, equity should not apply in situations where the reason of the law may be absent or not apparent, but the action required does not violate justice or the common good.[61] The will of the lawmaker alone is prima facie sufficient to oblige a morally neutral action because the lawmaker may have greater insight into a situation than the ordinary citizen.[62] Even if the lawmaker does not acknowledge a positively good reason, the lawmaker's will is still sufficient, because lacking anything to the contrary, the will is what makes the law oblige, not the potential reasons the lawmaker has.[63] In addition, often the law may require some action that is good in itself, even if the reason for the specific requirement of that law has ceased. For example, "a fast may be good, even though it is not necessary in order to mortify the flesh or to make satisfaction for one's sins; and the omission of the act could be good, even though the end of the law ceases that prohibited it, such as abstaining from contracting clandestine marriages."[64]

Suárez concludes with the argument that equity does not apply unless the law commands something unjust; even when the reason for a specific law ceases, there is usually a more universal reason to observe the law. "First, it would be against the common good if only [the absence of a reason] excused people from obeying the law. Secondly, because there is always an appropriate reason (*ratio honesta*) to observe the law universally with all parties, where without inconvenience it is possible to observe it."[65] This restriction means that even if the reason ceases in a particular instance, the general obligation of the law does not necessarily fail, absent other reasons to the contrary. Observing morally neutral laws, even those that lack a compelling reason, is actually in accordance with a higher justice (the natural equity noted earlier). It is derived from a respect for the perspective and authority of the lawmaker who, when issuing a general law, knows that the reason for the law would not necessarily apply in all cases but who can still justly desire that it be applied to all, generally.[66] Simply because a law lacks a reason for application in a certain sense does not mean that it necessarily falls short of the primary objective standard of justice required for the validity of all laws: to both advance the common good and not damage the private.[67] This distinction means that equity always respects the obliging value of the lawmaker's will—to the proper extent.

Suárez finds support for this claim in Aquinas's example of the sword placed on deposit. When determining whether to return the deposit, the person holding the deposit for the madman does not ask whether the sword will be used to accomplish anything positively good or simply be stored away. Rather, equity should only be applied when the sword should not be returned to the madman because it is clear that he will cause harm. The law requiring that the gates of the city be closed at night is not subject to the application of equity simply because citizens traveling late on the road request admission. Here, when there is no danger to the city that might require the gates to be open, the law would still oblige even if the reason does not seem clear. On the contrary, under the application of equity, the gates to the city should be opened to those escaping the enemy because their loss would be a significant damage to the city.[68] As Aquinas writes, equity should be applied "in this and in other cases it appears that it is bad to follow the law that has been given."[69] Aristotle too writes that equity is required where "the law sins"; in other words, where following the law as written would go against justice, not simply where it would have a neutral effect.[70]

This focus on contrary failure rather than negative failure goes against a number of jurists who claim that when the cause of the law ceases, the obligation of the law also ceases.[71] Suárez's insistence that the reason of the law is not necessary for law to oblige once again shows the way he always emphasizes the authority and importance of the rule of law. Although he actually extends equity farther than many of his contemporaries or predecessors, it is never done at the expense of the authority of the rule of law. Rather, he describes equity as upholding law's authority rather than diminishing it, because equity always grounds it in a higher standard of justice. Equity as a practice is always connected to natural equity as a standard. Thus, observing legal justice in and of itself is always important, because of what it achieves for the common good.[72] "In effect, even though the subject has not become involved in the general utility which the law intends, yet he is made to participate in the general utility which is given in the observance of the law and in the uniformity of its courts. And from this point of view, this law is just and is based in a more elevated reason."[73]

Three Modes of Equity

Having placed this restriction on the application of equity, Suárez then identifies three ways in which the law might cease contrarily, and equity alone would appropriately apply. "There are three modalities or motives in the use of the epikeia: one of these is to guard against something unjust, another is in order to avoid disagreeable and unjust obligations, another is through conjectures over the will of the legislator."[74] The first type—guarding against something unjust—is the standard and most widespread approach to equity. This is the approach of Cajetan and Soto, who argue for the strictest understanding: equity can be applied only when the reason for the law ceases in a way contrary to justice or when it would be sinful for the subject to actually obey the law, or even only when it would be "noxious for the entire community." Cajetan develops this line of reasoning based on Aristotle's claim that equity is a remedy when the law "sins by reason of its universality."[75] According to Cajetan, and accepted by his followers such as Soto, the only way to understand the description of law as sinning is when it actually requires a sinful act. Since equity is a part of justice, it can therefore be applied only to prevent the person obeying the law from falling into injustice.[76]

However, Suárez finds this understanding of what constitutes the law's sinfulness "excessively limited and rigid."[77] Of course, equity can and should apply when an individual does not obey a generally applicable law that would result in her sinning or doing something unjust. As Suárez points out, if the law obliges sin or an unjust action, then not obeying the law is in fact morally obligatory. But this approach would limit our understanding of equity to apply only to actions that are morally required of us. In addition, it limits our understanding of what constitutes justice and the common good to only that which is clearly a sinful action against God's law, rather than a full appreciation of the role of the virtue of prudence in discerning appropriate means to arrive at the good. Suárez argues that Aquinas's discussion of equity indicates additional modes in which equity is appropriate.

The second approach to equity that Suárez identifies focuses on the lawmaker's will. This mode takes into account that the limited lawmaker may not have issued the law with the intention that it would have had such a hard or rigorous application in a specific situation. "In effect, the superior does not always want to oblige with all the rigor and in all circumstances."[78] Suárez supports this claim with an argument from canon law. We know that the Church excuses Christians from fasting in the event of a grave illness. To do otherwise would be unjust. However, it is also assumed that the obligation to fast is not expected when a person is suffering from a minor illness. The Church has the ability to oblige in this instance, yet while the exemption is not explicitly listed, the equitable interpretation of the canons is that the Church, out of care for the well-being of Christians, would not want the letter of the law to be followed in situations of even minor illness.

This form of equitable interpretation, which requires interpretation of the lawmaker's intent against the letter of the law, is the form of interpretation

Suárez discusses at the end of the section on legal interpretation.[79] While it is justified by reasons other than those related to legal interpretation, the tools largely remain the same. The citizen seeking to interpret the lawmaker's will to understand whether the harsh outcome is desired still analyzes "other circumstances of time, place and persons and the normal mode of prescription, with this moderation understood, although it is not expressly said."[80]

The awareness of the double meaning of the lawmaker's intent has great significance here as well. It is assumed that the lawmaker desires above all to pass a valid law, so, therefore, could not have intended anything unjust. Equitable interpretation asks whether the lawmaker, who is presumed to be just, would want the law to be different if he or she was present. Suárez finds support for this second mode as well, in Aquinas and Aristotle: "And this without doubt seems to have been the moderation which Aristotle signaled to say that the epikeia amends the law, because the legislator himself, if he were present, would have said the same; that is, if he would have been moderate and also would have interpreted his own law. In this sense also St. Thomas said that the function of the equity is, *departing from the words of the law, to follow the intention of the legislator*."[81]

Suárez acknowledges that there are critics of this second mode. In fact, it might appear as though freedom to interpret the lawmaker's ideally just will against the lawmaker's actual will might contradict Suárez's own claims concerning the obliging quality of the lawmaker's will. Shouldn't Suárez be arguing that the lawmaker might will that the law continue, even if the reason for the law no longer applies?[82] However, although Suárez emphasizes the role of the will in making law, the will is never without bonds—bonds that are imposed both by divine law and natural law as discerned by the people. While the lawmaker's will is necessary for making an authoritative civil law, it is never without the limits applied according to the standards of natural equity.

The critiques raised by later scholars were based upon a similar concern to protect the lawmaker's power. While Suárez is considered as an extreme voluntarist in some contemporary theories, some of his predecessors were frightened because his theory of equity gives too wide a latitude to the individual to discern the lawmaker's intent. The perception was that Suárez's view of equity "tended to permit individuals to reach their own decisions on the basis of considerations extrinsic to any objective evidence manifesting the legislator's intention. To limit such subjectivism and relativity, the commentators tended to understand equity as a juridical principle written into the statute."[83] These critiques demonstrate how a strict view of law from above removes freedom of individual guidance and institutes much more of a top-down view than Suárez believes is theologically justifiable.

For the third modality of equity, Suárez presents his most innovative development of a theory of equity. Rather than simply confining his understanding of equity to laws that fail by contrary reason because they actively mandate sin, Suárez argues that equity can be applied even in a situation when obeying a law would be "excessively onerous or difficult."[84] Suárez grounds this claim in his earlier discussion regarding the law that does not oblige in cases of either "danger to life or other great inconvenience," even if the law does not require something by definition unjust. In this case it is not a moral obligation that equity should be applied, unlike in the first modality. Rather, in line with Suárez's emphasis upon the importance of prudent discernment, knowing whether to apply this mode of equity depends upon the person involved to determine if they want to "cede their right (*iui*)" to exercise equity, or if the person chooses to continue to obey the law and bear the cost of the inconvenience. "Thus, the excuse is not always united to the obligation of not realizing the act mandated, nor springing always from the injustice of the act, but from the other right (*iure*) that the person has: to not be obliged so servilely, so to speak."[85]

Suárez presents a number of clarifying examples, most helpfully around fasting. First, an ordinary layperson is licitly excused from required fasts in the event of illness or anything similar. However, that person may choose to observe the fast and cede their right to apply equity. In a similar way, Carthusians, by the rule of their order, are required to abstain from meat. However, if meat is the only option to prevent starvation, they can, without sin, leave off the observance of the rule in order to eat to preserve their lives. Still, if they chose to abide by the strict letter of the rule and not eat anything, they would also be without sin. In both examples, "if one, in spite of being excused, realized a required act, not only would he not sin, but at times might make a work of supererogation."[86] It would not be unjust to require the person to fast or to require the Carthusian to not eat meat. However, in both cases they are presented with the equitable option to avoid dire inconvenience (the ill effects of fasting, starvation, or both). They retain the option of making the choice to place themselves under the provision of the law or to claim the excusal of equity.[87]

In considering this sweeping expansion, Suárez argues Cajetan's view of what it means for the law to sin is too narrow with respect to what the law is meant to achieve. Rather than simply engaging justice, law must also promote the common good more broadly construed. Thus the law sins when it prescribes "things inhuman and more burdensome than the human condition can endure," not just when it requires that the person sins in obeying:

In other words, we have to understand what it means for the law to sin even more broadly than simply that it prescribes that which is unjust... Thus the law would not sin only by prescribing what was not owed, so to speak, the unjust, but prescribing what it should not, that is to say prescribing with more rigor than is just. The epikeia, therefore, comes to correct these two sins of the law, and in both takes place the definition of Aristotle and its exposition, and in the same way one should understand St. Thomas. In effect, the intention of the legislator is not only to prescribe what is correct but also to do it correctly. Thus, whoever observes the law as if submitted to her when she does not oblige because of some exculpatory cause, does not disagree with the intention of the legislator by more than that the act which is realized is not bad.[88]

This expansive view of equity, Suárez's most innovative contribution, makes understanding equity as a virtue, as well as a practice, even more essential, especially as far as understanding the role of prudence. Prudence not only discerns when the precept is bad, but determines when it is possible to not observe a precept without sinning, even though observance might also not be sinful. This does not mean, as Suárez points out, that equity is no longer a part of the virtue of justice. Rather, the person must determine, according to justice, whether or not the law obliges and whether or not it would be sinful to obey it. Then, using a special prudence, she may determine whether or not to take the additional step of disobeying it on grounds of inhumanity or grave inconvenience.[89]

The special prudence of equity assists the citizen in determining whether "it is sufficient that one is able in such a case to not comply with the law justly, and without being apart from rectitude, if this is what he wants, although he is not obliged to it... equal to the matter of the justice, at times we judge by equity that a person is not obliged to the restitution lowering his position, although, if he did it, he would not be accused of sin."[90] This position is significant when considering the connection Suárez draws between justice and the common good.

Suárez's virtue of prudence is normed and formed by precepts as well as practice and exemplary models.[91] He indicates three modalities for equity: not obeying the law that mandates something unjust; not obeying when it prescribes something hard or disagreeable; and not obeying when it is clearly contrary to the intention of the lawmaker if the lawmaker had known the circumstances. In determining whether the law is unjust, the citizen first has to consider the other precepts of natural and divine law, and whether the law requires something that "contradicts natural or divine law according to its words" or would mandate an act that "implicates malice or justice inseparable or at least contrary to a more serious precept."[92] The third modality, in which one considers whether or not the lawmaker might have intended something different *if* he or she had known of a specific circumstance, depends mostly on conjecture developed out of the specific circumstances, just as in the question of interpretation of laws.[93] The third modality, where one considers questions of inconvenience or grave burden, leads to equity being applied when it is clear that the action obliged would go beyond the authority of human law.

Equity and Authority

Given this sweeping view of the different possibilities of equitable action, it might seem that equity vacates the authority of law. Is it possible to both uphold law's authority and at the same time provide the people with the opportunity to engage with law to make it more just? This fear, that equity dilutes law's authority, was most concerning to Suárez's scholastic contemporaries and is specifically addressed by Aquinas in II–II q. 120, art. 1, ad 3. The final response to this question is that permitting the subject to pass judgment on the law would vacate the authority of the law. Is it not "the exclusive competency of the sovereign to declare if in some case, for reason of equity, the law does not need to be observed"?[94] Suárez's expansion of the applicability of equity to the other three modalities seems as though it would make this critique even more forceful.

However, the answer to this question, as with much of Suárez's view of law, is that equity, rightly understood, takes nothing away from the law's authority. Rather, he presents a theory of law that does not see engagement with the law from below as antagonistic to the rule of law, but rather as integral to its proper formation and function. Equity should be understood not as a suspension or disruption of the law, but rather as a further discovery of the content and authority of civil law through the individual's virtuous discernment of the relationship between natural law and civil law. The individual engaged in this sort of application of equity clearly cares deeply about the law and, by applying equity, is working to protect law's justice and authority in every situation.

Suárez demonstrates his concern about maintaining a balance between respect for authority and promoting justice through equity in his analysis of the question as to when the lawmaker's permission needs to be sought before equity can be applied. Suárez balances his emphasis on expanded power to the people with an acknowledgment of the lawmaker's importance. In his typical methodological and pragmatic approach, Suárez provides a decision tree to guide the citizen's evaluation of whether or not equity should be applied. If the injustice of the law is sure or "contrary to another precept that obliges more," the law's authority clearly ceases.[95] The citizen can, therefore, apply equity strictly based upon her own discernment, without appealing to a superior. Suárez finds clear support for this claim in II–II q. 120, where Aquinas writes, "In the clear questions interpretation is not needed, but execution."[96] The citizen simply chooses to obey the higher authority, that is, God's law. There is no need to ask for an excuse or permission from above, because the reigning authority's purview simply does not extend to this eventuality. While there might be reason to ask for permission from the superior so as to avoid scandal, this reason is completely accidental to circumstances and in no way establishes a general rule.[97]

Importantly, Suárez goes beyond what Aquinas explicitly confers on the citizen (although he claims that Aquinas allows room for this interpretation). In a situation in which it would not be possible to consult with a reigning authority, a citizen may apply equity "by a probable judgement if one judges that the exception of the case may escape the power of the legislator, or at least his will."[98] Suárez's statement is clear: he is not trying to vacate the moral authority of any type of fixed norm but rather is offering a realistic assessment of how moral discernment works. He acknowledges the reality that demanding certainty before any decision

> surpasses the condition and the human prudence, so that nearly all human knowledge is conjectural, over all in the ambit of the practical. In the same way, it could impose on humans a weight too heavy if it was never licit to them to make use of the *epikeia* by a probable judgement, when one does not have access to the superior. Thus, who would ever dare to consider himself excused from a positive law for an eventual necessity, feeling such that nobody is ever so certain—without a shadow of a doubt or fear—of what may be a sufficient cause? In the same way, in these cases the simple folks would not be able to follow the advice of a learned and pious man nor would he himself give such counsel, because almost never is it possible to lead without probable judgement.[99]

It is noteworthy that this judgment based on probable discernment is not without its limits. Since the judgment is only probable, it may be overridden by the lawmaker "if nevertheless the superior orders by certain knowledge declaring that he is able to do it and judging that such case is not improper or is not excessively burdensome, the subject will be obliged to obey, in so much as he does not have certainty, although he has probable judgement. The reason is that the right of the superior prevails and the subject ought to submit to his judgement, as is the common doctrine and necessary in practice."[100]

Lawrence Riley views this concession to the lawmaker's statement limiting the application of equity as a sign that Suárez is not willing to defend his theory against common practices that were more restrictive of the people's discernment.[101] However, this is Suárez's customary mode of engagement with law: attempting to balance the importance of individual human discernment with the necessity of communal unity and clarity regarding the law's content. The lawmaker is responsible for realizing the limitations of general law and taking into account how injustice and an excessive burden can affect the individual citizen. This realization places a much higher burden of proper discernment on the lawmaker than the probable standard of certainty required of the citizen. It does not give the citizen total freedom to make his or her own determinations as to when to obey the law, but it does emphasize that the lawmaker is still important for law. Suárez understands the content of law and its application as developed through a careful and gradual dialogical process of discernment between the lawmaker and the citizen, which characterizes all of his discussion of law.

Individual Freedom and the Common Good

Through his analysis of equity, Suárez also presents a theory in which individual freedom of conscience and the common good are intrinsically connected, not competitive or separate. He argues that giving the individual the freedom to discern when a law is unjust or unduly burdensome and to exempt herself from its authority also advances the common good of the community. This connection between the good of individual discernment and the communal good as articulated in the doctrine of equity complements Suárez's doctrine of the development of law by custom. The idea that customary practices of a community can make law in opposition to the ruler's will, because the community may at times be better able to discern the common good, is complementary to the theory that the individual may at times be better able to discern when a law is unduly burdensome in specific situations and thus better able to disregard the law under the doctrine of equity.

These two practices are connected. Suárez argues that leaving space for both individual and communal discernment in the end advances the common good. Just as communal development of custom has limits (since at times the ruler may have a better perspective on the common good), so also individual discernment is limited in its scope (since equitable practices cannot contradict the common good). Equity should be applied only in each individual case where the good of the individual would be threatened by the law "*and no other reason of the common good may oblige.*"[102] Suárez grounds this claim in the obligation of love for neighbor and justice. Love for neighbor and rendering each her due provide minimal standards of moral response and therefore take priority over advancing individual good. However, where no cost to others exists, there is no reason that an individual should not be free to discern when she may act according to her own judgment of prudence. According to Suárez this is the opinion of the "modern" theologians such as Soto, and is not contrary to Aquinas. Although Aquinas, in his discussion of equity in I–II q. 96, art. 6, does use an example that most clearly benefits the common good (i.e., the citizens being let back within the gate in opposition to the law in order to protect the city), Suárez claims that Aquinas does not exclude the individual good, since the good of the individual is included in the good of the whole.[103]

This commitment to protecting both the freedom of an individual's discernment and the common good explains why Suárez expands the scope of equity beyond the merely unjust to include the unduly burdensome. In addition, he expands the concept of what areas of life might be unduly burdened by the law. Many traditional readings permit the individual to apply equity only in the most grave circumstances, such as when the law threatens the rights that the individual is not able to cede (e.g., rights directly connected to the person's ability to sustain life). However, Suárez argues that the application of equity can also protect rights that can be ceded, such as rights related to property. For example, equity releases an individual from the burden of the law if her house is on fire and her acts to save it would violate a precept (such as, for example, the precept of Mass attendance). Although an individual is not obligated to violate the precept in order to protect the right, she does enjoy the freedom to protect that right and thus can discern whether violating the precept is acceptable when balanced against the common good. This right is not only related to present holding, but also includes the right to acquire goods at a later date. Thus if the profit that would be lost by observing a specific precept is sufficiently grave, equity might prevail even to protect future earnings and remove the authority of the law.[104]

In making this claim Suárez not only clears a wider space for individual determination as to how far the exception applies but also makes the important point that the individual good can never be understood without reference to the common good and the common good, is always indexed to the good of individuals.[105] Even regarding material goods, the community is invested in determining that the goods of the individual are able to be maintained in good repair. This is clear in other ecclesial practices as well: such as it being licit "to leave mass on a feast day to care for a gravely ill neighbor."[106] While the common good is more than the sum of individual goods, the protection of individual goods does contribute to the common good. Therefore equity preserves these individual goods but never at the expense of the common good. Contrarily, the common good, if truly understood, establishes the individual good and at certain times may lead to the justification of protecting the good of one individual. This is the reason that equity may not be applied, even if justified, out of respect for the lawmaker's superior ability to perceive the common good.

Suárez's acknowledgment of the intrinsic relationship between the freedom of individual discernment and the communal good leads to a theory of law that makes sense within a moral theological system founded on the idea that strict legal justice is not always the final and perfect solution to global issues of injustice. Thus, in considering equity, he writes that "it is improper for a prudent legislator not only to command unjust things, but also things which are inhuman and more burdensome than the human condition can bear."[107] The person possessing the virtue of equity is able to look not only at the terms of the law on its face but also at how it is applied in specific circumstances: "The law would not only sin by prescribing that which it should not, but also by prescribing when and how it should not, that is to say, obliging with more rigor than is just."[108] Through the lens of equity, Suárez ensures that the common good is understood most broadly—not simply granting somebody their due, but making sure that that due is understood in the appropriate situational context. This goes beyond Lon Fuller's description of the inner morality of the law (where laws are justly and properly enacted) to requiring that a subjective awareness of the impact on the individual, conceived as a whole person, is also part of the determination of the law's ultimate justness and therefore validity.[109]

This expansion of the common good is a reminder that there is more to a good life than simply preservation of life—and a much richer and fuller notion of law. An emphasis on lost opportunity is particularly important in our current political climate, where discussion of racial discrimination not only considers discrimination at the moment but, in addition, the lost opportunity costs resulting from past discrimination. It shows that the fullness of understanding law is achievement of the common good, since "this danger always redounds to the detriment of the community, which has an interest that the good of the citizens may be dilapidated."[110]

Equity in Scripture

Because the doctrine of equity is so intrinsically a part of the communal heritage, Suárez does not feel the need to provide explicit theological justifications. However, in our own culture, where the concept of theologically grounded equity is less well known, it is worth pausing to consider the theological grounding that Suárez broadly assumes. Turning to scripture, the story of Abigail, David, and Nabal in 1 Samuel 25: 1–44 provides a clear example of equity in action similar to that described by Suárez, particularly in the story's emphasis upon individual action and the role of equitable action in advancing the common good.

During his exile in the wilderness, David and his men come into contact with the shepherds of Nabal, who are shearing their sheep. Nabal is a very wealthy landowner, possessing "three thousand sheep and a thousand goats" (1 Sam. 25:2). Given the extent of his property and his apparent power, Jon Levenson argues that Nabal functions as the local Calebite chieftain.[111] Out of respect for Nabal, David and his men leave the shearers unmolested and in fact defend them from harm when they are in the fields. Later David sends emissaries to Nabal, asking for food. Nabal, in a manner befitting his name (it means "fool"), rudely sends David's emissaries away and denies them food. Generally, of course, denying food to brigands living near shepherds in the wilderness is not necessarily an unjust decision. However, in this situation, and given the unique care that David's men had taken to protect Nabal's shepherds and flocks—perhaps foreshadowing David's kingly protection of all of Israel—Nabal's edict is both foolish and unjust.

Filled with anger at the insult, David and his men prepare to attack Nabal and eliminate his entire household. Nabal's "clever and beautiful" wife, Abigail, hears of her husband's folly from his servants, who have run to her in distress and fear at the dangerous consequence of Nabal's declaration. Abigail realizes both the injustice of Nabal's actions and the immediate danger that his scornful rejection has created for their household. In the face of urgent necessity, and in obedience to the "higher principles" of justice, Abigail hurries out to meet David and his men with food and wine—but without telling her husband. Given Nabal's authority, it is fair to perceive Abigail's and the servants' rejection of Nabal's denial of goods to David and his men as on par with rejecting a legal edict. Abigail's quick action halts David in his quest for bloody revenge, saving David from bloodguilt and sparing the life of her foolish husband and all their household. David, who Abigail clearly identifies with the Lord, praises Abigail's "good sense" and, following Nabal's sudden death, marries her.

Abigail clearly displays the virtue of equity. She acts against a generally just precept in order to promote the common good in an exceptional situation. She displays gnome when she identifies the foolishness of Nabal's decision and the higher precept of justice that motivates the claims of David and his men. Her own desire to do justice is so strong that she puts herself at risk of harm in order to protect the other members of the community, seeking to save them from death and destruction at the hands of David's men. She upholds the more general common good by recognizing the importance of protecting the Lord's anointed from bloodshed. The surprise nuptial ending of the story, with David and Abigail united in marriage after Nabal's dramatic death, demonstrates that she is blessed, rather than condemned, for her actions.

Equity in a Contemporary Context

What, then, is the value of thinking of equity in a contemporary situation? How could it enrich our political discourse and the way Christians engage with the law? Such a discussion of equity is an approach that does not seem to have a place in contemporary American jurisprudence, where equity is seen only as judicially applied. Even the concept of burden, which arises in many rights-based cases, does not contain the fullness of Suárez's understanding of equity. Were a court to engage in a burden analysis, it would have to ask if a law infringes too far on a protected right and therefore should not be applied, rather than whether considering if the law burdens the individual good broadly conceived. In his discussion of equity, Suárez does engage with rights questions—the fact that one may put oneself under the authority of the law, if one so chooses, without falling into sin. His view of equity is that it applies when the law lacks authority because the law fails in its ultimate end: the promotion of justice and the common good. Equity applies whether a right granted by prior law is protected or not.

Suárez's approach to equity will not necessarily revitalize the idea that equity should be a branch of American law nor will it begin to be recognized by the courts. Rather, thinking of equity in this way may provide Christians and churches with a theologically robust way to discuss why and how they, at times, may feel obliged to act against the letter of a law. Specifically, it provides a way for discussing and analyzing how to address burdens on consciences that turn the dialogue away from claims of rights into a discussion of the common good *from both sides*. Thus, those who claim that their consciences are burdened must answer the question as to whether or not the weight of the burden is so great that obeying the law would be more unjust than the damages to the rule of law that would arise from the potential public scandal of disobedience and the damage to the community's recognition of the common good. On the other hand, courts and lawmakers should remember that the common good and justice are advanced when individual consciences are not too unduly burdened and that whatever specific community aim is gained from the universal application of the law may not be so great that there should not be openness to granting exceptions and waivers in the name of equity.

Returning to our opening examples of Joan Cheever's and Arnold Abbott's citations for feeding the homeless, their situations and a number of similar cases provide a perfect example of equity in action. In recent years multiple municipal regulations limiting food distribution to the homeless have become law. In opposition to these statutes, various individuals have engaged in equitable individual actions of public feeding because their consciences are burdened by the deprivation their neighbors are experiencing and out of a belief that their actions advance the common good while also serving individuals.

Recovering Suárez's concept of equity would empower advocates working in this field to develop their own approach to the law outside of a rights discourse to focus more on exactly how their individual actions advance justice and the common good. Such an approach would also change their posture from one of aggressive defensiveness and entrenched opinions to one of openness and a search for shared communality and conviction. Both the people claiming an exemption on the grounds of equity and the lawmakers and courts seeking to enforce the law would benefit from a shared commitment to the common good, rather than antagonism.

In a report released in 2014 by the National Coalition for the Homeless, three types of municipal laws are aimed at limiting food-sharing with the homeless. These three approaches are classified as 1) restrictions on public property use, 2) food safety actions, and 3) community attempts at relocation. One 2012 ordinance issued by the city of Houston limits public feedings to five people, citing care for the safety of food providers and recipients as well as a concern for the utilization and cleanliness of public and private property.[112] Although the first two categories of regulation might appear neutral, the coalition argues that they are often motivated by myths concerning homelessness, such as the belief that sharing food with the homeless contributes to homelessness as a systemic problem or simply an unwillingness to have homeless people present in one's own community.[113] The proponents of "Not in My Backyard" movements claim that they have the right to not have people they perceive as unsavory or unsafe in their neighborhoods. A proposed ban on panhandling in Portland, Maine, was allegedly motivated by neighborhood concerns about the dangers to the community posed by panhandlers.[114] Those arguing that food-sharing perpetuates homelessness claim that it is contrary to the common good to allow such practices to continue. On the other side, people committed to feeding the needy argue that their consciences would be unduly burdened, either for religious reasons or reasons of moral commitment, if they were prohibited from providing these food services.[115]

Religious institutions are often the target of municipal statutes.[116] One response has been for these institutions to bring suit for protection under the Religious Freedom Restoration Act, claiming that their rights of free exercise are unduly abrogated and that these regulations impose a substantial burden upon their exercise of crucial religious practices drawn from scriptural passages such as Matthew 25: 35–40.[117] For example, West Presbyterian Church has argued that "its program to feed the homeless ... constitutes religious activity protected by the First Amendment of the Constitution and the Religious Freedom Restoration Act of 1993, and that application of the District of Columbia's zoning regulations to the feeding program impermissibly infringes upon plaintiffs' right to free exercise of their religion."[118] As the debate over counsels and precepts during Suárez's time reveal, however, feeding the homeless through individual food distribution is not a clear mandate for all Christians, which does weaken a potential rights-based claim.[119]

Taking an equity-based approach to this issue would broaden the discussion beyond competing claims of rights of conscience versus rights of property owners. Based upon Suárez's three modalities of equity, we can see that these statutes are implicated under every mode. First, by prohibiting churches from feeding the homeless, they are requiring something unjust. Just as statutes should be relaxed to permit neighbors to help if somebody's house is on fire, they should be relaxed to permit those who want to help the hungry to give them food. Under the second modality, churches could also argue that while the lawmaker has a valid interest in protecting property values and the safety of the neighborhood, the need to make sure citizens are fed is an even more integral component of the common good. Under the third modality, food safety laws can be understood as placing too much of a burden on small nonprofits such as churches, which do not have the capacity to engage with a rigorous regulatory structure intended for much larger-scale organizations.

Regardless of which modality is considered for the application of equity, these statutes are clearly a relevant case for Suárez's theory of equity to be applied. There is no question that laws relating to property protection or food safety may be valid laws, and generally applicable. However, in the specific situation of regulating churches feeding the homeless, they clearly run contrary to justice and the common good, and thus churches do not have a moral obligation to obey them.

Considering these regulations through the lens of equity enables people engaged in food-sharing with the homeless to sustain three important goods. First, they must consider how they can still engage as responsible citizens in the public square and not be morally obligated to obey every single law. Solitary laws such as these, which clearly contradict a higher law and unduly burden consciences, can be understood not to oblige, without requiring a rejection of the entire system. This claim will always require a careful balancing act to determine how far the common good of the community is actually being destroyed. Are there other options for homeless people to receive food within a reasonable distance? Are neighbors merely uncomfortable or are they actually being threatened or facing property damage? Asking such questions will require the churches to interact with their neighbors, work with other nonprofits, and listen to the concerns of the homeless people themselves, rather than making unilateral decisions simply based on the claims of their own consciences.

Second, by claiming that they are acting under the doctrine of equity, individuals involved in food-sharing are also taking on a higher responsibility for their own behavior. The doctrine of probable certainty requires that churches are careful to see what parts of the statutes are reasonable and should be incorporated into their feeding practices. For example, food safety regulations may be unduly burdensome but some, such as requirements about food preservation, may be valid and should be adopted. In addition, even if they are pointless and somewhat burdensome, laws that are neutral, in that they do not inhibit the work, should still be obeyed. This is in accordance with Suárez's claim that priority should normally be granted to the lawmaker's superior insight as far as possible.

Churches, therefore, have to carefully consider statutory regulations in determining to which parts the practices of equity should be applied, and which ones should be adopted to the Church's practices. Because the entire body of the law is not being rejected—and only the specific parts are unjust and fail to advance the common good—the goods of the law can be received and appropriated. In addition, by considering equity as a virtue, churches engaged in this practice should be appropriately humble in assessing their own ability to prudently discern and act in accordance with justice. Claiming to act in contradiction to the words of the law in accordance with equity means that churches should commit to ensuring that they are actually cultivating the virtues of justice appropriately within their members, rather than using claims of burdened conscience as a shield to avoid engaging with the substance of the law.

Finally, differentiating between practices of equity and practices of rejection of the law can helpfully contribute to clarification of our theological dialogue. When is the law so clearly unjust that it needs to be rejected and reformed, and when should it be understood as not applying in a specific situation? When is it against justice and the common good, and when is it simply burdensome? If it is burdensome, churches need to discern whether or not it would advance the Church's mission more to fully comply with the law rather than applying equity. Might it be more effective for church members to practice sacrificial giving to fund another homeless feeding service rather than directly providing their own? How much are neighbors actually engaging with the Church or the underlying issues that contribute to homelessness in their community? Claiming that one's property rights or safety are being violated are valid claims and concerns, but they do not necessarily invalidate any other claims for other individual losses (such as hunger or unduly burdened consciences) that also detract from the common good.

While this is not necessarily a technique that results in law being changed, modified, or not enforced, the National Coalition for the Homeless does record that some groups have had success using just these types of techniques. For example, in Charlotte, North Carolina, a municipal ordinance was passed that prohibited people from giving away food outdoors, most likely to ensure that city parks weren't overrun and remained accessible by the whole community. The groups that had been involved in feeding the homeless mobilized in reaction to the ordinance. They expressed their commitment to continue feeding the homeless but also their willingness to comply with the parts of the statute that were just. The county has provided an indoor area for groups to continue feeding the homeless while at the same time requiring groups to register, follow food safety rules, and commit to continuing their programs. The results have been amazing for the community. One organizer noted, in particular, the number of children showing up to receive food in a safer venue had skyrocketed, from one per month to sixty-four.[120]

The practices of the virtue of equity can serve not only to remedy unjust applications of the law in individual instances but also provide a useful critique of the ways in which legal presumptions, understood generally, can work against the common good. A delightfully lucid and literary opinion issued by the Eleventh Circuit Court of Appeals is an example of how equitable practices can not only change the enforcement of a law in specific circumstances but also serve to provide broader societal critiques for protesting situations in which the good of individuals have been grievously burdened.[121] In 2018, Fort Lauderdale Food Not Bombs (FLFNB) filed suit challenging the same Fort Lauderdale city ordinance that Arnold Abbott had protested. Like Abbott, FLFNB had been repeatedly cited for violations of the city ordinances prohibiting publicly feeding the homeless. Like Abbott, this organization was involved in equitable action. FLFNB made a claim under 42 U.S.C. § 1983 arguing, among other causes, that the Fort Lauderdale ordinance restricted their free speech rights guaranteed by the First Amendment.

On appeal, the court overruled the district court's holding in favor of the city. FLFNB had argued that food-sharing in a public space was inherently expressive because these actions presented compelling evidence "that [ ] society can end hunger and poverty if we redirect our collective resources from the military and war and that food is a human right, not a privilege, which society has a responsibility to provide for all."[122] The court found that several key components of FLFNB's actions combined to provide a publicly protected expressive act: the group distributed literature explaining the organization's goals and it included all passersby in the communal meal. This latter action alone has significant social implications.[123] Third, they carried out the activity in a public park, a place that has been historically recognized as a key locus of individual and communal expression. The court expressly declined to consider whether the ordinance itself is unconstitutionally vague, and thus permitted it to stand as valid law. Although the holding was issued under a First Amendment claim, this case confirms Suárez's theory that equitable action, when individual consciences are burdened, may create an exception to an otherwise valid statute. The idea of expressive actions that are intended to promote the common good, even in opposition to an otherwise valid law, is nothing else than a description of equitable action. This is a contemporary description of Suárez's theory that practices of equity, in preserving the freedom for individuals to follow the discernment of their consciences, can be excepted from the law in order to contribute to the good of the entire community.

Notes

1. Joan Vinson, "Jury Trial Set for Cheever's Homeless Feeding Case," *Rivard Report*, July 9, 2015, https://sanantonioreport.org/jury-trail-set-for-cheevers-homeless-feeding-case/.
2. Kevin Conlon and Catherine E. Shoichet, "90-Year-Old Florida Man Charged for Feeding Homeless People," *CNN*, November 4, 2014, https://www.cnn.com/2014/11/04/justice/florida-feeding-homeless-charges/index.html.

3. On the other hand, Catholic political theology, as developed both in the Thomism of Jacques Maritain and in Catholic social teaching, holds a more positive view of the theological and civic value of rights discourse. See, e.g., Jacques Maritain, *Man and the State* (Washington, DC: Catholic University of America Press, 1998); and John Courtney Murray, SJ, *We Hold These Truths* (New York: Sheed & Ward, 2005).
4. Martin Luther King Jr., "Letter from Birmingham City Jail," in *The Essential Writings and Speeches of Martin Luther King, Jr.*, ed. James M. Washington (New York: Harper and Rowe, 1986), 289–302. Vincent Lloyd has raised important questions regarding how much of King's use of a European natural law theory in this letter was a rhetorical strategy intended to create a connection with white progressives. Lloyd also argues that concern and care for natural law were an important theme for King from the early days of his career. See Vincent Lloyd, *Black Natural Law* (Oxford: Oxford University Press, 2016), 88–89.
5. Martin Luther King Jr., *Where Do We Go from Here: Chaos or Community?* (Boston: Beacon, 1986), 210–12.
6. Dorothy Day, "On Pilgrimage—Our Spring Appeal," *Catholic Worker*, May 1970, 1, 2, 11, https://www.catholicworker.org/500-html on June 30, 2022.
7. Day, 1, 2, 11.
8. Dorothy Day, "Our Fall Appeal," *Catholic Worker*, November 1955, 2, https://www.catholicworker.org/dorothyday/articles/242.html.
9. Alastair Hudson, *Equity and Trusts*, 5th ed. (London: Routledge-Cavendish, 2007), 4–5 (emphases in original).
10. Jill E. Martin, *Hanbury and Martin: Modern Equity*, 14th ed. (Edinburgh, UK: Sweet & Maxwell, 1993).
11. Maurice Amen, CSC, "Canonical Equity before the Code (Concluded)," *The Jurist* 33 (1973): 264, citing Gratian, *Decretum*, C.35, C.XXIII, q. 4. For a more contemporary presentation of this same type of theological justification, see also Romanus Cessario, OP, "Epieikeia and the Accomplishment of the Just," in *Aquinas and Empowerment: Classic Ethics for Ordinary Lives*, ed. G. Simon Harak, SJ (Washington, DC: Georgetown University Press, 1997), 172.
12. Roger Shiner, "Aristotle's Theory of Equity," *Loyola of Los Angeles Law Review* 27, no. 4 (1993–94): 1251.
13. Shiner, 1252.
14. Hudson, *Equity and Trusts*, 5.
15. Jean Porter, *Justice as a Virtue: A Thomistic Perspective* (Grand Rapids, MI: Eerdmans, 2016), 272.
16. Porter, 272.
17. See Thomas Bushlack, *Politics for a Pilgrim Church: A Thomistic Theory of Civic Virtue* (Grand Rapids, MI: Eerdmans, 2015), 93n58. See also Cessario, "Epieikeia," 195n3.
18. See, for example, Josef Fuchs, SJ, *Personal Responsibility and Christian Morality* (Washington, DC: Georgetown University Press, 1983), 185–99; and James Keenan, SJ, *A History of Catholic Moral Theology in the Twentieth Century* (London: Bloomsbury, 2010), 154–55.
19. Aquinas, *Summa Theologiae*, II–II q. 120, art. 1. Aquinas, at least in the *Summa*, does not actually distinguish between epikeia and equity, but simply considers one as a translation of the other. For his differentiation between the terms in other works, and a discussion of the effect this differentiation has on other scholastic discussions of equity, see Lawrence Riley, *The History, Nature and Use of Epikeia in Moral Theology* (Lexington, KY: Christ the King Library, 2017), 31.

20. Aquinas, II–II q. 120, art. 2, ad 1.
21. Aquinas, II–II q. 120, art. 2, ad 2.
22. Cessario, "Epieikeia," 192.
23. Aquinas, I–II q. 92, art. 6.
24. Aquinas, *Summa*, II–II q. 120, art. 2, ad 1.
25. Aquinas, II–II q. 120, art. 2.
26. Aquinas, II–II q. 120, art. 2. A dispensation is not equity. Rather, it is simply the lawmaker using his or her executive power to ensure that the law does not apply in a specific situation.
27. Aquinas, I–II q. 96, art. 6.
28. Aquinas, I–II q. 96, art. 6, ad 2.
29. Aquinas, I–II q. 96, art. 6, ad 1.
30. Aquinas, I–II q. 96, art. 6, ad 3.
31. Aquinas, II–II q. 47, art. 8.
32. Bushlack, *Politics for a Pilgrim Church*, 97.
33. Francisco Suárez, *Tractatus de legibus ac Deo legislatore*, ed. Carlos Baciero (Madrid: Consejo Superior de Investigaciones Científicas, 2010), VI.vi.1.
34. Suárez, VI.vi.2.
35. Francisco Suárez, *Tractatus de legibus ac Deo legislatore*, ed. Luciano Pereña Vicente (Madrid: Consejo Superior de Investigaciones Científicas, 1972), I.ii.9.
36. Suárez, I.xvi.4. Suárez, like Aquinas in *Summa*, does not distinguish between epikeia and aequum, but simply views one as the Latin version of the word and the other as the Greek. Any difference in concept implied by the words is, he says, "differentiated little from it."
37. Suárez, I.ii.9.
38. Suárez., I.ii.9.
39. Suárez, I.ii.10.
40. Suárez, I.ii.10.
41. Suárez, VI.vi.6.
42. Suárez, VI.vi.4.
43. Suárez, VI.vi.2.
44. Suárez, VI.vi.2.
45. Suárez, II.xvi.4.
46. Suárez, II.xvi.5.
47. Suárez, II.xvi.7.
48. Suárez is quoting Cajetan's *Secundae Secundae Partis Summae Theologiae Sancti Thomae* in *Caietani Commentariis illustrata* (Augustae Taurinorum, 1581), q. 120, art. 1, p. 547.
49. Suárez, *De Legibus*, II.vi.7.
50. Suárez, II.xvi.9.
51. Suárez, II.vi.16.
52. Suárez, VI.vi.5.
53. Suárez, VI.vi.6.
54. Suárez, VI.vi.6.
55. Suárez, VI.vi.6.
56. Suárez, VI.vi.6.
57. Suárez, VI.vi.4.
58. Suárez, VI.vi.2.

59. Suárez, VI.vi.7.
60. Suárez, VI.vii.2.
61. Suárez, VI.vii.4.
62. See also Suárez, VI.vii.6.
63. Suárez, VI.vii.6.
64. Suárez, VI.vii.4.
65. Suárez, VI.vii.5.
66. Suárez, VI.vii.6.
67. Suárez, VII.vii.6.
68. Suárez, VII.vii.3.
69. Suárez, VII.vii.3, citing Aquinas, *Summa*, II–II, q. 120, art. 1.
70. Suárez, VII.vii.4.
71. Suárez, VII.vii.1.
72. Suárez, VI. vii.6.
73. Suárez, VI.vii.7.
74. Suárez, VI.vii.12.
75. Suárez, VI.vii.8.
76. Suárez, VI.vii.8.
77. Suárez, VI.vii.9.
78. Suárez, VI.vii.11.
79. Suárez, VI.vi.11.
80. Suárez, VI.vii.11.
81. Suárez, VI.vii.11. See also Aquinas, *Summa*, I–II q. 96, art. 6, ad 2.
82. Suárez, *De Legibus*, VI.vi.3.
83. John Coughlin, OFM, *Law, Person, and Community: Philosophical, Theological, and Comparative Perspectives on Canon Law* (Oxford: Oxford University Press, 2012), 112.
84. Suárez, *De Legibus*, VI.vii.9.
85. Suárez, VI.vii.9.
86. Suárez, VI.vii.9.
87. Suárez, VI.vii.10.
88. Suárez, VI.vii.10.
89. Suárez, VI.vii.10.
90. Suárez, VI.vii.10.
91. In this way Suárez makes the same argument regarding the importance of precepts for justice as Aquinas does in *Summa*, II–II, q. 122.
92. Suárez, *De Legibus*, VI.vii.12.
93. Suárez, VI.vii.12.
94. Suárez, VI.vi.3.
95. Suárez, VI.viii.1.
96. Suárez, VI.viii.1.
97. Suárez, VI.viii.1.
98. Suárez, VI.viii.6.
99. Suárez, VI.viii.6.
100. Suárez, VI.vii.6.
101. Riley, *History, Nature, and Use of Epikeia*, 79.
102. Suárez, *De Legibus*, VI.vii.13 (emphasis added).
103. Suárez, VI.vii.13.

104. Suárez, VI.vii.14.
105. Suárez, VI.vii.1.
106. Suárez, VI.vii.13.
107. Suárez, VI.vii.10.
108. Suárez, VI.vii.10.
109. Lon Fuller, *The Morality of Law*, rev. ed. (New Haven: Yale University Press, 1969), 39.
110. Suárez, *De Legibus*, VI.vii.13.
111. Jon D. Levenson, "1 Samuel 25 as Literature and History," *Catholic Biblical Quarterly* 40 (1978): 25. Part of Levenson's support for this claim is Abigail's later appearance in 2 Samuel, where she accompanies him, along with one other of Nabal's wives, as he assumes the kingship at the Calebite capital of Hebron (2 Sam. 2: 1–4). Levenson believes that Abigail's presence at this important moment in David's assumption of power is an indicator that through their marriage, David has assumed Nabal's political power.
112. City of Houston, Texas, Ordinance No. 2012–269, amending chapter 20 of the Code of Ordinances Houston, Texas, relating to feeding those in need, https://www.houstontx.gov/health/2012-269.pdf, retrieved June 28, 2019.
113. National Coalition for the Homeless, *Share No More: The Criminalization of Efforts to Feed People in Need*, ed. Michael Stoops (Washington, DC: National Coalition for the Homeless, 2014), http://www.nationalhomeless.org/wp-content/uploads/2014/10/Food-Sharing2014.pdf, 4.
114. Colin L. Anderson, "Median Bans, Anti-Homeless Laws and the Urban Growth Machine," *DePaul Journal of Social Justice* 8, no. 2 (2015): 406.
115. See, for example, *W. Presbyterian Church v. Bd. of Zoning Adjustment of D.C. (W. Presbyterian Church 1)*, 849. F. Supp. 77, 79 (D.D.C. 1994).
116. For a list of food-sharing claims brought against religious institutions, see Marc-Tizoc González, "Criminalizing Charity: Can First Amendment Free Exercise of Religion, RFRA, and RLUIPA Protect People Who Share Food in Public?," *UC Irvine Law Review* 7 (January 2017): 343–45.
117. For an analysis of RFRA-based legislation by churches related to civil legislation on feeding the homeless see González, 291–345.
118. *W. Presbyterian Church v. Bd. of Zoning Adjustment of D.C. (W. Presbyterian Church 2)*, 862. F. Supp. 538, 547 (D.D.C. 1994).
119. See for example the debate about the obligation to care for betters in Domingo de Soto, *Deliberation on the Cause of the Poor*, ed. Wim Decock, trans. Joost Possemiers and Jeremiah Lasquetey-Reyes (Grand Rapids, MI: CLP Academic, 2022).
120. National Coalition for the Homeless, *Share No More*, 18.
121. *Fort Lauderdale Food Not Bombs, et al. v. City of Fort Lauderdale*, Eleventh Circuit, No. 16–16808, August 22, 2018.
122. Page 4, citing D.E. 39 at 1.
123. The court supported this claim by citing anthropologist Mary Douglas, "Deciphering a Meal in Food and Culture," in *Implicit Meanings: Selected Essays in Case Anthropology* 231 (1975) ("Like sex, the taking of food has a social component, as well as a biological one," 12–13).

Conclusion

Francisco Suárez offers an innovate read on the traditional theological understanding of the way civil law is developed: rooted in theological conviction but bolstered by popular engagement with legal statutes. Suárez believes that all of civil law's authority rests on God's authority. However, this authority is dispersed in two different ways. First, it is dispersed to the people communally. Knowing the human need for social interaction, God gives lawmaking authority to humans when they come together in perfect community. The ends of this grant of power is for humans to develop the structures necessary for communal living, which advance justice and the common good. Once this lawmaking authority appears, the community has the ability to grant some degree of this authority to a leader or ruler. The ruler, therefore, can be said to rule with God's power, but only to a certain extent. The people always retain some amount of authority, and therefore always have the power to participate in adding or transforming the content of a law.

By emphasizing how God has distributed this lawmaking power, Suárez both upholds the importance of the lawgiver and leaves space for meaningful participation in lawmaking on the part of the people. An important part of the community's engagement is to bring civil law into conformity with the natural law. For Suárez, the natural law, while unchanging, is also primarily discerned through conventional structures and even individual experiences, and it may appear, to some degree, different in different societies and structures. The people, through their lived experiences, often have more insight than rulers into how the application of law actually advances the common good and is being applied justly, and thus how far they are in conformity with the natural law. On the other hand, the lawmaker, by virtue of the resources of her office, may have a better long-term perspective of how laws advance the common good. In addition, she may be better able to perceive how laws affect different communities differently and provide a protection against the possibility that community discernment of the common good forecloses the contributions of minorities or individuals.

For Suárez, both the ruler's lawmaking ability and the people's reception and response are crucial components in the development of law. Rather than perceiving law as rules that are static, Suárez views law as always in the process of change and development. He demonstrates this in his description of law's existence in three simultaneous phases: in the mind of the ruler, existing as a sign of the ruler's will, and received into the mind of the citizen. As law passes through each of these phases, it undergoes change and adaptation. This transmittal does not run just one way, from ruler through symbol to subject. Because of the law's content and the citizens' acceptance of it, the process of change runs the other way as well: from citizen to symbol to ruler. How citizens accept the law and respond to it can add or take away from it, can change the inflection and the meaning of the law as a sign and, often, can eventually change the lawmaker's mind as well. Thus, citizens' lawmaking power extends far beyond choosing representatives to determine a law's content, and rather shapes the law as a symbol and the law in the lawmaker's mind.

This acknowledgment, that popular reception can change law's content, does not in Suárez's view diminish the lawmaker's authority or the importance of the rule of law. Rather, under his theory of the "benign legislator," the citizens' response is always conditioned by an assumption that the lawmaker desired to issue a valid law—and thus advances justice and promotes the common good. Consequently, a citizen's action in engaging with law in the way that achieves the common good in the best way for that particular context is not a rejection, but rather a fulfillment of the lawmaker's original desire for making the law. Using this concept, Suárez is able to emphasize the importance of the lawgiver and the rule of law, as well as the crucial nature of the people's discernment and reception for shaping law's content through dialectical engagement.

Suárez's theory of law's development through this dialogue between lawmaker and the community provides Christian activists with a range of options for constructively engaging with law in order to have a positive impact on society. Suárez's theory of custom considers how the actions of the community can add to or subtract from existing law. This power to establish a law through custom cannot be surrendered by the people to any ruler but is always retained as part of the original grant of divine power. Although Suárez, like many contemporary Americans, has sound reasons for being concerned that the customs of the majority will become tyrannical, he argues that properly understanding how the search for the common good and justice limit the obligatory nature of unjust customs, as well as the importance of the ruler's approval, ensures that customs establishing law are understood to advance the good, not limit it.

Suárez builds upon his theory that customary actions can establish or abrogate law to explain how the community can limit or expand a specific law's meaning through interpretation of the words of a statute. Drawing upon theories of scriptural interpretation and sacramental theology, Suárez argues that the people and legal experts have the freedom to place the best potential interpretation upon statutory language. Although this interpretation may stretch the meaning of the statutory language, and even go beyond the most obvious meaning of the word, it may be the best way to ensure that the statute advances the common good even if this is not in alignment with what can be ascertained of the lawmaker's actual intention in drafting the statute. In both of these approaches Suárez uses the idea of the people's creative engagement with law as the linchpin that holds together a theologically grounded commitment to the rule of law and to the common good.

Suárez also considers situations in which general laws may not apply to specific individuals through the doctrine of equity. He follows Aquinas in defining equity as both a practice and a virtue which can be exercised by individual citizens in situations in which they have determined that an individual law does not apply. However, he goes beyond Aquinas's explicit claims to argue that equity applies not only when laws are unjust, but even when they are unduly burdensome. Equity can apply to ensure that a person's life is not in danger, but can also protect a wide range of other important elements of a life, including even property and future profit, which a problematic law might endanger for an individual. Suárez's theory of equity should also be understood as a tool for advancing civic discourse on how to balance the competing claims of individual rights and the common good.

Suarez's position can serve as a helpful corrective for several contemporary positions in political theology. As an Augustinian Thomist he provides helpful insights into how the role of individual citizens—and especially the development of their civic virtues—can supplement the Augustinian understanding of how the City of God and the City of Man can pursue certain shared goods. By focusing on how citizens can work to transform unjust laws through practices of creative custom, interpretation, and equity, Suarez provides a persuasive picture as to how citizens can engage in the *saeculum* without shedding their identity as citizens of the City of God, thus putting themselves at less risk of corruption than those who actually hold the reins of power.

Suarez's thought offers a useful corrective to classical liberalism's trend to individualism as well. Custom, interpretation, and equity offer powerful models for how citizens acting together in community can use their individual capacity to engage with law most powerfully to advance the common good in their own specific context.

Suarez's Jesuit ecclesiology provides a compelling vision of the Church's role within the public sphere. When considering the examples of practices and Suárez's understanding of law as developed from below, it is striking how many of them are carried out by Christians working within their church communities—providing perhaps a practical example of this Jesuit ecclesiology. This extends from the parish organization structure of COPs in San Antonio to the many churches that served as sanctuary churches and the church communities who responded to city ordinances by acting upon their gospel mandate to feed the homeless. These are striking, but not surprising, given that we should understand Suárez's work through the lens of his Jesuit incarnational and ecclesial theological commitments.

These ecclesial commitments do not negate the importance of practices of solidarity with people of goodwill who do not share Christian beliefs. Neither do they indicate that those acting to make civil laws more just must act in a way to bring them into accordance with supernatural rather than natural ends. However, the common occurrence of these practices arising from within church communities points to a special potentiality for this type of constructive engagement with law. Although understanding the role of the Church in Suárez's theology and philosophy would require at least another book, there are several relevant insights to highlight from his ecclesiology to explain why and how churches are so significant for this type of action.[1] Consider Suárez once again in dialogue with Pope Francis, a Jesuit pope who sees Suárez's insights as important for theology.

The first question that must be asked concerns how the Church can be capable of inculcating people in the virtues necessary to engage in this type of constructive action. Suárez would argue that, first and foremost, this formation must be rooted in the Church because the Church is the place where we learn how to pray. Suárez shares with the great Spanish mystical tradition, especially Teresa of Avila, a conviction that prayer changes us and changes the world. In his long discussion on the Lord's Prayer, he builds upon Augustine, Aquinas, and, arguably, Teresa, to argue that the Lord's Prayer provides a model for how the theological virtues of faith, hope, and love help us to understand and appropriately respond to the needs of everyday life. It is through prayer that we request God to make us just by filling us with God's love.[2] It is through prayer that we ask to be delivered from evil.[3] While prayer elevates our minds to God, it also changes how we engage here on earth and makes us people who can work for justice and deliver others from evil. Prayer does not separate us from nature, but makes it possible for us to engage with the natural order in a way that recognizes God's redemptive action, even in the natural goods.

In his recent apostolic letter on the liturgy, *Desiderio Desideravi*, Pope Francis describes the liturgy as the place where this type of "real existential engagement with the person of Christ" occurs.[4] It is through our attendance at the Supper of the Lamb that we encounter "the salvific power of Jesus" and make Christians into a people who live out the "missionary option" of inviting others to this supper who see the rest of the created order as containing, in their way, "the seed of the sanctifying grace of the sacraments."[5]

The second question concerns who in the Church must be involved for this type of communal action to be successful. In the example of COPS, both clergy and laypeople were crucial for the successful transformation of the San Antonio city ordinances. Suárez would not be surprised to learn that people from both states of life were crucial to this lawmaking endeavor because he believed that people from both states of life are equally crucial for discernment within the Church as well. In his discussion of empowering the people to make civil law, he gestures toward the authority of the people in constructive dialogue with pope, bishops, and priests to make canon law and shape Church practices. The Church needs both groups to accurately discern how God calls us to live in the world. Without both it is lost.

For Roman Catholics, the discussion of the role of the laity has been important since such documents as *Gaudium et Spes* from Vatican II and Paul VI's decree Apostolicam Actuositatem. However, laypeople have gained new significance under the pontificate of the current Spanish-speaking Jesuit pope. As Francis wrote to the Pontifical Council on the Laity in 2015, reflecting on the revival of the role of the laity at the time of the Council:

> The Council did not see the laity as if they were members of a "second order," at the service of the hierarchy and simple executors of higher orders, but as disciples of Christ who, by virtue of their Baptism and of their natural insertion "in the world," are called to enliven every environment, every activity, every human relationship according to the spirit of the Gospel (cf. *Lumen Gentium*, 31), bringing light, hope, and the charity received from Christ to those places that otherwise would remain foreign to God's action and abandoned to the misery of the human condition (cf. *Gaudium et Spes*, 37). There is no one more appropriate than they to carry out the essential task of seeing "that the divine law is inscribed in the life of the earthly city" (cf. *ibid.*, 43).[6]

However, despite the level of interest that has been aroused by the topic, understanding exactly what the role of the people can be in contributing to doctrine has resulted more often in controversy than clarity. Suárez's understanding of the importance of both the magisterial hierarchy and the people in developing doctrine and canon law—in a way that is faithful to natural law and divine law and also acknowledges particularity—could provide an important addition to these attempts to revitalize and reclaim the role of the laity.

This search for authority and the attempt to preserve the voice of the people is an equally important question for Protestants. Confronted with the challenges of modernity, including secularization and advancing technology, more Protestants are recognizing that "the center cannot hold" without some form of authority and oversight.[7] However, attempting to understand how an ecclesial authority can speak authoritatively without losing some key commitments to discernment by individuals and congregations is a more difficult question. It is possible that Suárez's understanding of how law within the Catholic Church is formed by laypeople and the magisterium might provide potential for finding ecumenical common ground in discussing both the role of Church hierarchy and the importance of the people.

The third insight is ecumenical. In examples such as the sanctuary movement and churches engaged in practices of feeding the hungry, one notable characteristic is Protestants and Catholics coming together to work toward the common good while also jointly acknowledging the presence of the Risen Christ in the poor whom they serve. In *Laudato Si* Francis describes the call to work for ecumenical unity as the same as the call to care for God's creation. He quotes approvingly the statement of Ecumenical Patriarch Bartholomew, when Bartholomew "asks us [all Christians] to replace consumption with sacrifice, greed with generosity, wastefulness with a spirit of sharing, an asceticism which 'entails learning to give, and not simply to give up. It is a way of loving, of moving gradually away from what I want to what God's world needs. It is liberation from fear, greed and compulsion.'"[8] In Francis's vision of this gradual transformation of both the surrounding natural world and the *person*, through obedient acts of service, there is hope for ecumenical reunion.

The theological crisis of the Reformation contributed just as much as the political crisis of early modernity to Suárez's development of his theory of law. Many of the same doctrinal questions he encountered remain five hundred years later. Without negating the importance of these questions and the need for substantive ecumenical analysis and discussion in order to resolve these differences, developing an understanding in greater detail will create a unifying power of solidarity in pursuit of the common good and continue to offer an important vision of how reunification can start to be effected from the ground up.

Notes

1. A volume related to this topic was published when this book was in the final stages of revision: see Eric DeMeuse, *Unity and Catholicity in Christ: The Ecclesiology of Francisco Suárez, S.J.* (Oxford: Oxford University Press, 2022).
2. Suárez, *De Religione,* in *Opera Omnia* (Paris: Apud Ludovicum Vives, 1856–78), VII.17.
3. Suárez, VII. 38.
4. Pope Francis, Desiderio Desideravi (2022) § 41, https://www.vatican.va/content/francesco/en/apost_letters/documents/20220629-lettera-ap-desiderio-desideravi.html, retrieved July 1, 2022.
5. Pope Francis, § 46.
6. "Message of His Holiness Pope Francis on the Occasion of the 50th Anniversary of the Decree 'Apostolicam Actuositatem,'" October, 11, 2015, https://www..vatican.va/content/francesco/en/messages/pont-messages/2015/documents/papa-francesco_20151022_messaggio-apostolicam-actuositatem.html.
7. Speaking of American Christians generally in his book *After Christendom* (Nashville, TN: Abingdon, 1991), Stanley Hauerwas writes: "In short, the great problem of modernity for the church is how we are to survive as disciplined communities in democratic societies. For the fundamental presumption behind democratic societies is that the consciousness of something called the common citizen is privileged no matter what kind of formation it may or may not have had" (97). For an example of Hauerwas's claims, see Tish Harrison Warren, "Who's in Charge of the Christian Blogosphere?," *Christianity Today,* April 2017, https://www.christianitytoday.com/women/2017/april-web-only/whos-in-charge-of-christian-blogosphere.html.
8. Pope Francis, *Laudato Si,* in *Catholic Social Thought: Encyclicals and Documents from Pope Leo XIII to Pope Francis,* ed. David J. O'Brien and Thomas Shannon (Maryknoll, NY: Orbis Books, 2016), §9.

Index

absolutism, 17–18, 55, 96, 101; absolute monarchy, 2–4, 28–29, 38, 49–52, 71; Hobbes on, 50–51; Suárez on, 9, 107n112
activism, 4, 35, 128, 132, 209
Agamben, Giorgio, 18–19
Alinsky, Saul, 131–33
Andrewes, Lancelot, 4, 50
anthropology, theological, 54
Aquinas, Thomas, 12–14; on authority, 14; on common good, 29–30, 60, 94–95, 178, 195; on custom, 115–16, 118; on equity, 177–79, 184–85, 187–89, 191–93, 195; on judgement, 154; on justice, 58; on natural law, 66, 81n112; Suárez and, 66, 84–86, 94–99, 154, 171n78, 177–78, 180; *Summa Theologiae*, 12, 29, 80n82, 84, 85–86, 177–79; on virtues, 94–95, 178, 179–80. *See also* Thomism
Aristotle: on equity, 177, 181, 184–85, 187–89, 191; on natural law, 81n112; Suárez on, 61, 84–86
asylum seekers, 166–68
Augustine of Hippo: on civic life, 24–27; on common good, 25–26, 28–29, 40; Elshtain on, 24–25; on evil, 54; Gregory on, 22, 26–27; on love, 22, 24, 25–27; on natural law, 66; and political theology, 20–21, 22–32; *saeculum*, 26–28, 210; on sin, 23, 25, 29, 54, 56; two cities, 26–27, 34, 40, 52–55, 88, 210; on virtue, 25–28, 40, 210

Augustinian Thomism, 21, 26–32
authoritarianism, 11, 18, 21, 28
authority: Aquinas on, 14; Bentham on, 111; and civil law, 49–51; and custom, 109, 111–12, 117–20; and divine law, 49; and equity, 179, 185–87, 192–94; and lawmaking, 20–21, 30, 49–50, 73–75; political, 9n13, 14–15, 16, 35; spiritual, 14
autocracy, 2, 18–19, 21, 52
autonomy, 31, 68

Balthasar, Hans Urs von, 37
baptism, 119, 121
Barr, William, 2–3, 4, 17
Barth, Karl, 21, 33–34, 36–37
Bederman, David, 113
Bejczy, István Pieter, 93
Bellarmine, Robert, 17, 87, 88, 164
Bentham, Jeremy, 109, 111–13, 120
Bergoglio, Jorge. *See* Francis, Pope
Black natural law, 32, 35–36, 204n4
Bloch, Ernst, 3
Bodansky, Daniel, 128–29
burden, 58, 192, 194–96, 198–203
Bushlack, Thomas, 180
business, and custom, 129–30

Cajetan, Thomas, 183, 185, 188, 190
Calvinism, 49, 55, 77n1
canon law: and custom, 115; and equity, 176, 188; on fasting, 59; and the role of

215

canon law (*continued*)
    the laity, 212–13; Suárez on, 87, 95, 97, 120, 188
Catholic Church, 134, 213
Catholicism/Catholics, 87, 88, 147, 164–66, 212–13
Catholic social teaching, 39, 204n3
Catholic Worker Movement, 33, 175
Cavanaugh, William, 34
charisms, 13, 92, 105n45
Chavez, Cesar, 110, 111
church and state, 27, 33–34, 37
citizenship, 26, 93–96
city of God, 25–27, 52
civic Augustinianism, 24–27
civic virtue, 28, 30, 40, 58, 96, 210
civil disobedience, 4–7, 18, 21, 36, 166, 174
civil law: and authority, 49–51; and canon law, 95; and custom, 112, 115; and equity, 177, 184, 192; interpretation, 148–51; and natural law, 31, 67–72; purpose, 55–57, 163; Suárez on, 90–95, 149
civil rights, 109, 166, 173
common good: Aquinas on, 29–30, 60, 94–95, 178, 195; Augustine on, 25–26, 28–29, 40; challenges to, 40–41; and community organizing, 135–37; content and context, 57–59; and custom, 121–22, 125, 135–36, 194–95; and equity, 175–82, 186–87, 194–203; and government, 30; and individual freedom, 194–97, 200, 210; and legal interpretation, 145, 152, 161–62, 168; Locke on, 22, 38; Suárez on, 40–41, 48, 55–61, 135–36, 161–63, 186, 191, 195–96
commonwealth, 21, 28, 38, 61–62, 118
communal engagement: Christians, 4, 20–21, 36, 49, 52, 209; feeding the homeless, 198–203, 211; and individualism, 211; in international environmental law, 129–30; with lawmaking, 11, 30, 208–9, 211, 212; with legal interpretation, 150–51. *See also* social movements
communitarianism, 39, 129
Communities Organized for Public Service (COPS), 132–36, 211, 212

community organizing, 110, 130–36
consent, 118, 119, 121–22, 123–24
conservativism, 17–18
constitutional law, 2, 6, 112, 140n81
COPS *see* Communities Organized for Public Service
counsel, 96–98
courts, of law, 20, 25, 129
critical theory, 35
custom: Aquinas on, 31, 115–16, 118; and authority, 109, 111–12, 117–20; Bentham on, 111–13; and business, 129–30; and civil law, 59, 112, 115; and common good, 121–23, 125, 135–36, 194–95; and community organizing, 130–36; defining, 116–17; and divine law, 121–22, 125; Gratian on, 115; historical background, 113–16; and international environmental law, 127–30; knowledge of, 120–22; and legal interpretation, 109; and modernity, 126–27; and morality, 122–25, 129; and natural law, 31, 122–23, 125; and rights, 117; and statutory law, 109, 112, 114–20; Suárez on, 110–11, 116–27, 129, 134–37, 138n15, 150, 209–10
customary law, 109, 127

Day, Dorothy, 175–76
Defensio catholicae fidei contra anglicanae sectae errores (1613), 1, 8, 48, 85, 87, 164–66, 168
De legibus (1612), 7, 48, 79n64; on changes to the law, 180; influences, 1; on lawmaking, 61; on legal interpretation, 144; on natural law, 54, 84; purpose of, 87; theological content, 89; on women, 14
de Lubac, Henri, 54, 90
democracy: Aquinas on, 29; Augustine on, 24; and the church, 214n7; and custom, 126, 131; liberal, 19, 126; Schmitt on, 17; Suárez on, 73–74
De religione (1608–1625), 8
De sacramentis (1593–1603), 8
dignity, human, 39
divine law: and authority, 49; and custom, 121–22, 125; and equity, 191–93;

human access to, 68; and legal interpretation, 146–49; Suárez on, 54, 56, 58–59, 72–73, 100–101
divine right, 1, 17, 49
doctrinal interpretation, 147–50
domination, law as instrument of, 2, 48, 51–52, 55, 124
Dominicans, 12, 13, 85
dominium, 56, 64, 101
Doyle, John, 147, 157
Duns Scotus, 185
duty, 100
Dworkin, Ronald, 17–18, 145–46, 158, 170n42

ecclesiology, 32–37, 88, 211
economic development, 135–36
ecumenism, 213
Elshtain, Jean Bethke, 24–25
Enlightenment, the, 39, 83, 84
environmental law, 127–30
epikeia, 177–78, 180, 183–84, 188–89, 191, 193
equity: Aquinas on, 177–79, 184–85, 187–89, 191–93, 195; Aristotle on, 177, 181, 184–85, 187–89, 191; and authority, 179, 185–87, 192–94; and civil law, 177, 184, 192; and common good, 175–82, 186–87, 194–203; defining, 180–83; and divine law, 191–93; and individual freedom, 194–97; legal theory, 176–80; and natural law, 183–84, 191–92; and nonviolent protest, 32; and prudence, 180, 184, 191; and the rule of law, 174–75, 182, 187; in scripture, 197–98; Suárez on, 173–74, 177, 180–201, 210; as virtue, 145, 177–83, 184–85, 191
eternal law, 66, 68, 89–90
ethics, 21, 26, 32–32
Eucharist, 157
evil, 54, 122–25

family, 24, 101
Farrell, Walter, 96
fasting, 59, 186, 188, 190
Figgis, John, 87, 92

Finnis, John, 30, 96, 100
Francis, Pope, 10–11, 37, 211–13
freedom: Christian, 49; and common good, 39–40, 175, 194–97, 200, 210; and moral obligation, 98; and the rule of law, 31, 53
free will, 54, 62, 77n1, 99
Fuller, Lon, 65, 112, 120, 196

Garzón Valdés, Ernesto, 161
Gilson, Étienne, 84
globalization, 13
gnome, 180, 184–85
Gordley, James, 81n112
grace, 54–55, 57, 90, 94
Graham, Franklin, 3–4
Granada (Spain), 11, 14, 15
Gratian, 31, 110, 115, 118, 119, 159
Gregory, Eric, 22, 26–27
Gutiérrez, Gustavo, 110, 111

Hadot, Pierre, 86
happiness, 54, 57, 90–91, 95–96, 163
Hart, H. L. A., 112–13, 119, 120, 139n60, 152, 163, 168
Hauerwas, Stanley, 33, 34, 39, 214n7
Hobbes, Thomas, 4, 17, 50–51, 96
Hollenbach, David, 40–41, 52
Holy Spirit, 92–93, 147–50
homelessness, 173–74, 199–203, 211, 213
Hooker, Richard, 21, 38
human rights. *See* rights

Ignatius of Loyola, 21, 36–37
imperialism, 13, 39
Incarnation, 10, 33–34, 36–37
individualism, 88, 146, 211
international law, 112, 119, 127–30
Irwin, Terence, 80n96, 84, 85, 89, 100
Islam, 169n25
ius gentium, 90, 127

James I (King of England): absolutism, 2, 3, 4, 49–50, 52, 71; Oath of Allegiance, 87, 164–66; Suárez and, 1, 12, 53, 87
Jesuits: and civil law, 92–93; ecclesiology, 211; education, 85–86; in Latin

Jesuits (*continued*)
America, 2; *limpieza de sangre* movement, 16; mission, 10–11, 13, 29, 36–37; political theology, 36–37, 87–89; Suárez's engagement with, 12, 16
Jews, 15–16
judges, 112, 120, 150, 153–55, 162, 176–77

Kaveny, Cathleen, 31
King, Martin Luther, Jr, 27, 32, 173, 175
knowledge, 120–22
Kubasek, Nancy, 127–29

Lambelet, Kyle, 35–36
language, legal, 152–58
Lantigua, David, 85
Las Casas, Bartolomé de, 42n10, 111
Latin America, 2, 14, 110
Latino community, 110, 132–37
lawmaking: and authority, 20–21, 30, 49–50, 73–75; communal engagement in, 11, 30, 208–9, 211, 212; and community, 72–76, 130–37; and custom, 116–19, 131; and equity, 179, 182, 185; and intellect, 102–3; and intention, 144, 146–47, 149–52, 158–64, 171n93; and interpretation, 144, 148–63, 182, 188–89; natural/supernatural ends, 53, 55, 83, 86–87, 89, 90–93, 211; and power, 61–66, 110–11, 118–19; role of ruler/subject, 61–66, 74; Suárez on, 61–66, 72–67, 135; and will, 185, 186, 188–89
law: abrogation, 124–25; as activity, 65–66; application of equity, 185–87, 193–94; Christian engagement with, 20–21, 36, 49, 52, 145; defining, 96–98, 103; as instrument of domination, 2, 48, 51–52, 55, 124; popular/communal engagement with, 1, 4, 5, 11, 18, 21, 72–76; promulgation, 60–61, 65, 98, 115, 120–21; purpose and intention, 159–64; reception, 150, 209; in Schmitt, 17; sinfulness of, 188, 190–91; theories of Suárez, 1, 5–6, 13, 29, 89–90; unjust, 11, 18, 20–21, 73–75, 111, 173–203. *See also* Black natural law; canon law; civil law; constitutional law; customary law; divine law; environmental law; eternal law; international law; natural law; positive law; Roman law; statutory law
legal interpretation: categories, 147–50; and civil law, 148–51; and common good, 145, 152, 161–62, 168; community engagement, 150–51; and custom, 109; defining, 145–46; and divine law, 146–49; doctrinal, 147–50; and equity, 188–89; James I's Oath of Allegiance, 164–66; meaning and language, 152–54, 155–58; and natural law, 148, 151; and reason, 149, 154–55; and sanctuary movement, 166–68; and scriptural interpretation, 146–51; Suárez on, 144–66, 210
legal positivism, 31, 58, 109, 111–12, 117
liberal democracy, 19, 126
liberalism, 18–22, 38–41, 93, 211
liberation theology, 110, 137
liturgy, 84, 93, 212
Lloyd, Vincent, 32, 35–36, 204n4
Locke, John, 21–22, 38, 40, 93
Louis XIII (King of France), 1
love, 22–27, 195
Lovin, Robin, 19, 33, 35, 41
Luther, Martin, 49, 52, 55
Lutherans/Lutheranism, 56, 59, 71, 77n1, 97, 102

MacCormick, Neil, 112, 171n76
Machiavelli, Niccolò/Machiavellian, 49, 51, 55, 72, 102
MacIntyre, Alasdair, 39, 83–86
Mahoney, John, 88
Maritain, Jacques, 29, 39, 204n3
Markus, Robert A., 27–28
martyrs/martyrdom, 10, 17, 36
Maryks, Robert, 16
messianism, 35–36
Metaphysics (Suárez), 83, 86, 88
Milbank, John, 19, 83, 87, 92, 93
Miner, Robert, 84, 85, 103n1
minority communities: organizing, 130–37; protection, 3, 20, 48, 126–27,

166–68; rights, 41, 111, 113; Suárez and, 15–16
mission, Jesuit, 10–11, 13, 29, 36–37
modernity, 126–27, 213
monarchy, 29, 38, 50, 71
morality, 31, 49, 67, 94, 122–25, 129
moral obligation, 98, 100–102, 190, 201
moral theology, 42n10, 89, 93–96, 150
moral virtues, 94–95, 174
Murphy, James B., 124, 140n80
Murphy, Paul, 93

nation-state, 4–5, 116, 126, 127–30
natural law: Augustine on, 52–53; and authority, 49–50; Bloch on, 3; and civil law, 31, 67–72; and custom, 122–23, 125; and equity, 183–84, 191–92; interpretation, 148, 151; Locke on, 38; permissive, 69, 70, 72, 101; Suárez's theory of, 54–55, 66–72, 84, 163, 183–84; and Thomism, 30, 31, 32, 37. *See also* Black natural law
natural rights, 25, 38–39, 115
Niebuhr, Reinhold, 23, 24

Obama, Barack, 19
obedience, religious, 36, 50, 53, 58–59, 117, 118
obligation, 98–100, 113, 150
O'Donovan, Oliver, 25–26

Pace, Paul, 80n101, 81n112, 163
Paraguay, 10, 36
Penner, Sydney, 81n112
Poindexter, Georgette, 136
political authority, 9n13, 14–15, 16, 35
Porter, Jean, 31–32, 115, 177
positive law, 50, 55–56, 90, 110, 151
Postema, Gerald, 112, 119, 121
poverty, 110, 175, 203
power: absolute, 2, 3, 4, 17, 28–29; and Christian realism, 22–24; and custom, 110–37; and lawmaking, 61–66, 118–19; political, 10–11, 16–17; popular, 110–11, 118–19, 132–37
prayer, 211–12
precept, 97–98, 99, 103, 191–92

promulgation, 60–61, 65, 98, 115, 120–21
property ownership, 69, 70, 195
proportionalism, 150
protest, nonviolent, 27, 32, 173–76
Protestantism/Protestants, 1, 116, 147, 213
prudence, 67, 94–95, 102, 121, 180, 184, 191
Pryzwara, Eric, 105n45
punishment, 76, 96, 99, 152

racial discrimination, 16, 18, 109, 196
Raz, Joseph, 112, 156, 158
realism, Christian, 22–24, 34
reason: Aquinas on, 96–98, 154; and legal interpretation, 155; and natural law, 66–68, 90, 101, 149; prudential, 102; right reason, 97, 124, 183–84; and will, 51, 71, 96–97, 103
reasonableness, 116, 122, 124–25
Reformation, 3, 13, 77n1, 87, 116, 168, 213
refugees, 166–68
right reason, 97, 124, 183–84
rights: and custom, 117; discourse, 39, 174, 199, 204n3; and equity, 195; human, 39, 41, 203; natural, 25, 38–39, 115
Riley, Lawrence, 177, 194, 204n19
ritual, 113, 121
Roman law, 64, 114
Ross, Richard, 140n68
Rutherglen, George, 109, 137

sacramental theology, 89, 157, 162, 210
saeculum, 26–28, 210
Salamanca, School of, 12, 13–14, 32, 85
Salas, Victor, 54
salvation, 22, 55, 93, 95
sanctuary movement, 166–68, 211, 213
Schaffner, Thomas, 89
Schauer, Frederick, 112–13, 120
Schmitt, Carl, 17, 19
Schneewind, Jerome, 106n96
Scholasticism, 12–13, 83–86, 125, 159
scripture, 55–57, 146–51, 197–98
sin: Augustine on, 23, 25, 29, 54, 56; Suárez on, 188, 190
slavery, 56, 64, 81n108, 109
Smith, Ted, 36

social contract, 21, 38
social movements: Catholic Worker Movement, 33, 175; Communities Organized for Public Service (COPS), 132–36, 211, 212; food sharing, 198–203; Latino community, 110; sanctuary movement, 166–68, 211, 213. *See also* communal engagement; community organizing
Sommerville, J. P., 9n13, 28
Soto, Domingo de, 13, 79n67, 85, 185, 188, 195, 207n119
South America, 11, 13–14
sovereignty, 22, 25, 38, 79n81, 116
spiritual authority, 14
state of exception, 18–19
statutory law, 60, 109, 112, 114–20, 152–56
Stern, Philip, 140n68
Stout, Jeffrey, 131
Suárez, Francisco: on absolutism, 9, 107n112; and Aquinas, 66, 84–86, 94–99, 154, 171n78, 177–78, 180, 185; and Aristotle, 61, 81n112, 84–86, 177, 181, 184–85, 189, 191; and Augustine, 28–32, 83; on canon law 87, 95, 97, 120, 188; on church and state, 37; on civil law, 90–95, 149; on common good, 40–41, 48, 55–61, 135–36, 161–63, 186, 191; *converso* descent, 15–16; on custom, 110–11, 116–27, 129, 134–37, 138n15, 150, 209–10; *Defensio catholicae fidei contra anglicanae sectae errores* (1613), 1, 8, 48, 85, 87, 164–66, 168; on democracy, 73–74; *De religione* (1608–1625), 8; *De sacramentis* (1593–1603), 8; on divine law, 54, 56, 58–59, 72–73, 100–101; and ecclesiology, 36–37, 88, 211; education and career, 11–14; on equity, 173–74, 177, 180–201, 210; on freedom, 40, 53, 79n67, 98, 99; on justice, 57–59, 74–75; on lawmaking, 61–66, 72–76, 135; on legal interpretation, 144–66, 210; lifestyle, 16; *Metaphysics*, 86, 88; moral theology, 89, 93–96; philosophy of law, 83–89, 91; on political authority, 9n13, 14–15; on pure nature, 54–55; on reception, 150; sacramental theology, 89, 210; scholasticism, 83–86, 125, 159; theological anthropology, 54; theological corpus, 12; theories of law, 1, 5–6, 13, 29, 89–90; theory of natural law, 66–72, 84, 163, 183–84; and Thomism, 1, 12, 42n10, 83, 85–86, 96–97; on two cities, 52–55; on tyranny, 64, 74; on virtues, 91, 92–96, 182; voluntarism of, 83, 96–100, 102–3, 160, 189; on women, 14–15, 16. See also *De legibus* (1612)
Summa Theologiae (Aquinas), 12, 29, 80n82, 84, 85–86, 177–79
supernatural ends, 53, 55, 83, 86, 87, 89, 90–93, 211

Teresa of Avila, 14–15, 211
terrorism, 2, 19, 31
theological anthropology, 54
Thomism: Augustinian, 21, 26–32; and equity, 177; influence on Suárez, 1, 12, 42n10, 83, 85–86, 96–97; and legal theory, 89, 91; natural law, 37; and rights discourse, 204n3; and virtues, 95
Trump, Donald, 3, 8n5, 19
trust, in institutions, 19–20
two cities, 26–27, 34, 40, 52–55, 88, 210
tyranny, 38, 64, 74, 114, 126, 209

violence, 36, 141n117, 175
virtue: Aquinas on, 94–95, 178, 179–80; Augustine on, 25–28, 40, 210; civic, 28, 30, 40, 58, 96, 210; equity as, 145, 177–83, 184–85, 191; moral, 94–95, 174; Suárez on, 91, 92–96, 182
Vitoria, Francisco de, 12, 13, 85
voluntarism, 83, 96–100, 102–3, 160, 189

Westerman, Pauline C., 65
will: and custom, 120–21; and equity, 185, 186, 188–89; free will, 54, 62, 77n1, 99; of the lawmaker, 156, 160; and reason, 51, 71, 96–97, 103; voluntarism, 83, 96–100, 102–3, 160, 189
Williams, Rowan, 27–28
women, 14–15, 16, 39, 140n78, 141n99

About the Author

ELISABETH RAIN KINCAID is Legendre-Soulé Chair of Business Ethics and director of the Center for Ethics and Economic Justice at Loyola University, New Orleans. She holds a PhD from the University of Notre Dame and a JD from the University of Texas at Austin School of Law.